The Israel/Palestine Reader

The Israel/Palestine Reader

ALAN DOWTY, EDITOR

Polity

First published in 2019 by Polity Press

Polity Press
65 Bridge Street
Cambridge CB2 1UR, UK

Polity Press
101 Station Landing
Suite 300
Medford, MA 02155, USA

ISBN-13: 978-1-5095-2733-5
ISBN-13: 978-1-5095-2734-2(pb)

A catalogue record for this book is available from the British Library.

Library of Congress Cataloging-in-Publication Data

Names: Dowty, Alan, 1940- author.
Title: The Israel/Palestine reader / Alan Dowty.
Description: Cambridge, UK ; Medford, MA : Polity Press, 2018. |
   Includes bibliographical references and index.
Identifiers: LCCN 2018019542 (print) | LCCN 2018028630 (ebook) |
   ISBN 9781509527373 (Epub) | ISBN 9781509527335 |
   ISBN 9781509527335q(hardback) | ISBN 9781509527342q(pbk.)
Subjects: LCSH: Arab-Israeli conflict–History–Sources. | Jewish-Arab relations–
   History–Sources. | Palestinian Arabs–Politics and government–Sources.
Classification: LCC DS119.7 (ebook) | LCC DS119.7 .D695 2018 (print) |
   DDC 956.04–dc23
LC record available at https://lccn.loc.gov/2018019542

Typeset in 9.5 on 13 pt Swift
by Toppan Best-set Premedia Limited
Printed and bound in the United Kingdom by Clays Ltd, Elcograf S.p.A.

For further information on Polity, visit our website: politybooks.com

Contents

Chapter 5   The Reemergence of the Palestinians   88

Chapter 6   The First Pass at Peace   111

Chapter 7   The Fourth Stage   132

Chapter 8   The Downward Spiral   155

Chapter 9   The Impasse that Remains   180

Chapter 10   The Perfect Conflict   205

Acknowledgments

Excerpt from "Ottoman Jerusalem in the Writings of Arab Travelers" by Abdul-Karim Rafeq, published in *Ottoman Jerusalem: The Living City, 1517–1917* by Sylvia Auld and Robert Hillenbrand, Altajir World of Islam Trust, 2000, pp. 71–72. Reproduced by permission of Altajir Trust; Excerpts translated from *Yawmiyat Khalil as-Sakakini Yawmiyat, Rasa'il, wa-Ta'amulat (Diaries of Khalil as-Sakakini: Diaries, Letters, and Thoughts)* by Khalil as-Sakakini, Vol. 2, 1914–1918, ed. Akram Musallem, Khalil Sakakini Center and the Institute of Palestine Studies, 2004, pp. 55–57, 61–61, 66. Reproduced by permission of Institute for Palestine Studies; Excerpts from *My Life* by Golda Meir, 1975. Reproduced with permission of The Orion Publishing Group, London and Naomi Samuel Wilf for the Estate of the author; Excerpts from "Nasser's Memoirs of the First Palestine War" by Gamal Abdul Nasser and translated by Walid Khalidi published in *Journal of Palestine Studies*, Vol. 2 (2), Winter 1973, pp. 3–32, copyright © 1973, University of California Press on behalf of the Institute for Palestine Studies. All rights reserved; Excerpts from *In Search of Identity: An Autobiography* by Anwar El-Sadat, copyright © 1977, 1978, the Village of Mit Abu el Kom. English translation copyright © 1978, Harper & Row Publishers, Inc. Reprinted by permission of HarperCollins Publishers; Excerpts from *The Battle for Peace* by Ezer Weizman, copyright © 1981 by Ezer Weizman. Used by permission of Bantam Books, an imprint of Random House, a division of Penguin Random House LLC. All rights reserved. Any third party use of this material, outside of this publication, is prohibited. Interested parties must apply directly to Penguin Random House LLC for permission; Excerpts from *Through Secret Channels* by Mahmoud Abbas, Garnet Publishing, 1995. Reproduced by permission of the publisher; Excerpts from *Touching Peace: From the Oslo Accord to a Final Agreement* by Yossi Beilin, 1999. Reproduced with permission of The Orion Publishing Group, London and the author Dr Yossi Beilin; Excerpts from "Camp David and After: An Exchange, (1. An Interview with Ehud Barak)" by Benny Morris, *The New York Review of Books*, 13/06/2002. Reproduced with permission of the author; Excerpts from "A Reply to Ehud Barak" by Robert Malley and Hussein Agha, *The New York Review of Books*, 13/06/2002, copyright © 2002 by Robert Malley and Hussein Agha. Reproduced by permission of The New York Review of Books; Excerpts from *Between the Lines: Israel, the Palestinians, and the U.S. War on Terror* by Tikva Honig-Parnass and Toufic Haddad, Haymarket Books, 2007, pp. 65–69. Reproduced by permission of the publisher; Abridgement of "Blaming the Victims" by Diana Buttu, published in

Journal of Palestine Studies, Vol. 44 (1), Autumn 2014, pp. 91–96, copyright © 2014, University of California Press on behalf of the Institute for Palestine Studies. All rights reserved; Abridgement of "Minding the Gaps: Territorial Issues in Israeli-Palestinian Peacemaking" by Michael Herzog, *Policy Focus*, No.116, December 2011, The Washington Institute for Near East Policy; Abridgement of "Apartheid, Settler Colonialism and the Palestinian State 50 Years On" by Walid Salem, published in *Palestine-Israel Journal*, Vol. 22 (2&3), 2017, pp. 112–118. Reproduced with permission; Abridgement of Hillel Halkin, "Why the Settlements Should Stay" by Hillel Halkin, *Commentary Magazine*, Vol. 113 (6), June 2002, pp. 21–27. Reproduced by kind permission of the author; Abridgement of "Attainable Justice: Elements of a Solution to the Palestinian Refugee Issue" by Rashid Khalidi, published in *International Journal*, Vol. 53 (2), Spring 1998, pp. 233–251, SAGE Publications, 06/01/1998, copyright © 1998, SAGE Publications; Abridgement of "The Palestinians and the 'Right of Return'" by Efraim Karsh, *Commentary Magazine*, Vol. 111 (5), May 2001, pp. 25–30. Reproduced by kind permission of the author; Abridgement of "The One-State Solution: An Alternative Vision for Israeli–Palestinian Peace" by Ghada Karmi, published in *Journal of Palestine Studies*, Vol. 40 (2), Winter 2011, pp. 62–76, copyright © 2011, the Institute for Palestine Studies. All rights reserved; Excerpt from "The Israel Stability Initiative" by Naftali Bennett, published in *Journal of Palestine Studies*, Vol. 41 (4), Summer 2012, pp. 195–196, copyright © 2012, the Institute for Palestine Studies. All rights reserved; Abridgement of "The Inevitable Two-State Solution" by David C. Unger, published in *World Policy Journal*, Vol. 25 (3), February 2002, pp. 59–67, copyright © 2008, World Policy Institute. All rights reserved. Republished by permission of the copyright holder, and the present publisher, Duke University Press, www.dukeupress.edu; and Abridgement of "Linking Justice to Peace in the Israeli–Palestinian Conflict: Looking for Solutions" by Yaacov Bar-Siman-Tov, published in *Justice and Peace in the Israeli-Palestinian Conflict*, ed. Arie M. Kacowicz, pp. 133–150, copyright © 2014, Routledge. Reproduced by permission of Taylor & Francis Books UK.

Preface

The introduction to any complex international conflict is enriched when the voices of the adversaries are heard. This collection of readings is designed to add a human dimension to study of the Israeli–Palestinian confrontation by drawing on the voices of leaders, thinkers, observers, and participants on both sides. It is structured to complement and coordinate with my own text, *Israel/Palestine* (4th edition, Polity 2017); but, with its contextual notes, it can be used to supplement any basic book on the conflict or to stand on its own as a representation of the dramatic range of voices in one of the world's most enduring and tortuous clashes.

But, in the Internet age, aren't these sources readily available from any keyboard? That might be the case with many conventional documents—treaties, speeches, official statements—but is much less so with the kind of personal testimonies and narratives featured in this volume. And, even when available online or elsewhere, these primary sources are seldom in a format or of a length that is useful or convenient for an introduction to the conflict. In this volume the "voices" have been tightly edited to highlight the most relevant aspects of the topic at hand and to keep the entire enterprise to a reasonable length.

I would like to thank Louise Knight, Nekane Tanaka Galdos, Manuela Tecusan, and all the others at Polity for their support in undertaking this somewhat unorthodox approach to a reader in a field where there is no lack of material in print.

Alan Dowty

Chapter 1

Two Worlds Collide

The origins of the modern Israeli–Palestinian and Arab–Israeli conflicts lie in the flow of Jewish settlers to Ottoman Palestine that began in the 1880s. These settlers—refugees by today's accepted international definition—were fleeing anti-Semitic attacks and official policies in tsarist Russia and elsewhere. Their aim was to renew a Jewish presence in the historic homeland that would not be subject to the will of others. This inevitably created a clash with the established Arab population, whose own historic roots in Palestine reached back well over a millennium.

This conflict is thus, in its essence, a conflict over the claim of two peoples to the same land. This immediately raises the issue of defining a "people" or a "nation" as a collective body that holds "national" rights to a certain territory, and then of determining whether Jews or Arabs meet this definition. At the outset neither side saw the other as a "nation" in this sense, and thus as a legitimate contender for territorial claims.

All of this was happening at a time when "nations," particularly in Europe, were discovering or rediscovering their identities and nationalism was emerging as the most powerful political current of the time. Jews—particularly those in Europe—and Arabs—targets of European influence—could hardly fail to be touched by these ideas.

One of the classic definitions of nationhood was offered in 1882—the very year when the flow of refugees from Russia began—by Ernest Renan, a renowned French scholar. Renan's famous lecture on the issue (Reading 1) tests the various ways in which a "nation" might be defined and reaches conclusions that continue to be hugely influential in debates on this matter today.

Apart from the ideological context in which the conflict arose, the geographical context is also critical. European influence and presence in the Middle East, and in Palestine, grew apace during the nineteenth century; the Jewish influx was part of a larger picture. Western perspectives on Palestine during this period bear, of course, the marks of the huge gap between East and West. Travelers from Europe or America saw late Ottoman Palestine as desolate and backward; but they had few means to appreciate the changes that were taking place. A typical—and colorful—portrait was provided by Mark Twain after his visit in 1867 (Reading 2). On the other hand, Nu'man al-Qasatli, a traveler from elsewhere in the Arab world, had a much less negative view when he visited Jerusalem a few years later (Reading 3).

Further online resources:

The Origins of Modern Palestine in Ottoman Documents: https://palestinesquare. com/2016/02/09/the-origins-of-modern-palestine-in-ottoman-documents.

Napoleon Bonaparte's Letter to the Jews, April 20, 1799: http://jewishliberation. blogspot.co.uk/2015/08/napoleon-bonapartes-letter-to-jews-in.html.

George Bush, *The Valley of Visions; Or, the Dry Bones of Israel Revived* (1844): https://books. google.co.uk/books?id=3TbDDxRB_t4C&printsec=frontcover&source=gbs_ge_ summary_r&cad=0#v=onepage&q&f=false.

Bernard Lewis, "The Ottoman Empire in the Mid-Nineteenth Century: A Review," *Middle Eastern Studies* 1.3 (1965): 283–295.

Edict of Gülhane, 1839 (beginning of Tanzimat reform): https://eudocs.lib.byu.edu/ index.php/History_of_Turkey:_Primary_Documents.

Ottoman Reform Edict of 1856: www.anayasa.gen.tr/reform.htm.

1. "What Is a Nation?"

*Ernest Renan**

EDITOR'S NOTE *Ernest Renan (1823–1892) was a noted philologist and expert on Semitic languages, though this plays no part in the lecture presented here. He also published landmark studies in history and philosophy, including a life of Jesus based on a scholarly approach that attracted considerable attention. At a time when nationalism seemed to be in the ascendant, he simply asks: what makes a nation into a nation? Is it race, ethnicity, language, religion, common interest, geography—or some combination of these "objective" elements? Or is it something that resides much more in the realm of "subjective" factors, such as perceptions of the past or of imagined commonalities, which are not necessarily "real"? Renan's answer is remarkably consistent with many contemporary theories of nationalism and national identity.*

What I propose to do today is to analyse with you an idea which, though seemingly clear, lends itself to the most dangerous misunderstandings. [...] Race is confused with nation and a sovereignty analogous to that of really existing peoples is attributed to ethnographic or, rather, linguistic groups. [...]

Since the fall of the Roman Empire or, rather, since the disintegration of Charlemagne's empire, western Europe has seemed to us to be divided into nations, some of which, in certain epochs, have sought to wield a hegemony over the others, without ever enjoying any lasting success. It is hardly likely that anyone in the future will achieve what Charles V, Louis XIV, and Napoleon I failed to do. The founding of a new Roman Empire or of a new Carolingian empire would now be impossible. Europe is so divided that any bid for universal domination would very rapidly give rise to a coalition, which would drive any too ambitious nation back to its 'natural frontiers'. A kind of equilibrium has long been established. France, England, Germany, and Russia will, for centuries to come, no matter what may befall them, continue to be individual historical units, the crucial pieces on a checkerboard whose squares will forever vary in importance and size but will never be wholly confused with each other.

---

* Abridgement of a lecture delivered at the Sorbonne on March 11, 1882: "Qe'est-ce qu'une nation?" in *Oeuvres complètes de Ernest Renan*, vol. 1 (Paris: Calmann-Levy, 1958), pp. 887–890; translated by Martin Thom in Homi K. Bhabha, ed., *Nation and Narration* (London: Routledge, 1990), pp. 8–22.

Nations, in this sense of the term, are something fairly new in history. Antiquity was unfamiliar with them; Egypt, China, and ancient Chaldea were in no way nations [...] France, Germany, England, Italy, and Spain made their way, by often circuitous paths and through a thousand and one vicissitudes, to their full national existence, such as we see it blossoming today.

What in fact is the defining feature of these different states? It is the fusion of their component populations. In the above-mentioned countries, there is nothing analogous to what you will find in Turkey, where Turks, Slavs, Greeks, Armenians, Arabs, Syrians, and Kurds are as distinct today as they were upon the day that they were conquered. Two crucial circumstances helped to bring about this result. First, the fact that the Germanic peoples adopted Christianity as soon as they underwent any prolonged contact with the Greek or Latin peoples. When conqueror or conquered have the same religion or, rather, when the conqueror adopts the religion of the conquered, the Turkish system—that is, the absolute distinction between men in terms of their religion—can no longer arise. The second circumstance was the forgetting, by the conquerors, of their own language. [...]

The crucial result of all this was that, in spite of the extreme violence of the customs of the German invaders, the mould which they imposed became, with the passing centuries, the actual mould of the nation. 'France' became quite legitimately the name of a country to which only a virtually imperceptible minority of Franks had come. In the tenth century, in the first *chansons de geste*, which are such a perfect mirror of the spirit of the times, all the inhabitants of France are French. [...]

It is [only] by contrast that these great laws of the history of western Europe become perceptible to us. Many countries failed to achieve what the king of France, partly through his tyranny, partly through his justice, so admirably brought to fruition. Under the crown of Saint Stephen, the Magyars and the Slavs have remained as distinct as they were 800 years ago. Far from managing to fuse the diverse [ethnic] elements to be found in its domains, the House of Hapsburg has kept them distinct and often opposed the one to the other. In Bohemia [for instance], the Czech and German elements are superimposed, much like oil and water in a glass. The Turkish policy of separating nationalities according to their religion has had much graver consequences, for it brought about the downfall of the East. If you take a city such as Salonika or Smyrna, you will find there five or six communities each of which has its own memories and which have almost nothing in common. [...]

If one were to believe some political theorists, a nation is above all a dynasty, representing an earlier conquest, one which was first of all accepted and then forgotten by the mass of the people. [...] Is such a law, however, absolute? It undoubtedly is not. Switzerland and the United States, which have formed themselves, like conglomerates, by successive additions, have no dynastic basis. [...] It must therefore be admitted that a nation can exist without a dynastic principle, and even that nations which have been formed by dynasties can be separated from them without therefore ceasing to exist. The old principle, which only takes account of the right of princes, could no longer be maintained; apart from dynastic right, there is also national right. Upon what criterion, however, should one base this national right? By what sign should one know it? From what tangible fact can one derive it?

Several confidently assert that it is derived from race. The artificial divisions, resulting from feudalism, from princely marriages, from diplomatic congresses are, [these authors assert], in a state of decay. It is a population's race, which remains firm and fixed. This is what constitutes a right, a legitimacy. The Germanic family, according to the theory I am expounding here, has the right to reassemble the scattered limbs of the Germanic order, even when these limbs are not asking to be joined together again. The right of the Germanic order over such and such a province is stronger than the right of the inhabitants of that province over themselves. There is thus created a kind of primordial right, analogous to the divine right of kings; an ethnographic principle is substituted for a national one. This is a very great error, which, if it were to become dominant, would destroy European civilization. The primordial right of races is as narrow and as perilous for genuine progress as the national principle is just and legitimate. [...]

Ethnographic considerations have therefore played no part in the constitution of modern nations. France is [at once] Celtic, Iberic, and Germanic. Germany is Germanic, Celtic, and Slav. Italy is the country where the ethnographic argument is most confounded. Gauls, Etruscans, Pelasgians, and Greeks, not to mention many other elements, intersect in an indecipherable mixture. The British Isles, considered as a whole, present a mixture of Celtic and Germanic blood, the proportions of which are singularly difficult to define. [...]

What we have just said of race applies to language too. Language invites people to unite; but it does not force them to do so. The United States and England, Latin America and Spain speak the same languages yet do not form single nations. Conversely, Switzerland—so well made, since she was made with the consent of her different parts—numbers three or four languages. [...] Let me repeat that these divisions of the Indo-European, Semitic, or other languages, created with such admirable sagacity by comparative philology, do not coincide with the divisions established by anthropology. Languages are historical formations, which tell us very little about the blood of those who speak them and which, in any case, could not shackle human liberty when it is a matter of deciding the family with which one unites oneself for life or for death. [...]

Religion cannot supply an adequate basis for the constitution of a modern nationality either. Originally, religion had to do with the very existence of the social group, which was itself an extension of the family. Religion and the rites were family rites. [...] In our own time, the situation is perfectly clear. There are no longer masses that believe in a perfectly uniform manner. Each person believes and practices in his own fashion what he is able to and as he wishes. There is no longer a state religion; one can be French, English, or German and be either Catholic, Protestant, or orthodox Jewish, or else practice no cult at all. Religion has become an individual matter; it concerns the conscience of each person. [...]

A community of interest is assuredly a powerful bond between men. Do interests, however, suffice to make a nation? I do not think so. Community of interest brings about trade agreements, but nationality has a sentimental side to it; it is both soul and body at once; a customs union is not a fatherland.

Geography, or what is known as natural frontiers, undoubtedly plays a considerable part in the division of nations. Geography is one of the crucial factors in history. Rivers have led races on; mountains have brought them to a halt. The former have favoured movement in history, whereas the latter have restricted it. Can one say, however, that, as some parties believe, a nation's frontiers are written on the map and that this nation has the right to judge what is necessary to round off certain contours, in order to reach such and such a mountain and such and such a river, which are thereby accorded a kind of a priori limiting faculty? I know of no doctrine which is more arbitrary or more fatal, for it allows one to justify any or every violence. [...]

We have now seen what things are not adequate for the creation of such a spiritual principle, namely race, language, material interest, religious affinities, geography, and military necessity. What more, then, is required? [...]

A nation is a soul, a spiritual principle. Two things, which in truth are but one, constitute this soul or spiritual principle. One lies in the past, one in the present. One is the possession in common of a rich legacy of memories; the other is present-day consent, the desire to live together, the will to perpetuate the value of the heritage that one has received in an undivided form. Man, gentlemen, does not improvise. The nation, like the individual, is the culmination of a long past of endeavours, sacrifice, and devotion. Of all cults, that of the ancestors is the most legitimate, for the ancestors have made us what we are. A heroic past, great men, glory (by which I understand genuine glory)—this is the social capital upon which one bases a national idea. To have common glories in the past and to have a common will in the present; to have performed great deeds together, to wish to perform still more—these are the essential conditions for being a people. [...]

A nation is therefore a large-scale solidarity, constituted by the feeling of the sacrifices that one has made in the past and of those that one is prepared to make in the future. It presupposes a past; it is summarized, however, in the present by a tangible fact, namely consent, the clearly expressed desire to continue a common life. A nation's existence is, if you will pardon the metaphor, a daily plebiscite, just as an individual's existence is a perpetual affirmation of life. That, I know full well, is less metaphysical than divine right and less brutal than so-called historical right. According to the ideas that I am outlining to you, a nation has no more right than a king does to say to a province: 'You belong to me, I am seizing you.' A province, as far as I am concerned, is its inhabitants; if anyone has the right to be consulted in such an affair, it is the inhabitant. A nation never has any real interest in annexing or holding on to a country against its will. The wish of nations is, all in all, the sole legitimate criterion, the one to which one must always return.

We have driven metaphysical and theological abstractions out of politics. What, then, remains? Man, with his desires and his needs. The secession, you will say to me, and, in the long term, the disintegration of nations will be the outcome of a system which places these old organisms at the mercy of wills which are often none too enlightened. It is clear that, in such matters, no principle must be pushed too far. Truths of this order are only applicable as a whole in a very general fashion. Human wills change; but what is there, here below, that does not change? The nations are not something eternal. They had their beginnings and they will end. A European confederation will very probably replace them. But such is not the law of the century in which we are living. At the present time, the existence of nations is a good thing, a necessity even. Their existence is the guarantee of liberty, which would be lost if the world had only one law and only one master.

Through their various and often opposed powers, nations participate in the common work of civilization; each sounds a note in the great concert of humanity, which, after all, is the highest ideal reality that we are capable of attaining. Isolated, each has its weak point. I often tell myself that an individual who had those faults which in nations are taken for good qualities, who fed off vainglory, who was to that degree jealous, egotistical, and quarrelsome, and who would draw his sword on the smallest pretext would be the most intolerable of men. Yet all these discordant details disappear in the overall context. Poor humanity, how you have suffered! How many trials still await you! May the spirit of wisdom guide you, in order to preserve you from the countless dangers with which your path is strewn!

Let me sum up, gentlemen. Man is a slave neither of his race nor his language, nor of his religion, nor of the course of rivers, nor of the direction taken by mountain chains. A large aggregate of men, healthy in mind and warm of heart, creates the kind of moral conscience which we call a nation. So long as this moral consciousness gives proof of its strength by the sacrifices which demand the abdication of the individual to the advantage of the community, it is legitimate and has the right to exist. If doubts arise regarding its frontiers, consult the populations in the areas under dispute. They undoubtedly have the right to a say in the matter. This recommendation will bring a smile to the lips of the grand theorists of politics, these infallible beings who spend their lives deceiving themselves and who, from the height of their superior principles, take pity upon our mundane concerns. 'Consult the populations, for heaven's sake! How naive! A fine example of those wretched French ideas which claim to replace diplomacy and war by childishly simple methods.' Wait a while, gentlemen; let the reign of the grand theorists pass; bear the scorn of the powerful with patience. It may be that, after many fruitless gropings, people will revert to our more modest empirical solutions. The best way of being right in the future is, in certain periods, to know how to resign oneself to being out of fashion.

2. Innocents Abroad

*Mark Twain**

EDITOR'S NOTE Mark Twain (1835–1910) was at the beginning of his literary career in 1867, when, at the age of 31, he boarded a ship for a five-month pilgrimage focused on the Holy Land. His travelogues during the trip were published as newspaper articles and then collected in The Innocents Abroad, published in 1869. Twain's reactions to what he saw were similar to those of other western visitors during the period, who were struck by what they saw as the rocky aridity, the sparse population, the pervasive venality, the general backwardness, and the rampant lawlessness of the late Ottoman Palestine. To this general picture Twain brought his own brand of wit and humor, as well as his skepticism of the religious icons venerated by his fellow travelers. The reader should ask: does such an account provide any hint of the changes that were then taking place, or of the even more momentous transformations that would soon occur?

A fast walker could go outside the walls of Jerusalem and walk entirely around the city in an hour. I do not know how else to make one understand how small it is. The appearance of the city is peculiar. It is as knobby with countless little domes as a prison door is with bolt-heads. Every house has from one to half a dozen of these white plastered domes of stone, broad and low, sitting in the center of, or in a cluster upon, the flat roof. Wherefore, when one looks down, from an eminence, upon the compact mass of houses (so closely crowded together, in fact, that there is no appearance of streets at all, and so the city looks solid), he sees the knobbiest town in the world, except Constantinople. It looks as if it might be roofed, from center to circumference, with inverted saucers. The monotony of the view is interrupted only by the great Mosque of Omar, the Tower of Hippicus [Tower of David], and one or two other buildings that rise into commanding prominence. [...]

The population of Jerusalem is composed of Moslems, Jews, Greeks, Latins, Armenians, Syrians, Copts, Abyssinians, Greek Catholics, and a handful of Protestants. One hundred of the latter sect are all that dwell now in this birthplace of Christianity. The nice shades of nationality comprised in the above list,

---

* Excerpts from Mark Twain, *Innocents Abroad, or, The New Pilgrims' Progress* (New York: Harper & Brothers, 1869).

and the languages spoken by them, are altogether too numerous to mention. It seems to me that all the races and colors and tongues of the earth must be represented among the fourteen thousand souls that dwell in Jerusalem. Rags, wretchedness, poverty, and dirt, those signs and symbols that indicate the presence of Moslem rule more surely than the crescent flag itself, abound. Lepers, cripples, the blind, and the idiotic, assail you on every hand, and they know but one word of but one language apparently—the eternal "bucksheesh." To see the numbers of maimed, malformed, and diseased humanity that throng the holy places and obstruct the gates, one might suppose that the ancient days had come again, and that the angel of the Lord was expected to descend at any moment to stir the waters of Bethesda. Jerusalem is mournful, and dreary, and lifeless. I would not desire to live here.

One naturally goes first to the Holy Sepulchre. It is right in the city, near the western gate; it and the place of the Crucifixion, and, in fact, every other place intimately connected with that tremendous event, are ingeniously massed together and covered by one roof—the dome of the Church of the Holy Sepulchre.

Entering the building, through the midst of the usual assemblage of beggars, one sees on his left a few Turkish guards—for Christians of different sects will not only quarrel, but fight, also, in this sacred place, if allowed to do it. Before you is a marble slab, which covers the Stone of Unction, whereon the Savior's body was laid to prepare it for burial. It was found necessary to conceal the real stone in this way in order to save it from destruction. Pilgrims were too much given to chipping off pieces of it to carry home. Near by is a circular railing which marks the spot where the Virgin stood when the Lord's body was anointed.

Entering the great Rotunda, we stand before the most sacred locality in Christendom—the grave of Jesus. It is in the center of the church, and immediately under the great dome. It is inclosed in a sort of little temple of yellow and white stone, of fanciful design. Within the little temple is a portion of the very stone which was rolled away from the door of the Sepulchre, and on which the angel was sitting when Mary came thither "at early dawn." Stooping low, we enter the vault—the Sepulchre itself. It is only about six feet by seven, and the stone couch on which the dead Savior lay extends from end to end of the apartment and occupies half its width. It is covered with a marble slab, which has been much worn by the lips of pilgrims. This slab serves as an altar, now. Over it hang some fifty gold and silver lamps, which are kept always burning, and the place is otherwise scandalized by trumpery, gewgaws, and tawdry ornamentation. [...]

It is a singular circumstance that, right under the roof of this same great church, and not far away from that illustrious column, Adam himself, the father of the human race, lies buried. There is no question that he is actually buried in the grave which is pointed out as his—there can be none—because it has never yet been proven that that grave is not the grave in which he is buried.

The tomb of Adam! How touching it was, here in a land of strangers, far away from home, and friends, and all who cared for me, thus to discover the grave of a blood relation. True, a distant one, but still a relation. The unerring instinct of nature thrilled its recognition. The fountain of my filial affection was stirred to its profoundest depths, and I gave way to tumultuous emotion. I leaned upon a pillar and burst into tears. I deem it no shame to have wept over the grave of my poor dead relative. Let him who would sneer at my emotion close this volume here, for he will find little to his taste in my journeyings through Holy Land. Noble old man—he did not live to see me—he did not live to see his child. And I—I—alas, I did not live to see him. Weighed down by sorrow and disappointment, he died before I was born—six thousand brief summers before I was born. But let us try to bear it with fortitude. Let us trust that he is better off where he is. Let us take comfort in the thought that his loss is our eternal gain. [...]

And so I close my chapter on the Church of the Holy Sepulchre—the most sacred locality on earth to millions and millions of men, and women, and children, the noble and the humble, bond and free. In its history from the first, and in its tremendous associations, it is the most illustrious edifice in Christendom. With all its clap-trap side-shows and unseemly impostures of every kind, it is still grand, reverend, venerable—for a god died there; for fifteen hundred years its shrines have been wet with the tears of pilgrims from the earth's remotest confines; for more than two hundred, the most gallant knights that ever wielded sword wasted their lives away in a struggle to seize it and hold it sacred from infidel pollution. Even in our own day a war,[1] that cost millions of treasure and rivers of blood, was fought because two rival nations claimed the sole right to put a new dome upon it. History is full of this old Church of the Holy Sepulchre—full of blood that was shed because of the respect and the veneration in which men held the last resting-place of the meek and lowly, the mild and gentle, Prince of Peace! [...]

At nine in the morning the caravan was before the hotel door and we were at breakfast. There was a commotion about the place. Rumors of war and bloodshed were flying every where. The lawless Bedouins in the Valley of the Jordan and the deserts down by the Dead Sea were up in arms, and were going to destroy all comers. They had had a battle with a troop of Turkish cavalry and

---

[1] The Crimean War.

defeated them; several men killed. They had shut up the inhabitants of a village and a Turkish garrison in an old fort near Jericho, and were besieging them. They had marched upon a camp of our excursionists by the Jordan, and the pilgrims only saved their lives by stealing away and flying to Jerusalem under whip and spur, in the darkness of the night. Another of our parties had been fired on from an ambush and then attacked in the open day. Shots were fired on both sides. Fortunately there was no bloodshed. We spoke with the very pilgrim who had fired one of the shots, and learned from his own lips how, in this imminent deadly peril, only the cool courage of the pilgrims, their strength of numbers and imposing display of war material, had saved them from utter destruction. It was reported that the Consul had requested that no more of our pilgrims should go to the Jordan while this state of things lasted; and, further, that he was unwilling that any more should go, at least without an unusually strong military guard. Here was trouble. But with the horses at the door and every body aware of what they were there for, what would you have done? Acknowledged that you were afraid, and backed shamefully out? Hardly. It would not be human nature, where there were so many women. You would have done as we did: said you were not afraid of a million Bedouins—and made your will and proposed quietly to yourself to take up an unostentatious position in the rear of the procession. [...]

We had had a glimpse, from a mountain top, of the Dead Sea, lying like a blue shield in the plain of the Jordan, and now we were marching down a close, flaming, rugged, desolate defile, where no living creature could enjoy life, except, perhaps, a salamander. It was such a dreary, repulsive, horrible solitude! It was the "wilderness" where John preached, with camel's hair about his loins—raiment enough—but he never could have got his locusts and wild honey here. We were moping along down through this dreadful place, every man in the rear. Our guards—two gorgeous young Arab sheiks, with cargoes of swords, guns, pistols, and daggers on board—were loafing ahead.

"Bedouins!"

Every man shrunk up and disappeared in his clothes like a mud-turtle. My first impulse was to dash forward and destroy the Bedouins. My second was to dash to the rear to see if there were any coming in that direction. I acted on the latter impulse. So did all the others. If any Bedouins had approached us, then, from that point of the compass, they would have paid dearly for their rashness. We all remarked that, afterwards. There would have been scenes of riot and bloodshed there that no pen could describe. [...]

The new-comers were only a reinforcement of cadaverous Arabs, in shirts and bare legs, sent far ahead of us to brandish rusty guns, and shout and brag, and carry on like lunatics, and thus scare away all bands of marauding Bedouins that might lurk about our path. What a shame it is that armed white Christians must travel under guard of vermin like this, as a protection against the prowling vagabonds of the desert—those sanguinary outlaws who are always going to do something desperate, but never do it. I may as well mention here that on our whole trip we saw no Bedouins, and had no more use for an Arab guard than we could have had for patent leather boots and white kid gloves. The Bedouins that attacked the other parties of pilgrims so fiercely were provided for the occasion by the Arab guards of those parties, and shipped from Jerusalem for temporary service as Bedouins. They met together in full view of the pilgrims, after the battle, and took lunch, divided the bucksheesh extorted in the season of danger, and then accompanied the cavalcade home to the city! The nuisance of an Arab guard is one which is created by the Sheiks and the Bedouins together, for mutual profit, it is said, and no doubt there is a good deal of truth in it. [...]

The commonest sagacity warns me that I ought to tell the customary pleasant lie, and say I tore myself reluctantly away from every noted place in Palestine. Every body tells that, but with as little ostentation as I may, I doubt the word of every he who tells it. I could take a dreadful oath that I have never heard any one of our forty pilgrims say any thing of the sort, and they are as worthy and as sincerely devout as any that come here. They will say it when they get home, fast enough, but why should they not? [...] It does not stand to reason that men are reluctant to leave places where the very life is almost badgered out of them by importunate swarms of beggars and peddlers who hang in strings to one's sleeves and coat-tails and shriek and shout in his ears and horrify his vision with the ghastly sores and malformations they exhibit. One is glad to get away. [...]

We visited all the holy places about Jerusalem which we had left unvisited when we journeyed to the Jordan and then, about three o'clock one afternoon, we fell into procession and marched out at the stately Damascus gate, and the walls of Jerusalem shut us out forever. We paused on the summit of a distant hill and took a final look and made a final farewell to the venerable city, which had been such a good home to us.

For about four hours we traveled down hill constantly. We followed a narrow bridle path which traversed the beds of the mountain gorges, and when we could we got out of the way of the long trains of laden camels and asses, and when we could not we suffered the misery of being mashed up against perpendicular walls of rock and having our legs bruised by the passing freight. [...] One horse had a heavy fall on the slippery rocks, and the others had narrow escapes. However, this was as good a road as we had found in Palestine, and possibly even the best, and so there was not much grumbling.

Sometimes, in the glens, we came upon luxuriant orchards of figs, apricots, pomegranates, and such things, but oftener the scenery was rugged, mountainous, verdureless, and forbidding. Here and there, towers were perched high up on acclivities which seemed almost inaccessible. This fashion is as old as Palestine itself and was adopted in ancient times for security against enemies.

We crossed the brook which furnished David the stone that killed Goliath, and no doubt we looked upon the very ground whereon that noted battle was fought. We passed by a picturesque old gothic ruin whose stone pavements had rung to the armed heels of many a valorous Crusader, and we rode through a piece of country which we were told once knew Samson as a citizen.

We staid all night with the good monks at the convent of Ramleh, and in the morning got up and galloped the horses a good part of the distance from there to Jaffa, or Joppa, for the plain was as level as a floor and free from stones, and besides this was our last march in Holy Land. These two or three hours finished, we and the tired horses could have rest and sleep as long as we wanted it. This was the plain of which Joshua spoke when he said, "Sun, stand thou still on Gibeon, and thou moon in the valley of Ajalon." As we drew near to Jaffa, the boys spurred up the horses and indulged in the excitement of an actual race—an experience we had hardly had since we raced on donkeys in the Azores islands.

We came finally to the noble grove of orange-trees in which the Oriental city of Jaffa lies buried; we passed through the walls, and rode again down narrow streets and among swarms of animated rags, and saw other sights and had other experiences we had long been familiar with. We dismounted, for the last time, and out in the offing, riding at anchor, we saw the ship! I put an exclamation point there because we felt one when we saw the vessel. The long pilgrimage was ended, and somehow we seemed to feel glad of it. [...]

So ends the pilgrimage. We ought to be glad that we did not make it for the purpose of feasting our eyes upon fascinating aspects of nature, for we should have been disappointed—at least at this season of the year. A writer in *Life in the Holy Land*[2] observes:

> Monotonous and uninviting as much of the Holy Land will appear to persons accustomed to the almost constant verdure of flowers, ample streams and varied surface of our own country, we must remember that its aspect to the Israelites after the weary march of forty years through the desert must have been very different.

Which all of us will freely grant. But it truly is "monotonous and uninviting," and there is no sufficient reason for describing it as being otherwise.

---

[2] William Cowper Prime, *Tent Life in the Holy Land* (New York: Harper and Brothers, 1865).

Of all the lands there are for dismal scenery, I think Palestine must be the prince. The hills are barren, they are dull of color, they are unpicturesque in shape. The valleys are unsightly deserts fringed with a feeble vegetation that has an expression about it of being sorrowful and despondent. The Dead Sea and the Sea of Galilee sleep in the midst of a vast stretch of hill and plain wherein the eye rests upon no pleasant tint, no striking object, no soft picture dreaming in a purple haze or mottled with the shadows of the clouds. Every outline is harsh, every feature is distinct, there is no perspective—distance works no enchantment here. It is a hopeless, dreary, heart-broken land.

Small shreds and patches of it must be very beautiful in the full flush of spring, however, and all the more beautiful by contrast with the far-reaching desolation that surrounds them on every side. I would like much to see the fringes of the Jordan in spring-time, and Shechem, Esdraelon, Ajalon, and the borders of Galilee—but even then these spots would seem mere toy gardens set at wide intervals in the waste of a limitless desolation.

Palestine sits in sackcloth and ashes. Over it broods the spell of a curse that has withered its fields and fettered its energies. Where Sodom and Gomorrah reared their domes and towers, that solemn sea now floods the plain, in whose bitter waters no living thing exists—over whose waveless surface the blistering air hangs motionless and dead—about whose borders nothing grows but weeds, and scattering tufts of cane, and that treacherous fruit that promises refreshment to parching lips, but turns to ashes at the touch. Nazareth is forlorn; about that ford of Jordan where the hosts of Israel entered the Promised Land with songs of rejoicing, one finds only a squalid camp of fantastic Bedouins of the desert; Jericho the accursed, lies a moldering ruin, to-day, even as Joshua's miracle left it more than three thousand years ago; Bethlehem and Bethany, in their poverty and their humiliation, have nothing about them now to remind one that they once knew the high honor of the Savior's presence; the hallowed spot where the shepherds watched their flocks by night, and where the angels sang "Peace on earth, good will to men," is untenanted by any living creature, and unblessed by any feature that is pleasant to the eye. Renowned Jerusalem itself, the stateliest name in history, has lost all its ancient grandeur, and is become a pauper village; the riches of Solomon are no longer there to compel the admiration of visiting Oriental queens; the wonderful temple, which was the pride and the glory of Israel, is gone, and the Ottoman crescent is lifted above the spot where, on that most memorable day in the annals of the world, they reared the Holy Cross. The noted Sea of Galilee, where Roman fleets once rode at anchor and the disciples of the Savior sailed in their ships, was long ago deserted by the devotees of war and commerce, and its borders are a silent wilderness; Capernaum is a shapeless ruin; Magdala is the home of beggared Arabs; Bethsaida and Chorazin have vanished from the earth; and the "desert places" round about them, where thousands of men once listened to the Savior's voice and ate the miraculous bread, sleep in the hush of a solitude that is inhabited only by birds of prey and skulking foxes.

Palestine is desolate and unlovely. And why should it be otherwise? Can the curse of the Deity beautify a land?

Palestine is no more of this work-day world. It is sacred to poetry and tradition—it is dream-land.

3. "Nu'man al-Qasatli's Travels in Palestine"

Abdul-Karim Rafeq[*]

EDITOR'S NOTE *Nu'man al-Qasatli (1856–1920) was an Arab scholar in Damascus, known primarily as the author of an authoritative history of his native city. In 1874 he traveled to Palestine and published his observations as part of a book that also covered Syria and Egypt. Apparently this book has been lost, but sections from it dealing with Palestine were discovered in the Asad National Library in Damascus by the Syrian American historian Abdul-Karim Rafeq (1931–). In the selection offered here, Rafeq describes al-Qasatli's account of late nineteenth-century Jerusalem. As an observer who was at home in Arab and Middle Eastern society, al-Qasatli provides an informative contrast with western travelers such as Mark Twain. At the same time, his picture of the Jewish community in Jerusalem meshes fairly well with other contemporary sources.*

A new type of travel account appears with the journey to Palestine of the Arab Christian historian from Damascus, Nu'man al-Qasatli (1856–1920). What establishes al-Qasatli's reputation as an historian rather than a chronicler is the history of Damascus which he wrote under the title of *al-Rawda al-Ghanna' fi Dimashq al-Faya* [*The Blooming Garden in Great Damascus*], in which he dealt with almost all aspects of life in the city, with much insight and analysis. He mentions at the end of this book that he will follow it with another book, entitled *Mir'at Suriyya wa Misr* [*The Mirror of Syria and Egypt*]. Sadly, nothing is known about the whereabouts of this volume. However, some of al-Qasatli's account of travel in Palestine, which seems to be part of it, has recently been found. Two of its three sections (al-Qasatli refers to them as *defters*) have been discovered.

Al-Qasatli's new approach, especially in the description of his voyage in Palestine, and the way he looked at events, interpreted them and reached logical conclusions based on them, constitutes a major change in Syria's traditional historiography. Al-Qasatli apparently acquired much insight from his work with scholars sent to Palestine by the Palestine Exploration Fund who published their research in the Fund's publication, *The Quarterly Statement*. In his travel account on Palestine, al-Qasatli refers, for instance, to Captain C. R.

* Excerpt from Abdul-Karim Rafeq, "Ottoman Jerusalem in the Writings of Arab Travelers," in Sylvia Auld and Robert Hillenbrand, eds., *Ottoman Palestine: The Living City, 1517–1917* (London: Altajir World of Islam Trust, 2000), pp. 71–72.

Conder, who was a noted scholar and member of the Fund. The experience thus acquired by al-Qasatli shows in his travel account, in which he includes both architectural sketches and plans of ancient sites in Palestine.

Al-Qasatli departed from 'my town' (*madinati*—Damascus—as he refers to it) on Saturday, 26 September 1874, heading toward Palestine by way of Beirut. He toured many towns and sites before arriving at Jerusalem. His account of Jerusalem, where he says he stayed for three months and one day, is unfortunately rather fragmentary and incomplete compared to what he wrote about the other Palestinian towns. It could be that the third missing *defter* of his account would fill this gap.

Unlike the earlier Arab travellers who never gave any figures concerning the number of inhabitants, al-Qasatli, in the style of European travellers, gives a reasonably accurate estimate of their number. To judge by the accuracy of what he has written about Damascus, he seems to have had access to Ottoman and European sources on population figures and other details. Chief among the Ottoman sources to which he had access is the *Salname* (yearbook) of Syria of the year 1288/1871–2, which is extremely important, given the varied information and statistics it offers for that early period. After giving a brief survey of the ancient history of Jerusalem (*Urshalim* and *al-Quds al-Sharif*), al-Qasatli estimates its population at the time of his visit in 1874, at 40,000 inhabitants, of whom 6,000 were Muslims, 12,000 Christians of different denominations, both foreign and native (*min jami' al-tawa'if Afranj wa wataniyyin*), and the remainder 22,000, Jews, made up of natives (*wataniyyin*, apparently Oriental and Sephardic Jews) and *Siknaj* (Ashkenazim—German Jews—and affiliates). Al-Qasatli records his insight that probably after a short time the population of this city will increase considerably because of the influx of Jews to it from all over the world.

Al-Qasatli describes the population of Jerusalem as being composed of different nations with different languages and tastes. The houses of the city are, he says, built of stone, and the population enjoys a good life. Crafts there are limited in number, with the exception of the profession of construction, which is almost monopolised by Christian builders. The building activity is concentrated mainly outside the walls of the city. Al-Qasatli estimates that 5,000–6,000 of Jerusalem's 40,000 inhabitants live outside the walls and suffer from lack of water. He estimates that in the past the circumference of the city had been nine or more miles but in his day it was a mere three miles.

The craft of carpenters, catering for the new buildings, and that of shoemakers were both making good progress at the time, according to al-Qasatli. Wood was also used in making religious souvenirs for tourists. Soap-making was mainly the profession of peasants. Candle-making and the icon industry were also flourishing because of demand by tourists, and for religious occasions. Al-Qasatli, however, laments the small number of crafts in Jerusalem overall and he urges the population to introduce a greater variety. He also encourages them to teach mathematics in the schools to avoid calamities awaiting them in the future. He refers to the poor commercial activity in Jerusalem, which is in the hands of Europeans and Jews. The only commodities Jerusalem exports, according to al-Qasatli, are soap and a limited number of icons and rosaries, most of which were made in Bethlehem.

The perspective of the Arab travellers, whether Muslim or Christian, visiting Jerusalem differs from that of the European travellers who came more frequently to Jerusalem. In much the same way as Muslim travellers were primarily interested in describing the holy places of Islam, the European travellers were mainly interested in describing the Christian religious establishments. However, the Muslim travellers, for their part, also visited those Jewish and Christian shrines which were cited in the Quran. The accounts of both groups of travellers thus complement each other.

Chapter 2

The Jewish Story

Jews have one of the longest histories, if not the longest one, as a people with a distinct identity marked by language, culture, genealogy, and religious practices. In the late nineteenth century, Jews, like other peoples, derived from this a distinct national identity based on perception of a shared past and present (to use Renan's formulation).

The puzzle of Jewish survival has intrigued historians; most explanations revolve around the Jews' role in shaping monotheism and in their relations with the other monotheistic religions. An important element in Jewish religious thought is the theme of exile from and return to a homeland. Thus the idea of a return to Zion is woven into tradition and across space and time. For example, we have the medieval poetry of Yehuda Halevi, from eleventh-century Spain (Reading 4), expressing the deep yearning to return—a yearning that Halevi realized at the end of his life.

A second constant in Jewish history was the fear of persecution, a reality that, more than any other, shaped Jewish population movements over the centuries. In this regard the nineteenth century promised deliverance through the "emancipation" of Jews in most western nations. Yet that was also a century of nationalism, which left Jews in an ambivalent position. The outbreak of a new, racial anti-Semitism late in the century sharpened their dilemma. A younger generation of Jews in Russia, who had sought to become assimilated, felt themselves betrayed and were drawn to the radical solution of reconstituting Jewish life in the historic homeland. An early expression of this desperation was the Bilu Manifesto of 1882 (Reading 5), which angrily rejected assimilation and asked the Ottoman sultan for a home in Palestine. A few years later a "western" Jew, Theodor Herzl, put the same ideas in more refined language when he issued a dramatic proposal for Jewish statehood in *The Jewish State* (Reading 6).

The continuation of vicious pogroms, mainly in Russia, guaranteed a persistent push to rebuild Jewish life in Ottoman Palestine. The intensity of the anger produced by anti-Jewish violence is captured in Chaim Nachman Bialik's classic poem "On the Slaughter" (Reading 7), written in response to the Kishinev pogrom of 1903. Bialik himself was soon to find his way to Palestine.

The early Jewish settlers in Ottoman Palestine had numerous clashes with their Arab neighbors over land disputes, grazing rights, and other such "ordinary" sources of conflict. They told themselves that these problems would pass with time and that no deeper source of opposition was at work. It was only in 1905 that a veteran settler, Yitzhak Epstein, challenged this assurance—which he did in a lecture at the Seventh Zionist Congress ("A Hidden Question," Reading 8). The Arab question, Epstein asserted, outweighed all the others. At the time few within the movement agreed with him, as can be seen from a rebuttal that appeared shortly afterwards in the same journal and was written by the author Nehama Pukhachewsky ("Open Questions," Reading 9).

Further online resources:

Bible Verses about the Land of Israel: https://www.kingjamesbibleonline.org/Bible-Verses-About-The-Land-Of-Israel.
Edict of Expulsion of the Jews from Spain, 1492: http://www.sephardicstudies.org/decree.html.
The May Laws (Russia), May 3, 1882: jewishencyclopedia.com (search under M)
Leon Pinsker, Auto-Emancipation, 1882: http://www.jewishvirtuallibrary.org/quot-auto-emancipation-quot-leon-pinsker.
Early Zionist writings: jewishvirtuallibrary.org/texts-concerning-zionism.
Program of the First Zionist Congress: mideastweb.org.
Letter from Dr. Theodor Herzl to M. Youssuf Zia al-Khalidi, March 19, 1899, aldeilis.net/english.
Theodor Herzl, Altneuland: http://www.mideastweb.org/basleprogram.htm.
Ber Borochov, texts on socialist Zionism: angelfire.com/il2/borochov.

4. Two Poems by Yehuda Halevi*

EDITOR'S NOTE *Yehuda Halevi (1025–1141) was a Jewish poet, philosopher, and physician who lived under both Christian and Muslim rulers in Spain. His poetry reflected his devotion to the deep-seated Jewish belief that true fulfillment could only be found in Eretz Yisrael ("the Land of Israel"). In the first poem here, the "grip of Edom" refers to crusader rule in Palestine after the First Crusade (1095–1099). In the second poem, the image of becoming "a harp for your songs" was later incorporated into the modern unofficial Israeli anthem, Jerusalem of Gold, by composer Naomi Shemer. The entire poem also became an integral part of Jewish prayers on Tisha B'Av, the Jewish day of mourning commemorating the destruction of the First and Second Temples. Halevi himself finally arrived in Jerusalem in 1141, where according to legend he was killed by an Arab horseman in front of the city gate.*

My Heart Is in the East

My heart in the East
and I am on the far edge of the West.
How can I taste what I eat
or find pleasure in it?
How can I fulfill my vows and pledges
while Zion is in the grip of Edom
and I am in the yoke of Arabia?
I would easily leave the treasures of Spain;
I long to see the dust of the ruined shrine.

Zion, Will You Not Ask?

Zion, will you not ask of the welfare of your captives,
those who seek your comfort, the remnant of your flocks?
From west and east, from north and south, near and far,
blessings come from all directions,
and the blessing of this captive of desire,

---

* Translated by the editor. For the Hebrew text, see T. Carmi, ed. and trans., *The Penguin Book of Hebrew Verse* (New York: Penguin, 1981), pp. 347–349.

who sheds his tears like the dew of Hermon
and yearns to have them fall on your hills!
When I weep over your distress, I am a jackal,
But when I dream of the return from exile
I become a harp for your songs.

My heart aches for Bethel and Peniel
and for Mahanaim and for all your holy shrines.
There the Almighty dwelt within you, and your Creator
opened your gates facing the gates of heaven,
and the splendor of God was your only light;
neither sun, nor moon, nor stars shone over you.
I would have my soul spill over in the place
where the spirit of God spilled over your chosen ones.
You are the house of royalty and the throne of God,
even if slaves sit on your rulers' seats.

If only I could wander through those places
where God was revealed to your prophets and messengers.
Who will craft me wings that I might roam afar?
I would carry my broken heart over your broken hills.
I would put my face in your earth, would treasure
your stones, and would pardon your dust.
I would weep over my forefathers' graves
and would grieve over the Patriarchs' tombs in Hebron.
I would pass through your forests and meadows
and sojourn in Gilead and wonder at Mount Abirim
and Mount Hor, where lie two great lights [Moses and Aaron]
who enlightened and led you.
The air of your land is the life of the soul,
the grains of your earth are flowing myrrh,
and your rivers are the finest nectar.
My soul will delight to walk naked and barefoot
among the bleak ruins where your shrines once stood,
where your Ark was hidden,
and where your cherubim inhabited your innermost chambers. [...]

Happy the one who waits and lives to see
your light rise and your dawn break over him,
to see your chosen people flourish,
and to rejoice in your joy when
you return to the days of your youth.

5. The Bilu Manifesto, 1882*

EDITOR'S NOTE *The Bilu Society was organized by Jewish students in the Kharkov area, in reaction to the wave of pogroms that swept Russia. It took its name from the Hebrew initials of Isaiah 2:5: "House of Jacob, come, let us go." The movement spread quickly to other Jewish communities. There was widespread agreement that assimilation to Russian society would not work, but debate over whether emigration should be directed toward America or toward the ancestral homeland of Palestine. Bilu adherents were in no doubt; on their way to Palestine, one group of "Biluim" issued this manifesto from Constantinople, asking the sultan to grant them a "home," at least in the framework of a state within the Ottoman state.*

To our brothers and sisters in exile!

"If I do not help myself, who will help me?"

Nearly two thousand years have passed since, in an evil hour, after an heroic struggle, the glory of our Temple vanished in fire and our kings and chieftains exchanged their crowns and diadems for the chains of exile. We lost our country, where our beloved ancestors had lived. Into the exile we took with us, of all our glories, only a spark of the fire by which our Temple, the abode of the Great One, was engirdled; and this little spark kept us alive while the towers of our enemies crumbled into dust, and this spark leapt into the celestial flame and illuminated the heroes of our race and inspired them to endure the horrors of the dance of death and the tortures of the autos-da-fé. And this spark is again kindling and will shine for us, a true pillar of fire going before us on the road to Zion, while behind us is a pillar of cloud, the pillar of oppression threatening to destroy us. Are you asleep, O our nation? What have you been doing until 1882? Sleeping and dreaming the false dream of assimilation. Now thank God, you have awaked from your slothful slumber. The pogroms have awakened you from your charmed sleep. You eyes are open to recognize the obscure and delusive hopes. Can you listen in silence to the taunts and mocking of your enemies? [...]

Where is your ancient pride, your old spirit? Remember that you were a nation possessing a wise religion, a law, a constitution, a celestial Temple whose wall is still a silent witness to the glories of the past. [...]

---

* Issued by Bilu Central Office in Constantinople in mid-1882; translation available at http:// www.jewishvirtuallibrary.org/bilu-manifesto.

Your state in the West is hopeless: the star of your future is gleaming in the East. Deeply conscious of all the foregoing and inspired by the true teaching of our great master Hillel—"If I do not help myself, who will help me?"—we propose to form the following society, for national ends:

1 The society will be named "BILU," according to the motto "House of Jacob, come, let us go." It will be divided into local branches according to the numbers of its members.
2 The seat of the Committee will be Jerusalem.
3 Donations and contributions shall be unfixed and unlimited.

WE WANT:

1 A home in our country. It was given to us by the mercy of God; it is ours as registered in the archives of history.
2 To beg it of the sultan himself, and if it be impossible to obtain this, to beg that we may at least possess it as a state within a larger state; the internal administration to be ours, to have our civil and political rights, and to act with the Turkish Empire only in foreign affairs, so as to help our brother Ishmael in his time of need.

We hope that the interests of our glorious nation will rouse the national spirit in rich and powerful men, and that everyone, rich or poor, will give his best labors to the holy cause.

Greetings dear brothers and sisters!

HEAR O! ISRAEL! The Lord is our God, the Lord is one, and our land Zion is our only hope.

GOD be with us!

The Pioneers of BILU

6. The Jewish State

*Theodor Herzl**

EDITOR'S NOTE Theodor Herzl (1860–1904) was a Viennese journalist and playwright and an assimilated Jew with little previous attachment to Judaism. But the new racial anti-Semitism in Western Europe toward the end of the century shocked him into publishing a passionate plea for the establishment of a Jewish state, whether in Palestine or elsewhere. Herzl's little pamphlet Der Judenstaat *(1896) was quickly translated into many other languages and caused a sensation throughout the Jewish world, and especially in Eastern Europe, where most Jews lived. Herzl's arguments that assimilation was doomed to failure and that only an independent Jewish state could solve the problem found a ready audience among those who had borne the brunt of both old and new anti-Semitism. The following year (1897) Herzl organized the First Zionist Congress and founded the World Zionist Organization.*

The Jewish question still exists. It would be foolish to deny it. It is a remnant of the Middle Ages, which civilized nations do not even yet seem able to shake off, try as they will. They certainly showed a generous desire to do so when they emancipated us. The Jewish question exists wherever Jews live in perceptible numbers. Where it does not exist, it is carried by Jews in the course of their migrations. We naturally move to those places where we are not persecuted, and there our presence produces persecution. This is the case in every country, and will remain so, even in those highly civilized—for instance, France—until the Jewish question finds a solution on a political basis. The unfortunate Jews are now carrying the seeds of anti-Semitism into England; they have already introduced it into America.

I believe that I understand anti-Semitism, which is really a highly complex movement. I consider it from a Jewish standpoint, yet without fear or hatred. I believe that I can see what elements there are in it of vulgar sport, of common trade jealousy, of inherited prejudice, of religious intolerance, and also of pretended self-defence. I think the Jewish question is no more a social than a religious one, notwithstanding that it sometimes takes these and other forms.

---

* Excerpts from Theodor Herzl, *The Jewish State: An Attempt at a Modern Solution to the Jewish Question*, trans. Sylvie D'Avigdor (London: Rita Searl, 1946), 2–46.

It is a national question, which can only be solved by making it a political world question, to be discussed and settled by the civilized nations of the world in council.

We are a people—one people.

We have honestly endeavoured everywhere to merge ourselves in the social life of surrounding communities and to preserve the faith of our fathers. We are not permitted to do so. In vain are we loyal patriots, our loyalty in some places running to extremes; in vain do we make the same sacrifices of life and property as our fellow citizens; in vain do we strive to increase the fame of our native land in science and art, or her wealth by trade and commerce. In countries where we have lived for centuries we are still cried down as strangers, and often by those whose ancestors were not yet domiciled in the land where Jews had already had experience of suffering. The majority may decide which are the strangers; for this, as indeed every point which arises in the relations between nations, is a question of might. I do not here surrender any portion of our prescriptive right, when I make this statement merely in my own name as an individual. In the world as it now is and for an indefinite period will probably remain, might precedes right. It is useless, therefore, for us to be loyal patriots, as were the Huguenots who were forced to emigrate. If we could only be left in peace. [...]

But I think we shall not be left in peace.

Oppression and persecution cannot exterminate us. No nation on earth has survived such struggles and sufferings as we have gone through. Jew-baiting has merely stripped off our weaklings; the strong among us were invariably true to their race when persecution broke out against them. This attitude was most clearly apparent in the period immediately following the emancipation of the Jews. Those Jews who were advanced intellectually and materially entirely lost the feeling of belonging to their race. Wherever our political well-being has lasted for any length of time, we have assimilated with our surroundings. I think this is not discreditable. Hence, the statesman who would wish to see a Jewish strain in his nation would have to provide for the duration of our political well-being; and even a Bismarck could not do that.

For old prejudices against us still lie deep in the hearts of the people. He who would have proof of this need only listen to the people where they speak with frankness and simplicity: proverb and fairy tale are both anti-Semitic. A nation is everywhere a great child, which can certainly be educated; but its education would, even in most favourable circumstances, occupy such a vast amount of time that we could, as already mentioned, remove our own difficulties by other means long before the process was accomplished.

Assimilation, by which I understood not only external conformity in dress, habits, customs, and language, but also identity of feeling and manner—

assimilation of Jews could be effected only by intermarriage. But the need for mixed marriages would have to be felt by the majority; their mere recognition by law would certainly not suffice. [...]

The whole plan is in its essence perfectly simple, as it must necessarily be if it is to come within the comprehension of all.

Let the sovereignty be granted us over a portion of the globe large enough to satisfy the rightful requirements of a nation; the rest we shall manage for ourselves.

The creation of a new state is neither ridiculous nor impossible. We have in our day witnessed the process in connection with nations which were not, largely, members of the middle class, but poorer, less educated, and consequently weaker than ourselves. The governments of all countries scourged by anti-Semitism will be keenly interested in assisting us to obtain the sovereignty we want. [...]

Should the powers declare themselves willing to admit our sovereignty over a neutral piece of land, then the Society [of Jews] will enter into negotiations for the possession of this land. Here two territories come under consideration, Palestine and Argentine. In both countries important experiments in colonization have been made, though on the mistaken principle of a gradual infiltration of Jews. An infiltration is bound to end badly. It continues till the inevitable moment when the native population feels itself threatened and forces the government to stop a further influx of Jews. Immigration is consequently futile, unless we have the sovereign right to continue such immigration.

The Society of Jews will treat with the present masters of the land, putting itself under the protectorate of the European powers, if they prove friendly to the plan. We could offer the present possessors of the land enormous advantages, assume part of the public debt, build new roads for traffic, which our presence in the country would render necessary, and do many other things. The creation of our state would be beneficial to adjacent countries, because the cultivation of a strip of land increases the value of its surrounding districts in innumerable ways.

Shall we choose Palestine or Argentine? We shall take what is given us and what is selected by Jewish public opinion. The Society will determine both these points. [...]

Palestine is our ever memorable historic home. The very name of Palestine would attract our people with a force of marvellous potency. If His Majesty the Sultan were to give us Palestine, we could in return undertake to regulate the whole finances of Turkey. We should there form a portion of a rampart of Europe against Asia, an outpost of civilization as opposed to barbarism. We should, as a neutral state, remain in contact with all Europe, which would have to guarantee our existence. The sanctuaries of Christendom would be safeguarded by assigning to them an extraterritorial status such as is well known to the law of nations. We should form a guard of honour about these sanctuaries, answering for the fulfilment of this duty with our existence. This guard of honour would be the great symbol of the solution of the Jewish question after eighteen centuries of Jewish suffering. [...]

The land which the Society of Jews will have secured by international law must, of course, be privately acquired. Provisions made by individuals for their own settlement do not come within the province of this general account. But the Company will require large areas for its own needs and ours, and these it must secure by centralized purchase. It will negotiate principally for the acquisition of fiscal domains, with the great object of taking possession of this land 'over there' without paying a price too high, in the same way as it sells here without accepting one too low. A forcing of prices is not to be considered, because the value of the land will be created by the Company through its organizing the settlement in conjunction with the supervising Society of Jews. [...]

Here it is, fellow Jews! Neither fable nor deception! Every man may test its reality for himself, for every man will carry over with him a portion of the Promised Land—one in his head, another in his arms, another in his acquired possessions.

Now, all this may appear to be an interminably long affair. Even in the most favourable circumstances, many years might elapse before the commencement of the foundation of the state. In the meantime, Jews in a thousand different places would suffer insults, mortifications, abuse, blows, depredation, and death. No; if we only begin to carry out the plans, anti-Semitism would stop at once and forever. For it is the conclusion of peace.

The news of the formation of our Jewish Company will be carried in a single day to the remotest ends of the earth by the lightning speed of our telegraph wires.

And immediate relief will ensue. The intellects which we produce so superabundantly in our middle classes will find an outlet in our first organizations, as our first technicians, officers, professors, officials, lawyers, and doctors; and thus the movement will continue in swift but smooth progression.

Prayers will be offered up for the success of our work in temples and in churches also; for it will bring relief from an old burden, which all have suffered.

But we must first bring enlightenment to men's minds. The idea must make its way into the most distant, miserable holes where our people dwell. They will awaken from gloomy brooding, for into their lives will come a new significance. Every man need think only of himself, and the movement will assume vast proportions.

And what glory awaits those who fight unselfishly for the cause!

Therefore I believe that a wondrous generation of Jews will spring into existence. The Maccabeans[1] will rise again.

Let me repeat once more my opening words: the Jews who wish for a state will have it. We shall live at last as free men on our own soil, and die peacefully in our own homes.

The world will be freed by our liberty, enriched by our wealth, magnified by our greatness.

And whatever we attempt there to accomplish for our own welfare will react powerfully and beneficially for the good of humanity.

---

[1] Ancient Jewish rebels against alien rule.

7. "On the Slaughter"

*Chaim Nachman Bialik**

EDITOR'S NOTE *Chaim Nachman Bialik (1873–1934) is often considered the poet of the "Hebrew renaissance," as Hebrew was being reborn as a national language. Born in Russia, he became a key member of the Zionist literary circle centered in Odessa. In 1903 he was sent to Kishinev, site of a particularly bloody pogrom, to investigate and report on the event. He poured his anger into this poem, whose title echoes the blessing for slaughter of animals. The poem conveys the intensity of Zionist reactions to the atrocities of the time.*

> Heaven, beg mercy for me! If there is
> a God in you, a pathway through
> you to this God—which I have not
> discovered—then pray for me! For my
> heart is dead, no longer is there prayer
> on my lips; all strength is gone,
> and hope is no more.
> Until when, how much longer, until when?
> You, executioner! Here's my neck—go
> to it, slaughter me! Behead me like a
> dog, yours is the almighty arm and the
> axe, and the whole earth is my scaffold
> and we, we are the few! My blood is
> fair game—strike the skull, and
> murder's blood, the blood of nurslings
> and old men, will spurt onto your
> clothes and will never, never be wiped off.
> And if there is justice—let it show
> itself at once! But if justice show itself
> after I have been blotted out from
> beneath the skies—let its throne be
> hurled down forever! Let heaven rot
> with eternal evil! And you, the arrogant,

* T. Carmi, ed. and trans., *The Penguin Book of Hebrew Verse* (New York: Penguin, 1981), pp. 512–513.

go in this violence of yours, live by
your bloodshed and be cleansed by it.
And cursed be the man who says:
Avenge! No such revenge—revenge for
the blood of a little child—has yet been
devised by Satan. Let the blood pierce
through the abyss! Let the blood seep
down into the depths of darkness, and
eat away there, in the dark, and breach
all the rotting foundations of the earth.

8. "A Hidden Question"

Yitzhak Epstein[*]

EDITOR'S NOTE *Yitzhak Epstein (1862–1943) was a Russian-born teacher and writer who immigrated to Palestine in 1886 and settled in Rosh Pina, the first Zionist settlement in the Upper Galilee. Over the next two decades, Epstein had considerable contact with Arabs in the region, as is clear in his writing. In the context of the Seventh Zionist Congress in 1905 he delivered the lecture below (published two years later) warning that "the Arab question" would be the biggest problem facing the Zionist enterprise. Many other Zionists disputed this claim, but it remains the first serious analysis within the movement to put Arab relations at the center of concerns.*

Among the difficult questions linked to the idea of the rebirth of our people on its land, there is one question that outweighs all the others: *the question of our attitude toward the Arabs.* This question, upon whose correct solution hangs the revival of our national hope, has not been *forgotten*, but has been completely *hidden* from the Zionists and in its correct form is scarcely mentioned in the literature of our movement. [...] The Zionists certainly did not intentionally ignore one of the main conditions of settlement; they did not recognize its reality because they did not know the country and its inhabitants—and, even more, they lacked human and political sensitivity.

The fact that it was possible to avoid such a fundamental question and that, after thirty years of settlement activity, it must be addressed as a new inquiry—this depressing fact is sufficient demonstration of the superficiality that dominates our movement and shows that we skim over the surface of things without entering into their content or core.

From the day the national movement began, and to this moment, Zionist activists have lost interest in the procedures and laws of Eretz Israel, while the question of the people who dwell there—its true workers and rulers—still does not arise either in the arena of actions or in theory. We all saw the prominent splinter and did not sense the hidden beam. Governmental procedures,

[*] Originally published in *HaShiloah* 17 (1907): 193–206. Abridged version from the translation in Alan Dowty, "'A Question That Outweighs All Others': Yitzhak Epstein and Zionist Recognition of the Arab Issue," *Israel Studies* 6.1 (2001): 34–54.

restrictions imposed on buying land or building houses, the prohibition of Jewish entry and other such matters strike at all who come to Eretz Israel, while from the Arab side there are not, at first glance, many obstacles. And if our brothers in Eretz Israel did not realize the seriousness of the question, it certainly never arose among Zionists far from the scene. We pay close attention to all the affairs of our land, we discuss and debate everything, we praise and curse everything, but we forget one small detail: that there is in our beloved land an entire people that has been attached to it for hundreds of years and has never considered leaving it.

For many years we have heard that the number of inhabitants in Eretz Israel is six hundred thousand. If we assume this number is correct and subtract the eighty thousand Jews, we find that in our land there are now more than half a million Arabs, of whom 80 percent live off the land and occupy all the areas suitable for farming without further improvement. The time has come to dismiss the discredited idea, spread among Zionists, that there is in Eretz Israel uncultivated land as a result of lack of working hands and the indifference of the inhabitants. [...]

We buy the lands, for the most part, from the owners of large estates; these owners, or their predecessors, acquired their land by deceit and exploitation and lease it to the *fellahin* [Arab farmers]. Sometimes we buy it from villages that sell part of their property. The *fellah* who leases land is no stranger to it, but a permanent resident who stays in place; and there are *fellahin* whose grandfathers tilled the fields that they, the grandsons, are leasing. It is customary in Eretz Israel for the estate to pass from one owner to another while the tenants remain in their place. But when we buy such a property, we evict the former tillers from it. To be sure, we do not send them away empty-handed, but we pay them well for their hovels and gardens, and in general we are not stingy with money during "the dismissal." From the viewpoint of customary justice and official honesty we are completely righteous, even beyond the strict letter of the law. But, if we do not want to deceive ourselves with a conventional lie, we must admit that we have driven impoverished people from their humble abode and taken bread out of their mouths. [...] The work that we give to an Arab will never be seen, in his eyes, as indemnity for the field that was taken from him; he will take the good but not forget the bad.

In general we are making a flagrant error in human understanding toward a great, resolute, and zealous people. While we feel the love of homeland, in all its intensity, toward the land of our fathers, we forget that the people living there now also has a feeling heart and a loving soul. The Arab, like any person, is strongly attached to his homeland. [...] The lament of Arab women on the day that their families left Ja'uni—Rosh Pina—to go and settle on the Horan east of the Jordan still rings in my ears today. The men rode on donkeys and the women followed them weeping bitterly, and the valley was filled with their lamentation. As they went they stopped to kiss the stones and the earth.

The question of land purchase can be a problem even when the *fellahin* themselves sell part of the village land. Indeed, in the farmer's distress, crushed [as he is] by the burden of debts that have accumulated when he was forced to pay heavy taxes, he decides, in a moment of desperation (and often in response to urgings of village elders who receive a decent cut), to sell his field; but this sale leaves in his heart a wound that will never heal, and he will always remember the cursed day in which his property fell into alien hands. I knew *fellahin* who, after selling their land, worked together with their wives for the Jews and, given their good wage and low expenses, saved money. So long as they earned a good income they kept their silence, but the moment the work stopped they began to grumble about the Jews and to challenge the land sale.

Can we really rely on this way of acquiring land? Will it succeed, and does it suit our purpose? One hundred times, no. The children of a people that first decreed the principle that "the land will never be sold" and limited the rights of the buyer in favor of the cultivator need not and cannot themselves expropriate their land from cultivators who were innocently settled on it. They cannot uproot from it people who, with their ancestors, devoted to it their utmost vigor and their best labor. If there are farmers who water their fields with their own sweat and their own mother's milk, it is the Arabs. Who can appreciate the toil of a *fellah* plowing in torrential rains, harvesting on a summer day in our country, loading and transporting the produce? And what does he get for his labor? A ramshackle house, lowly and dingy, which serves as a general shelter for his family, his ox, and his donkey, the bread of poverty, a worn-out shirt and cloak—these are his clothes, day and night. And his wife and children— how meager is their portion! From her youth until her final days the Arab woman never stops silently bearing her yoke of heavy labor; she draws the water and sometimes also hews the wood, a beast of burden. With a nursing baby on her shoulders, a bundle in her robe, and a jug of water on her head, she goes to the shearing and to the gleaning and from morning to evening she works bent under the heat of the blazing sun, and upon her return home, with the sun soon to return, immersed in smoke, she bakes the humble bread and boils the thin broth. Yet these we will dispossess, these we will harm, their poverty we will increase?

But let us leave aside for a moment justice and sentimentality and look at the question from the viewpoint of practicality alone. Let us assume for now that in the land of our fathers we need not be concerned with others and that we are permitted—or even also obligated—to buy any land that comes into our hands. Can such a way of buying land last for long? Will those evicted really hold their peace and calmly accept what was done to them? Will they not in the end rise up to take back with their fists what was taken from them by the power of gold? Will they not press their case against the foreigners who drove them from their land? And who knows if they will not then be both the prosecutors and the judges [...] And they are brave, all armed, wonderful marksmen, excellent horsemen, devoted to their nation and in particular to their religion. And this people, as yet untouched by the Enlightenment that enervates men's strength, is only a small part of the great nation that occupies all the surrounding areas: Syria, Mesopotamia, Arabia, and Egypt. [...]

What follows from all this is that, when we come to buy lands in Eretz Israel, we must thoroughly check whose land it is, who works it, and what the rights of the latter are, and we must not complete the purchase until we are certain that no one will be worse off. In this way we will have to forswear most cultivated land. What is left for us, therefore, in our land? Here we reach the critical question to which all the other important questions are secondary: how can we establish ourselves in Eretz Israel without sinning against justice and without harming anyone?

An answer to this question of questions can be found in a basic principle that we must place before ourselves in everything, as a guideline for our undertakings in Eretz Israel: *we come to our land to take possession of what is not already possessed by others, to find what others have not found, to reveal for our benefit and for the happiness of all the inhabitants the hidden wealth under its soil and the concealed blessing in its skies and sun.* Regarding settlement, we will try first of all to acquire all the land that is not being cultivated because it requires improvement that is more or less difficult and expensive. [...]

And above all doubt, after we have made efforts like these in various districts of our land, hundreds of villagers will come to request the Jews to take over their land, and other land buyers in Eretz Israel will not be able to compete with us. Then the government as well will see the great benefit that we have brought to the country's inhabitants, and even our opponents—and they are many—will have to admit that our settling in Eretz Israel brings only benefit. [...]

We must, therefore, enter into a covenant with the Arabs and conclude an agreement that will be of great value to both sides and to all humankind. We will certainly agree to such a covenant, but the agreement of the other side is also necessary; this we will obtain gradually, by means of practical action that benefits the land, us, and the Arabs. In this practical way our neighbors will little by little understand the great blessing that they can derive from the partnership between the Jewish people and the Arab people. Every new factory and every settlement that we found, every public institution that we establish, if we but share the benefit with the residents of Eretz Israel, brings us closer to our goal. Achievement of this living charter, which needs to be inscribed not on paper or on parchment, but on the heart and mind of an entire people, is an

immense undertaking that has no like in the chronicles of humankind's progress and liberation, because its outcome is the rebirth of two ancient Semitic
peoples, talented and full of potential, who complement each other. It must be
admitted that up to now we had the "wrong address"; in order to acquire our
land we turned to all the powers that had some link to it, we negotiated with
all the in-laws but forgot about the groom himself: we ignored the true masters
of the land. Without belittling all those who have an interest in our land, and
particularly in its government, we must deal mostly with the Arab people, and
among them mostly with the *fellahin* faction, which is more straightforward
and more numerous than the other factions. The most important thing we can
do in this regard is to improve the condition of the tenants and the *fellahin* who
live on the lands that we buy. The more we continue to buy land and to benefit
those who work it, the more numerous will be those wanting to sell their land
to us, the more influential we will be in Eretz Israel, and the more recognition
there will be of our beneficence and indispensability.

But also in the cities there we have broad scope for action. Let us open our
public institutions wide to residents of Eretz Israel: hospitals, pharmacies,
libraries, reading rooms, inexpensive restaurants, savings and loan funds; let
us arrange popular lectures, plays, and musical performances to their taste and
in their language; let us give an important place to the Arabic language in our
schools and willingly enroll Arab children in them; let us open our kindergar-
tens to their younger children and in so doing bring great benefit to poor families: an economic, hygienic, but, more importantly, spiritual and moral benefit.
And through the children we will exercise an enormous influence on the
adults. [...]

And when we come to educate our ally and to deal with him, let us not forget
another principle. As a teacher must know his student's inner soul and inclina-
tions, so it is not enough for us to pose the final goal, but we have a duty to
become properly acquainted with the Arab people, their attributes, their incli-
nations, their aspirations, their language, their literature, and especially to
gain a deep understanding of their life, their customs, their sufferings, and
their torments. Let us not make the mistake that has inflicted endless damage
on children's education. For thousands of years educators have seen their
pupils as short adults; that is to say, they saw childhood in the body but not
in the spirit, which, when it confronted the material, was—in the opinion of
educators of old—already sufficiently formed, ready, and prepared and armed
with all the skills to understand, to be educated, and to feel. We are entering
an environment that is now living in the sixteenth century, and we must take
into account in all our actions the spiritual condition of this people at the
moment. If we want to lead a person to a known place, we must take him from
where he is *now*: otherwise he cannot follow us. We need, therefore, to study

the psyche of our neighbors and to understand its differences. It is a disgrace that, to date, *nothing whatsoever has been done in this regard*, that so far not even one Jew has devoted himself to this topic, so that we are *complete illiterates in anything concerning the Arabs* and all of our knowledge about them is folk wisdom. It is time to get smart! [...]

The prophet of exile, when he came to speak on the division of the land, said: "You shall allot it as a heritage for yourselves and for the strangers who reside among you, who have begotten children among you. You shall treat them as Israelite citizens; they will receive allotments along with you among the tribes of Israel. You shall give the stranger an allotment within the tribe where he resides" (Ezekiel 47:22–23). And the great prophet from Anatot, who came before Ezekiel, when he came to prophesy bad tidings for the evil neighbors who were encroaching on Israel's heritage, said at the end: "I will restore them each to his own inheritance and his own land. And if they learn the ways of my people [...] then they shall be built up in the midst of my people" (Jeremiah 12:15–16).

Let us teach them the good ways, let us build them—and we will also be built.

9. "Open Questions"

*Nehama Pukhachewsky**

EDITOR'S NOTE Nehama Pukhachewsky (1869–1934) arrived in the new settlement of Rishon LeTsion in 1889, from Russia. She was active in public life—especially as an early advocate of women's rights and as an author of short stories—and is sometimes described as the first women writer in modern Hebrew literature. When Yosef Klausner, editor of HaShiloah, published Yitzhak Epstein's article (Reading 8), he indicated his disagreement with much of it and promised publication of a rejoinder in the near future. For this he turned to Pukhachewsky, whose views clearly matched his own and who wrote the following critique of Epstein's arguments. This can be seen as the beginning of the debate among Zionists between integration and separation, a debate that remained at the center of Jewish politics in Palestine and Israel.

In Mr. Epstein's article "A Hidden Question," light and darkness are intermingled. It has a great measure of humanity and superior morality, but it is not constructed on those perspectives, the fruit of practical logic that a nation being revived needs, so that it can acquire its land and maintain itself on this land.

Mr. Epstein warns us not to plunder the property of others, but apart from the purchase of Metula—where only the administration [of Baron Edmond de Rothschild] was guilty—there were no dishonest or unjust purchases and, despite the attitude of the *fellahin* [Arab farmers], Mr. Epstein supports the rights of tenants; but, if it is a question of rights, according to who came first, then our rights come first!

Mr. Epstein dwells on the miserable condition of the Arab, and from his words one might conclude that we are guilty for this misfortune—as though we robbed and wronged this poor soul, while even Mr. Epstein knows that it is the government that robs the Arab blind, while the Jews never brought him anything but benefits; because Jewish settlement increased the value of the land, something that no one can deny. Arab villages were strengthened and grew; the *fellah* exchanged his hut for a stone house with a tile roof, after earning so much in the Jewish settlement near his village. The town dwellers

---

* Nehama Pukhachewsky, "She'elot geluyot" ["Open Questions"], *HaShiloah* 18 (1908): 67–69. Translated by the editor.

in the land profited from the impetus that the Jew brought to their commerce; and the various tradesmen also profited greatly from Jewish settlement. And, after all that, someone comes to charge us with exploiting the Arab, and to threaten that in the end we will arouse his hard fist against us for our malicious conduct?

Fear of the fist is still far away for us, and if a day comes when relations with the living Arab also deteriorate, this will not be because of our method of land purchase, but rather the eternal hatred toward a people exiled from its land.

Mr. Epstein warns us not to provoke *a sleeping lion*; what is our provocation? Who sees us provoking malevolence? Indeed neither the *fellah* nor the government deny the benefit that Jewish settlement has brought to the land. And in his heart the *fellah* honors the Jew, who surpasses him in knowledge, and the elders among the *fellahin* believe in an ancient Jewish tradition according to which the Jews will ultimately return to their homeland and become its masters, as in days of old.

Mr. Epstein said, correctly, that it is very hard to buy the love of the Arabs; but if so, why should we toil in vain? There are no lovers of Israel. The more we grovel, the more they hate us; the more we continue to submit and to enslave ourselves, the heavier our yoke and the more they continue to press us. How the people Israel tried to find favor, for example, in the eyes of the Russian people and to buy its love! The best of our sons we sent to slaughter for the freedom of the country's inhabitants, and how did they pay us back? The payback was "generous," whether from the government, the peasant, or even the worker. So please let us abandon this path of defeat and proceed by a straight track to our rebirth; let us begin to think about ourselves, our existence and our happiness.

Mr. Epstein begins his second chapter, once again, with warnings about land purchases; and in this he suggests a condition for purchase that deprives us of any hope of expanding Jewish settlement in line with our potential. Mr. Epstein demands that we only buy lands not already occupied by Arabs and not already cultivated; but these lands—something not known to everyone—will not be of any use, because of their aridity and climate. He expands on the valleys of the Land of Israel, its skies and sun, but apparently did not sense how far this was from giving us even a glimmer of hope. How will we penetrate, with our feeble powers, the *valleys* of the land, if we have no right to acquire what is on the *surface* of the land? And the skies with the sun are tremendous support to the man who works more or less good land; but if we set out to transform the arid and the stony into fertile land, then these two great forces will laugh at us. And if it is possible with the aid of science to transform the arid and the stony into fields of grain and charming vineyards, where are the billions needed for this?

Further on, Mr. Epstein constructs an entire system of "the wolf (or the lion, as he previously called the country's inhabitants) shall dwell with the lamb." But here as well he transcends reality and ignores the limits of what is possible. He says that we need to teach the Arab modern farming methods, to better his situation, to open schools to his children, to impart culture to them; and before I ask wherefrom will come the bountiful means needed for this, I will ask whether *we ourselves* have learned to work the land properly, whether *we* already know how to better our situation; whether we have already founded sufficiently many good schools for our own children. Indeed this is unfinished among us, in every corner we turn to; how can a man of Israel require us now to attend to the material and spiritual development of the Arab? And if these words are meant for "the future yet to come," then the path of *our* development should have been set out *first*.

Mr. Epstein says that the reborn people of Israel should be a brother to every people, that it is coming to life, and therefore also—and especially—to the Arab people; and Mr. Epstein forgot that he had said previously that the Arab people never ceased living for a moment and doesn't require revival. If this is true, how can we unite with the Arabs? We, a people driven from our land, persecuted and hated everywhere, aspire to return to the land of our fathers and to build therein a secure haven; and they live on this land without challenge. Why, then, do they merit our brotherly love, and our mercy, which Mr. Epstein tries to stir in our hearts toward them?

"What we can give to the Arabs, they could not get from any other people." Our fathers in heaven! Why do we always have to just give and give? To this one—the soul, to that one—the body, and to these—the remnant of the hope to live as a free people on its historic homeland!

Out of unbounded idealism, Mr. Epstein forgot the clear lesson taught by experience. He resolves that, if we better the Arab's situation, lift him from his lowly position and create good working conditions for him, he will sell us his land or give us rights of usage. But he does not seem aware that the Arab sells his land only when the government crushes him with taxes until he can no longer bear them, or when the *effendi* squeezes him until he truly has nothing to lose by selling his land. His work is so primitive, so grueling, that it yields him nothing; were it not for the Jewish settlements, which give him work and, consequently, a chance to survive, undoubtedly many villages would have withered away in the last quarter century. But, if we create better living conditions for the Arab, then he will not sell his land for any price. We are being asked to better the Arab's situation so that there will never be a chance for us to acquire the land of our forefathers.

But, even if we become extreme "altruists," do we have the material means to fulfill Mr. Epstein's demands? Because he requires that we uplift the Arabs with all the advances of modern civilization: in public institutions, in schools, in low-cost food shops, in savings institutions, in theater, in songfests—and so on and so on. A lovely program! But have we yet managed to build all these things for *ourselves*, so that we can extend them to others? *We* still have nothing— yet we have among us those who dream of bounties that we will bestow on others!

It is especially disheartening to hear such things about *schools*. Mr. Epstein says that, if we were to understand the value of education in our land, we could compete for educational influence on the Arabs with the French and the Anglo-Americans, who have opened high-level schools for Palestinians and Syrians. Yes, a people that cannot manage *its own* primary schools properly is told to compete in founding universities for others. And this from a dedicated teacher, who has devoted his best days to the children of Israel and knows the sad story of education in this land!

Chapter 3
The Arab Story

Arabs have a pre-Islamic history going back well into biblical times; the earliest mention of Arab tribes, in the Arabian peninsula, is from 853 BCE. But it was the rise of Islam in the seventh century CE and its rapid spread, within a century, from Spain to India that made Arabs and the Arabic language major actors in world history. In the earlier period of this expansion, historical Palestine fell under Muslim rule: Jerusalem was conquered by a Muslim army under the Caliph Umar (successor to Muhammad) in 638 CE. Over the following centuries most of the largely Christian population became Muslim and, as in other core areas of the Islamic world, Arabic became the dominant language.

The intertwining of Arab and Jewish histories is also of ancient origin, though that in itself does not explain the modern conflict. Muhammad's revelations, as recorded in the Quran, dealt at length both with Judaism and Christianity and with their connection to the new faith of Islam. On the one hand, Jews and Christians are regarded as "people of the book," whose right to their own beliefs is protected; on the other hand, there is severe criticism of these beliefs. This ambivalence, inherent in Islam, can be seen in a representative selection of Quranic verses that deal with the Jews (Reading 10).

Another important dimension of Arab history is a long and complicated relationship with the West, that is, with the European Christian world. This was the world from which late nineteenth-century Jewish settlers in Palestine came, and it is therefore an important part of the picture. The crusades, better remembered in the Middle East than in the West, are etched in Arab historical memory and—together with more recent European colonialism—help to explain Arab attitudes toward the West. An early illustration of this claim is the twelfth-century Arab warrior and writer Usamah ibn Munqidh, who expressed Arab and Muslim views on the invaders that remained relevant for centuries afterward (Reading 11).

At the time when the first Zionists began arriving in Palestine, the latter was part of the Ottoman Empire. For centuries, most Arabs had been ruled by their fellow Muslims, the Turks. But, almost simultaneously with the challenge of Jewish nationalism, the first glimmers of Arab nationalism also appeared, as chronicled by George Antonius shortly afterward (Reading 12). The first "text" of Arab nationalism appeared in 1905 and was written by Najib Azuri, who, like Antonius, had experience as a government official in Palestine (Reading 13). For both Antonius and Azuri, the goal of Arab statehood ran counter to the Jewish program for statehood in the same territory. The reader will ask: could it have been otherwise?

Further illustration of the evolution of Arab thinking, namely on the eve of World War I, is provided by the diaries of Khalil as-Sakakini, a Palestinian educator (Reading 14). By this time the Zionist presence in Palestine was much more visible than it had been when the first wave of Jewish immigrants arrived 30 years earlier. Sakakini also demonstrates the appeal of Arab nationalism among western-oriented Arab intellectuals, many of them Christian, who saw it as a force that could counter both Muslim revivalism and European imperialism.

Further online resources:

Pact of Umar, seventh century: https://sourcebooks.fordham.edu/source/pact-umar. asp.

Sheikh Hasan al-Kafrawi, "The Status of Jews and Christians in Muslim Lands," 1772: https://sourcebooks.fordham.edu/jewish/1772-jewsinislam.asp.

Beshara Doumani, "Rediscovering Ottoman Palestine: Writing Palestinians into History," *Journal of Palestine Studies* 21.2 (1992): 5–28. doi: 10.2307/2537216.

Yuval Ben-Bassat, "Translation of 10 Petitions Sent to Istanbul from Ottoman Palestine": https://www.academia.edu/24210326/Translation_of_10_petitions_sent_to _Istanbul_from_Ottoman_Palestine.

Ibrahim al-Yaziji, "Awake! Arab Be Awake" (nationalist poem), 1868: https:// www.poemhunter.com/poem/awake-arab-be-awake.

Emanuel Beška, "Responses of Prominent Arabs towards Zionist Aspirations and Colonization prior to 1908," *Asian and African Studies* 16.1 (2002): 22–44.

The Young Turks: Proclamation for the Ottoman Empire, 1908: https:// sourcebooks.fordham.edu/mod/1908youngturk.asp.

Hasan Kayali, *Arabs and Young Turks: Ottomanism, Arabism, and Islamism in the Ottoman Empire, 1908–1018* (Berkeley: University of California Press, 1997): publishing.cdlib .org/ucpressebooks/view?docId=ft7n39p1dn&brand=u.

10. References to Jews in the Quran*

EDITOR'S NOTE The Quran (lit. Recital) is a collection of revelations in the voice of God, conveyed orally by the prophet Muhammad and transcribed into an authoritative written version soon after his death in 632 CE. It is divided into 114 chapters (suras). Those reading the Quran for the first time are often struck by the number of familiar names and events from Jewish and Christian scriptures: clearly Muhammad was conversant with these monotheistic faiths and saw his own message as a completion of theirs. Relations with Jews and Judaism were therefore a central focus in Islam from the outset. But those who look for a simple guide to this relationship in the Quran itself will not find it. The attitude is neither uniformly hostile nor uniformly sympathetic. Like all religions, Islam has room for ambivalence and disputed interpretations. The reader will have to ask which verses seem to support a particular interpretation and which ones lend support to seemingly contradictory readings.

2.40: Children of Israel! Call to mind the (special) favor which I bestowed upon you and fulfill your Covenant with Me as I fulfill My Covenant with you, and fear none but Me.

2.47: Children of Israel! Call to mind the (special) favor which I bestowed on you, and that I preferred you to all others.

2.62: Those who believe and those who follow Jewish scriptures and the Christians and the Sabians—any who believe in God and the Last Day, and work righteousness, shall have their reward with their Lord: on them shall be no fear, nor shall they grieve.

2.83: And remember We took a Covenant from the Children of Israel: worship none but God; treat with kindness your parents and kindred, and orphans and those in need; speak fair to the people; be steadfast in prayer; and practice regular charity. Then did ye turn back, except a few among you, and ye backslide even now.

2.120: Never will the Jews or the Christians be satisfied with thee unless thou follow their form of religion. Say: "The Guidance of God—that is the only

---

* Selected verses from *The Holy Qur'an*, translated by Abdullah Yusuf Ali (Elmhurst, NY: Tahrike Tarsile Qur'an), 2001.

Guidance." Wert thou to follow their desires after the knowledge which hath reached thee, then wouldst thou find neither Protector nor Helper against God.

2.12: Those to whom We have sent the Book study it as it should be studied: they are the ones that believe therein: those who reject faith therein—the loss is their own.

2.211: Ask the Children of Israel how many clear signs we have sent them. But if any one after God's favor has come to him, substitutes something else, God is strict in punishment.

3.67: Abraham was not a Jew nor yet a Christian. But he was true in Faith, and bowed his will to God's, which is Islam, and he joined not gods with God.

4.47: O ye People of the Book! Believe in what We have revealed, confirming what was with you, before We change the face and fame of some beyond recognition, and turn them hindwards, or curse them as We cursed the Sabbath breakers, for the decision of God must be carried out.

4.160: For the iniquity of the Jews, we made unlawful for them certain foods good and wholesome which had been lawful for them—in that they hindered many from God's Way.

5.12: God did aforetime take a Covenant from the Children of Israel, and We appointed twelve Captains among them. And God said: "I am with you: if ye establish regular Prayers, practice regular Charity, believe in My apostles, honor and assist them, and loan to God a beautiful loan, verily I will wipe out from you your evils and admit you to Gardens with rivers flowing beneath; but if any of you, after this, resisteth faith, he hath truly wandered from the path of rectitude."

5.13: But because of their breach of their Covenant, We cursed them, and made their hearts grow hard: they change the words from their right places and forget a good part of the Message that was sent them, nor wilt thou cease to find them—barring a few—ever bent on new deceits: but I forgive them, and overlook their misdeeds: for God loveth those who are kind.

5.32: On that account: We ordained for the Children of Israel that, if any one slew a person—unless it be for murder or for spreading mischief in the land—it would be as if he slew the whole people. And if anyone saved a life, it would be as if he saved the life of the whole people. Then, although there came to them Our Apostles with Clear Signs, yet, even after that, many of them continued to commit excesses in the land.

5.33: The punishment of those who wage war against God and His Apostle, and strive with might and main for mischief through the land, is: execution, or crucifixion, or the cutting off of hands and feet from opposite sides, or exile from the land: that is their disgrace in this world, and a heavy punishment is theirs in the Hereafter.

5.44: It was We who revealed the Law to Moses; therein was guidance and light. By its standard have been judged the Jews, by the Prophets who bowed as in Islam to God's Will, by the Rabbis and the Doctors of Law: for to them was entrusted the protection of God's Book, and they were witnesses thereto: therfore fear not men, but fear Me, and sell not My Signs for a miserable price. If any do fail to judge by the light of what God hath revealed, they are no better than Unbelievers.

5.51: O ye who believe! Take not the Jews and the Christians for your friends and protectors: they are but friends and protectors to each other. And he among you that turns to them for friendship is of them. Verily God guideth not a people unjust.

5.59: Say: "O People of the Book! Do ye disapprove of us for no other reason that that we believe in God, and the revelation that hath come to us and that which came before, and that most of you are rebellious and disobedient?"

5.69: Those who believe, those who follow the Jewish scriptures, and the Sabians and the Christians—any who believe in God and the Last Day, and work righteousness—on them shall be no fear, nor shall they grieve.

5.72: They do blaspheme who say: "God is Christ the son of Mary." But said Christ: "O Children of Israel! Worship God, my Lord and your Lord." Whoever joins other gods with God—God will forbid him the Garden, and the Fire will be his abode. There will, for the wrongdoers, be no one to help.

5.73: They do blaspheme who say: God is one of three in a Trinity: for there is no god except One God. If they desist not from their word, verily a grievous penalty will befall the blasphemers among them.

5.78: Curses were pronounced on those among the Children of Israel who rejected Faith, by the tongue of David and of Jesus the son of Mary: because they disobeyed and persisted in Excesses.

5.82: Strongest among men in enmity to the Believers wilt thou find the Jews and Pagans; and nearest among them in love to the Believers wilt thou find those who say, "We are Christians": because among these are men devoted to learning and men who have renounced the world, and they are not arrogant.

7.137: And We made a people, considered weak, inheritors of lands in both East and West—lands whereon We sent down Our blessings. The fair promise of thy Lord was fulfilled for the Children of Israel, because they had patience and constancy, and We levelled to the ground the great Works and fine Buildings which Pharaoh and his people erected.

9.30: The Jews call Uzair [Ezra] a son of God, and the Christians call Christ the Son of God. That is a saying from their mouth; in this they but imitate what the Unbelievers of old used to say. God's curse be on them: how they are deluded away from the Truth!

17.4: And We gave warning to the Children of Israel in the Book, that twice would they do mischief on the earth and be elated with mighty arrogance and twice would they be punished.

17.5: When the first of the warnings came to pass, we sent against you Our servants given to terrible warfare: they entered the very inmost parts of your homes: and it was a warning fulfilled.

17.6: Then did We grant you the Return as against them: we gave you increase in resources and sons, and made you the more numerous in manpower.

17.7: If ye did well, ye did well for yourselves; if you did evil, ye did it against yourselves. So when the second of the warning came to pass, we permitted your enemies to disfigure your faces, and to enter your Temple as they had entered it before, and to visit with destruction all that fell into their power.

17.104: And We said thereafter to the Children of Israel, "Dwell securely in the land": but when the second of the warnings came to pass, We gathered you together in a mingled crowd.

61.6: And remember, Jesus, the son of Mary, said: "O Children of Israel! I am the apostle of God sent to you, confirming the Law which came before me, and giving Glad Tidings of an Apostle to come after me, whose name shall be Ahmad [Muhammad]." But when he came to them with Clear Signs, they said, "This is evident sorcery!"

61.14: O ye who believe! Be ye helpers of God: as said Jesus the son of Mary to the Disciples, "Who will be my helpers in the work of God?" Said the Disciples, "We are God's helpers!" Then a portion of the Children of Israel believed, and a portion disbelieved; but we gave power to whose who believed, against their enemies, and they became the ones that prevailed.

11. "On the Franks"

Usamah ibn Munqidh[*]

Editor's Note Usamah ibn Munqidh (1095–1188) was a Muslim poet, author, knight, and official who served various rulers, including Saladin, during the period of crusader states after the First Crusade. Born in what is now Syria, he spent much time in Palestine, where he was able to observe the Franks—the label applied by Muslims to all European crusaders. Usamah published his observations around 1175, in the Book of Contemplation, which survived in a single manuscript that was rediscovered in the nineteenth century. His comments on the crusaders whom he encountered convey a sense of how Europeans were seen at the time by educated natives of the Middle East.

Their lack of sense. Mysterious are the works of the Creator, the author of all things! When one comes to recount cases regarding the Franks, he cannot but glorify Allah (exalted is he!) and sanctify him, for he sees them as animals possessing the virtues of courage and fighting, but nothing else; just as animals have only the virtues of strength and carrying loads. I shall now give some instances of their doings and their curious mentality.

In the army of King Fulk, son of Fulk, was a Frankish reverend knight who had just arrived from their land in order to make the holy pilgrimage and then return home. He was of my intimate fellowship and kept such constant company with me that he began to call me "my brother." Between us were mutual bonds of amity and friendship. When he resolved to return by sea to his homeland, he said to me: "My brother, I am leaving for my country and I want you to send with me thy son (my son, who was then fourteen years old, was at that time in my company) to our country, where he can see the knights and learn wisdom and chivalry. When he returns, he will be like a wise man."

Thus there fell upon my ears words which would never come out of the head of a sensible man; for even if my son were to be taken captive, his captivity could not bring him a worse misfortune than carrying him into the lands of the Franks. However, I said to the man: "By thy life, this has exactly been my idea. But the only thing that prevented me from carrying it out was the fact that his grandmother, my mother, is so fond of him and did not this time let

[*] Excerpts from Usamah ibn-Munqidh, *Memoirs of an Arab-Syrian Gentleman: Memoirs of Usamah ibn-Munqidh*, trans. Philip K. Hitti (New York: Columbia University Press, 2000), pp. 161–70.

him come out with me until she exacted an oath from me to the effect that I would return him to her." Thereupon he asked, "Is thy mother still alive?" "Yes." I replied. "Well," said he, "disobey her not." [...]

Franks lack jealousy in sex affairs. The Franks are void of all zeal and jealousy. One of them may be walking along with his wife. He meets another man who takes the wife by the hand and steps aside to converse with her while the husband is standing on one side waiting for his wife to conclude the conversation. If she lingers too long for him, he leaves her alone with the conversant and goes away. Here is an illustration which I myself witnessed.

When I used to visit Nablus, I always took lodging with a man named Mu'izz, whose home was a lodging house for the Muslims. The house had windows which opened to the road, and there stood opposite to it on the other side of the road a house belonging to a Frank who sold wine for the merchants. He would take some wine in a bottle and go around announcing it by shouting: "So and so, the merchant, has just opened a cask full of this wine. He who wants to buy some of it will find it in such and such a place." The Frank's pay[ment] for the announcement made would be the wine in that bottle. One day this Frank went home and found a man with his wife in the same bed. He asked him: "What could have made you enter into my wife's room?" The man replied: "I was tired, so I went in to rest." "But how," asked he, "didst thou get into my bed?" The other replied: "I found a bed that was spread, so I slept in it." "But," said be, "my wife was sleeping together with you!" The other replied: "Well, the bed is hers. How could I therefore have prevented her from using her own bed?"

"By the truth of my religion," said the husband, "if thou shouldst do it again, thou and I would have a quarrel." Such was for the Frank the entire expression of his disapproval and the limit of his jealousy. [...]

Another illustration. [...] I entered the public bath in Sur [Tyre] and took my place in a secluded part. One of my servants thereupon said to me: "There is with us in the bath a woman." When I went out, I sat on one of the stone benches and behold! the woman who was in the bath had come out all dressed and was standing with her father just opposite me. But I could not be sure that she was a woman. So I said to one of my companions: "By Allah, see if this is a woman"—by which I meant that he should ask about her. But he went, as I was looking at him, lifted the end of her robe and looked carefully at her. Thereupon her father turned toward me and said: "This is my daughter. Her mother is dead and she has nobody to wash her hair. So I took her in with me to the bath and washed her head." I replied: "Thou hast well done! This is something for which thou shalt be rewarded [by Allah]!" [...]

Ordeal by water. I once went in the company of al-Amir Mu'in-al-Din (may Allah's mercy rest upon his soul!) to Jerusalem. We stopped at Nablus. There a blind man, a Muslim, who was still young and was well dressed, presented himself before al-Amir carrying fruits for him and asked permission to be admitted into his service in Damascus. The Amir consented. I inquired about this man and was informed that his mother bad been married to a Frank whom she had killed. Her son used to practice ruses against the Frankish pilgrims and cooperate with his mother in assassinating them. They finally brought charges against him and tried his case according to the Frankish way of procedure.

They installed a huge cask and filled it with water. Across it they set a board of wood. They then bound the arms of the man charged with the act, tied a rope around his shoulders and dropped him into the cask, their idea being that, in case he was innocent, he would sink in the water and they would then lift him up with the rope so that he might not die in the water; and in case he was guilty, he would not sink in the water. This man did his best to sink when they dropped him into the water, but he could not do it. So he had to submit to their sentence against him—may Allah's curse be upon them! They pierced his eyeballs with red-hot awls. [...]

Among the Franks are those who have become acclimatized and have associated long with the Muslims. These are much better than the recent comers from the Frankish lands. But they constitute the exception and cannot be treated as a rule.

Here is an illustration. I dispatched one of my men to Antioch on business. There was in Antioch at that time al-Ra'is Theodoros Sophianos, to whom I was bound by mutual ties of amity. His influence in Antioch was supreme. One day he said to my man: "I am invited by a friend of mine who is a Frank. Thou shouldst come with me so that thou mayest see their fashions." My man related the story in the following words:

> I went along with him and we came to the home of a knight who belonged to the old category of knights who came with the early expeditions of the Franks. He had been by that time stricken off the register and exempted from service, and possessed in Antioch an estate on the income of which he lived. The knight presented an excellent table, with food extraordinarily clean and delicious. Seeing me abstaining from food, he said: "Eat, be of good cheer! I never eat Frankish dishes, but I have Egyptian women cooks and never eat except their cooking. Besides, pork never enters my home." I ate, but guardedly, and after that we departed.

12. The Arab Awakening

*George Antonius**

Editor's Note George Antonius (1891–1942) was a Lebanese-born Orthodox Christian Arab who served in a senior position in the British Mandate of Palestine during the 1920s. A graduate of Cambridge University, he later gained a reputation as the first scholar of Arab nationalism. His 1938 book The Arab Awakening *was his major work, based on his research in the earliest sources of Arab nationalism in the late nineteenth century. As the first definitive statement on the movement's origins, the book assumed great importance as a key document at a pivotal moment in its history, functioning practically as a primary source in its own right.*

The first organised effort in the Arab national movement can be traced back to the year 1875—two years before Abdul-Hamid's accession—when five young men who had been educated at the Syrian Protestant College in Bairut formed a secret society. They were all Christians, but they saw the importance of getting Moslems and Druzes to join, and managed after some time to enlist the membership of some twenty-two persons belonging to the different creeds and representing the enlightened elite of the country. [...]

The centre of their organization was Bairut, and they established branches in Damascus, Tripoli, and Sidon. Their aims being frankly revolutionary, they could scarcely indulge in any of the pleasures of publicity, and their procedure was at first entirely confined to secret meetings at which they would exchange views and discuss plans, and to the dissemination of their political ideas through personal channels. At last, after three or four years of whispered conspiracy, they realised that to continue preaching to themselves would serve only to increase their own ardour, and they decided to broaden their appeal. The method they chose—the only one open to them under a vigilant Turkish bureaucracy—was that of posting anonymous placards in the streets.

Once this decision was taken, they set to work with the agility of youthful conspirators. Having drafted the text of an appeal, they would spend long nightly vigils making out innumerable copies of it in disguised handwritings. Then, at an agreed hour at dead of night, the younger members would go out,

---

* Excerpts from George Antonius, *The Arab Awakening* (London: Hamish Hamilton, 1938).

with pots of glue in their pockets, and stick as many placards as they found time for on the walls of the city. In the morning, a crowd would collect around each poster while someone read it out aloud, until the police would come, tear it down, and make arrests among the innocent bystanders. Before the excitement had died down in Bairut, reports would come in of the appearance of similar placards in Damascus, Tripoli, or Sidon. Their contents furnished a topic of hushed conversation at private gatherings; and the members of the society, carefully guarding their secret, would circulate among their friends and acquaintances, take part in the discussions, and inwardly note the comments. They would then compose their next appeal in the light of the effect caused by the last. By a refinement of the art of disguise, they varied the style and literary standard of their compositions, and committed deliberate errors of grammar, thus rendering conjecture as to authorship still more uncertain.

The placards contained violent denunciations of the evils of Turkish rule, and exhorted the Arab population to rise in rebellion and overthrow it. The authorities, in Constantinople as well as in Syria, were puzzled and perturbed, and the Sultan despatched secret emissaries of his own to Bairut to investigate. Houses were searched and a number of people imprisoned on suspicion. Rumour had it that the Governor-General of Syria, who was none other than Midhat Pasha, the former Grand Vizir and author of the Constitution of 1876, was privy to the existence of the society and, if he had not actually created it, was at any rate shielding it. The intention was even assigned to him of wishing to foment trouble in Syria in the hope of wresting it from the Sultan's rule and, like Mehemed Ali in Egypt, founding a dynasty of his own. The available evidence can hardly support this accusation. Yet such was the effervescence caused by the proclamations of the Bairut society that the Sultan recalled Midhat. It is pretty certain that he was innocent of any connection with it. The society remained in existence for three or four years after his recall, until the weight of Abdul-Hamid's tyranny became so heavy that it was thought prudent to suspend its activities. Its scanty records were destroyed, and several of its most active members emigrated to Egypt. The secret was well kept to the end, and the identity of the conspirators was never known to the government or to the public. [...]

The programme announced in the third of its placards stands out as a model for those which came later. It is the first statement of political aims of which there is any record in the history of the movement, and it merits attention as the only document of the period that provides us with an authentic picture of the nature and the tendencies of Arab nationalism in its earliest days. [...]

The first plank in that programme aims at the achievement of independence based upon the unity of Syria and the Lebanon. The special regime of local autonomy established in the Lebanon by the *Règlement organique* of 1864 had endowed that province with an administration of its own, which had virtually detached it, in point of political structure, from the rest of Syria. Whatever its beneficial effects in other directions may have been, this disseverance was altogether hostile to the spirit of Arab revival, to its hatred of barriers and divisions, and to its fervent belief in the virtues of unison and concord, which it regarded as the principle of salvation. The fact that the Arab character, with its strongly individualistic strain, was conspicuously deficient in those virtues and had proved an easy prey to the dangers of clannishness and faction gave added stimulus to the zeal of the leaders in extolling their merits. In the Bairut programme, the emphasis put upon the community of interests and the political identity of the Lebanon with the rest of Syria was only the natural reflection of that revulsion against the mere idea of partition and separation. Here, too, is the root of the idea of Arab unity, which, spreading outward from Syria, has embraced the whole of the Arab nationalist world and taken a place in the forefront of Arab aspirations. It was in the pursuit of that idea as it bore on the problem of Syria that the authors of the programme of 1880 adopted, for the first time on record, the plank of an independent state embodying the national (as against the sectarian) concept of a political entity.

In the same way, the second point in the programme is the direct reflection of the earliest phases of the revival, namely the rehabilitation of Arabic as a medium of literary expression and the campaign against ignorance and fanaticism. From 1864 onwards, as the policy of greater centralisation in the Ottoman Empire developed, the use of Turkish as the language of government became more widely imposed in Syria. The higher officials were all Turks, and the majority of them totally unacquainted with Arabic. The business of administration, in the law courts and the principal public services, was conducted in Turkish; and [...] that language, which had remained a foreign tongue despite centuries of Ottoman sovereignty, was now becoming an indispensable medium for official transactions. This change was taking place at a time when, as we have seen, the educational efforts of the foreign missions and the activities of scholars who were resuscitating the forgotten culture of the past had led to the regeneration of Arabic as a vehicle of thought and to a vigorous movement of literary and scientific production in the national language. The spreading imposition of Turkish ran counter to this movement and wounded the pride of its enthusiastic adherents. Nor was this all: there was also the censorship, introduced by Abdul-Hamid soon after the suspension of the constitution, which was gradually growing in severity and stupidity, extending its withering hand to ban foreign books as well as stifle local expression. To none could such shackles appear more galling than to the members of the Bairut secret society, with its varied membership of scientists and men of letters. [...] Like their appeal for unity, their plea for language and intellectual freedom was but the echo of the impassioned doctrines of their masters and was destined, likewise, to be the battle-cry of the coming generations.

Unlike the first two, the third point in the programme deals with a matter of incidental rather than fundamental origin. It was a protest against the newly introduced practice of detailing the Arab troops recruited in Syria to fight the Arabs of the Yaman. The reconquest of that province by the Ottoman forces in 1872 had opened a long and costly chapter of enmity between Turk and Arab, and the imperial troops in occupation of it could scarcely, from the very start, hold their own against a hostile population. It was thought that regiments formed of Arab troops might meet with less determined resistance, and orders were issued to draft the conscripts enlisted in Syria for service in the peninsula. The first batch, amounting to several thousands, had been forcibly embarked in 1874 amid general consternation. Three years later, battalions recruited in Syria had been despatched to the theatres of the Russo-Turkish War, to fight for a cause with which they had not the remotest connexion.

The publication of the programme was the outward climax of the society's activities. It[1] continued to exist over the next three or four years and, according to oral report, it issued further appeals. But, of these, no trace has yet come to light; and in any case, on the testimony of one of the society's founders, they did not add materially to the earlier ones. The agitation had served its main purpose: to translate racial sentiment into a political creed, and in doing so had not merely unfurled a flag, but, what was more needed still, had set an arrow to point the way.

---

[1] Presumably the society is meant here.

13. The Awakening of the Arab Nation

Najib Azuri*

EDITOR'S NOTE *Najib Azuri (1873–1916) was a Maronite Christian Arab, born in what is now Lebanon, who worked from 1898 as an official for the Ottoman governor of Jerusalem. Falling out with the Ottomans, in 1904 he fled Jerusalem for Cairo and then went to Paris, publishing harsh denunciations of Turkish rule. For this Azuri was condemned to death in absentia. He also tried to organize a movement for an independent Arab state, publishing Le Réveil de la nation arabe [The Awakening of the Arab Nation] in 1905. The book was written in French; its principal thrust is an appeal to western nations—France in particular—to support the Arabs against the Turks. Nevertheless, it is usually considered to be the first serious text of modern Arab nationalism. Reflecting Azuri's experience in Palestine, it also features highly negative observations on early Zionist activity and on Jews as a people. This is the focus of the passages quoted here.*

We advise the reader that this volume is also intended to complement another, more extensive work that we will soon publish under the title *The Universal Jewish Peril: Revelations and Political Studies* [...]. We therefore urge the public to read both, if they wish to know in depth the advantages that the awakening of nationalities in the Ottoman Empire will confer on Europe.

One might ask how we have been impelled to speak of the Jews in a political book on the Asian component of the Eastern Question. It is because our movement comes at the very moment when Israel is so close to success, in order to defeat its projects of universal domination.

In order to facilitate awareness of "the Jewish Peril," as well as to spare our readers a lengthy description of Arab countries, in this book we will look only at the detailed geography of Palestine, which constitutes a miniature version of the future Arab empire. [...]

Two important phenomena, of the same nature yet opposed, which have not yet attracted anyone's attention, are evident at this moment in Asian Turkey: these are the awakening of the Arab nation and the veiled effort of Jews to reconstitute, on a very large scale, the ancient monarchy of Israel. These two

* Excerpts from Negib Azouri [Najib Azuri], *Le Réveil de la nation arabe dans l'Asie turque* (Paris: no publisher listed, 1905). Translated by the editor.

movements are destined to fight continually until one vanquishes the other. The fate of the entire world will depend on the final outcome of this battle between these two peoples, which represent two contrary principles. What is more, this is not the first time that Europe's interests in the Mediterranean are stirred up in Arab countries; because this territory, which connects three continents and three seas, has at different times been a stage where political or religious events have taken place that altered the course and destiny of the universe. [...]

The Palestine that Jews want to reconstitute today would be much larger than what they possessed in different phases of their historical existence. Neither during the time of Joshua nor under the monarchy of David and Solomon were the Jews able to gain control of the natural borders of the country in order to block conquerors and invaders. Even in the period of the two kings, Palestine never sheltered in its bosom a single people, one that spoke the same language, had the same historical origins, professed the same beliefs, and practiced the same customs, because the Jews could not exterminate or enslave the diverse nations dwelling in the Jordan Valley and in the land of Canaan. The Philistines occupied the coastal plain that extends from the Oja [Yarkon] River to Gaza; the Amalekites, the Idumeans, and the Midianites lived in the fertile plateau between Gaza, Beersheba, the southern point of the Dead Sea, and the Suez Isthmus; the Edomites, the Amorites, and the Hivites occupied the magnificent Transjordanian plateau from Mount Hermon to the Sinai desert; and the Canaanites cultivated the entire coastal plain from the Oja River to the Leontes [Litani] River in the north, with the best part of the Plain of Esdrelon [Jezre'el Valley]. The Israelites did not succeed in assimilating these peoples or in living in peace with them, but were always on guard against one or another. The dozen tribes of Israel, collectively, never outnumbered any one of the races among which they were situated; and each of these peoples in turn subjected the Jews to its domination. The fact that neither the Jews were able to assimilate these different nations nor they to absorb the Jews shows that they were all equal in terms of civilization. Thus, apart from the religious issue, the Jews are no more interesting for a historian than any nomadic tribe: the Amalekites or the Moabites, for example.

In the end, the Jews possessed in Palestine only the west bank of the Jordan and the mountain range that extends west of the river, from Hebron to Lake Hula. However, the Bible shows us that, even in this part of the country, Jews were mixed with considerable numbers of Canaanites.

Palestine was therefore exposed everywhere to foreign invasions; coming from the north, conquerors could penetrate through the Jordan Valley or on the Mediterranean coast, since from the two sides they could be sure of finding allies among indigenous populations who detested the Jews. Armies of the south had only to undertake a campaign against Israel to obtain from the Amalekites and the Idumeans, mortal enemies of the Jews, all indispensable support for crossing the desert. This state of affairs explains perfectly the frequent incursions of the Egyptians, Syrians, and Assyrians into Palestine. Nor did the Jews enjoy peace of mind on their eastern front: the various peoples of the plateau joined together on occasion, to launch raids on the people of Israel. But these pillagers were not very dangerous, thanks to the quarrels that divided them and the natural barriers that separated them from the Jews: the Jordan and the Dead Sea. Moreover, on the east bank of the river the Jews had an avant-garde composed of the tribes of Reuben, Gad, and Manasses, which settled there. Perhaps if the Jews had known how to absorb the Canaanite races and extend their borders to Mount Hermon and the Leontes Valley while establishing an avant-garde to occupy Coelo-Syria [the Beqaa Valley] up to Sidon, and if they had less corruption and internal disorder and more loyalty and wisdom in their relations with northern and southern neighbors, they would still exist today as an independent kingdom, and they might even have thwarted the flowering of Christianity.

The Jews of our time have understood perfectly well the faults of their ancestors; they also are seeking carefully to avoid them in the reconstitution of their ancient homeland, by acquiring the part of Palestine that their forefathers were never able to occupy, and above all by gaining control of the natural borders of the country; these are the two most important points in the Zionist plan of action.

For them, these natural borders are Mount Hermon, which encloses the sources of the Jordan and the Leontes Valley of the north, with the territory between Rashaya and Saida [Sidon] for an avant-garde; the Suez Canal and the Sinai Peninsula to the south; the Arabian Desert to the east; and the Mediterranean to the west. Thus constructed, Palestine becomes an impregnable country in the hands of a people who knows how to defend it.

14. "My View of Zionism"

Khalil as-Sakakini*

EDITOR'S NOTE Khalil as-Sakakini (1878–1953) was a Palestinian Christian educator, literary figure, and early supporter of Arab nationalism. He is primarily known through his
voluminous diaries, which cover the period 1907–1952 and were published after his death.
The diaries reveal a complex dialogue between Sakakini's appreciation of western culture
and his support of Arab independence and unity. They also demonstrate the strong and
consistent opposition to Jewish settlement in Palestine that was a central part of his public
activities. The following selections from the diaries, near the end of the Ottoman era, represent the thinking of many in the Palestinian Arab intellectual elite, even among those
attracted to European ideals and even when Jewish settlement was still on a relatively
small scale.

Tuesday, February 17, 1914

I went downtown and saw that the Jews were preparing to receive Rothschild.
Many of them were standing in front of the Katz Hotel, from which Rothschild
would depart for the train station. Schoolchildren came out with flags to greet
him at the station. But I did not see in this spectacle anything encouraging or
worth watching. The Arab world needs someone like Rothschild, who would
spend money for its revival.

Despite the despair that seizes me sometimes regarding the success of the
Arab nation, and despite the decreased honor that I see in belonging to it, I
cannot be other than nationalistic. To the contrary: I prefer to belong to the
nation even in its current decline, and not to lack citizenship and be deprived
of any nationality. It's true that mankind is marching toward unity and that
national and religious differences will sooner or later disappear. But, so long
as the nation takes pride in its nationality, works to better its condition, creates
for itself hopes that fill its horizon, rules over its emotions, stirs its hearts, and
arouses its spirit, I cannot be indifferent to my nation, even in its stagnation.

* Excerpts from Khalil as-Sakakini, Yawmiyat Khalil as-Sakakini: Yawmiyat, Rasa'il, wa-Ta' amulat
[Diaries of Khalil as-Sakakini: Diaries, Letters, and Thoughts], vol. 2: 1914–1918, ed. Akram Musallem
(Ramallah: Khalil Sakakini Center and the Institute of Palestine Studies, 2004), pp. 55–57,
61–61, 66. Translated by the editor.

More than that: if I were the heir of a noble nationality, such as English, French, or American, I would devote my life to furthering the Arab nation, I would invest efforts to arouse it so that it would catch up with other nations. Because it is not right that some nations will rise to the peak of glory while others descend to the depths of humiliation and disgrace.

If I hate the Zionist movement, it is only because it is building its existence and its independence on the ruins of others. I wonder only about the Ottoman government, which sees this and does nothing, and about the European governments that try to get rid of the Jews at the expense of others. I am not opposed to the Jewish nation's striving for its independent existence; to the contrary, I commend every dispersed and depressed nation to stir itself and become free; but I oppose the precept on which the movement arose, which was to bring down another in order for it to hold its head high, to destroy an entire nation in order to live. In doing so, it is as if it tries to take its independence by theft and deceit, from the hands of time. This is no wonder, since it is its way in all matters and what made it hated and scorned by all nations. What's so special if it achieves its independence this way? What's more, this independence, achieved with money and by exploiting the inertia of other nations, their weakness and frailty, is nothing but a weak independence, built on sand. What will the Jews do if the national spirit awakens in the Arab nation? Will they be able to hold on against it? [...]

Monday, February 23, 1914

I went to the Fast Hotel to teach my student—Mr. Ivri is his name and he is a Jew. Today we immediately took up the subject of Zionism.

I said to him: "If I work for the Arab nation and dedicate myself to its service, I do not do that because I hate other nations or because I put the Arab nation ahead of others, but because this is my duty, first of all as one of the sons of this nation and, secondly, as one of the sons of mankind. And if I hate Zionism, I do not do so because I am opposed to the Jewish nation's revival and escape from the pit of misery and the depths of weakness, but because I hate the precept upon which the Zionist movement stands: it tries to build its nationhood on the ruins of another. Because conquering Palestine is like conquering the heart of the Arab nation, since Palestine is the link connecting the Arabian peninsula to Egypt and Africa; and, if the Jews conquer it, they will separate the Arab nation and even divide it into two parts with no link between them, and this will weaken the Arab cause and block the unity of the nation and its solidarity."

He said: "The Arab nation need not fear this, because no more than two or three hundred thousand will immigrate to Palestine. The idea of founding a Jewish nation in Palestine is dead, because Jews know that the land will not be sufficient."

I said: "In that case, what's the point of two or three hundred thousand coming to Palestine?"

He said: "The aim is cultural and spiritual: the world needs a new Torah. The Jews who come to this land come only because a religious and spiritual force drives them; if they come to the land of their forefathers and take shelter under the skies of the prophets, a holy one such as Moses or Jesus or Muhammad will appear among them, and he will shake the world and will add pages of glory to the chronicles of history."

I said: "This is not an era of prophets."

He said: "There is no difference between this era and past ones. There were splendid cultures already in the past, sages and philosophers and poets, and prophets appeared; and they were not men of wisdom or philosophy, and not men of power and authority either, but their power was great by virtue of their spirit and their character, and they overcame everything."

I said: "If the prophet is the one who brings a new idea to the world, the one who guides the world to a new way of life, the one who reduces the misery, the one who expands human knowledge, the one who opens eyes, the one who arouses the nations and leads them to progress and prosperity, the one who eases their agony, the one who gives them vital force—if so, then there are many prophets in our age and they have many Torahs and covenants. It is not important that a person arises whom public opinion follows because of his knowledge or his smooth tongue, or because of his spiritual power or his excellent character—since such a thing is not impossible or far from reality; what's important is: will he lead them forward or not? Moreover, not everyone needs a prophet, and there are nations that need one more than others. The prophecy will not come from above, but rather people will get it from one another, and the prophet of the East will get the vital prophecy from the West and will pass it on to his people. It seems to me that you, the Jews, are the people most in need of a Torah, but I fear that the fate of the prophet among you will be like the fate of his predecessors, whom you burned and killed. And your condition in this age will be as it was in all eras: the prophets and the Torah come from you, but not to you. If you feel that you need a new Torah, you need to obtain it from your fellow man; if you are fading stars, you need to search for your sun and move around it; you are a star that has faded, and you must not wait for the whole world, with its suns and moons, to revolve around you."

Afterward we spoke about nationalism, and I said to him: "The world marches toward unity. From many small pieces multinational bodies will be built, and nations and languages will decline. And perhaps one of these large bodies will prevail over the others and will swallow them, and then there will be only one nation in the world. This is better for mankind, because people will be brothers, and wars and quarrels among them will decrease. Every person should help to achieve this outcome." [...]

Saturday, February 28, 1914

At 7:30 in the morning I went to teach Mr. Ivri. We spoke about the Zionist movement and the return of the Jews to the land.

He said: "Since the land fell into the hands of the Arabs, it became wilderness, the shadow of death hovers over it, and it became naked and barren. All the nations that settled on the land before the Arabs left their marks on it, all except for the Arabs. And if one should ask you: "By what right do you possess the land?"—what will you say? You had this land and you lived in it for many generations, and you did nothing in it. True, the Jewish nation was not eager to build and had no material culture, but in spirit it surpassed all nations and created for Palestine a glorious history, and thus the glorious history of the Jews and their eternal yearning for this land; give them the right to return to it. And, as for you, you have only one vindication, which is that you have lived in this land for many generations. If so, Jews have the historic right and the right of attachment, and you have the right of life; and, since the land is broad and fertile, you have no right to prevent the Jews from returning to it and living in it with you. The Jews do not want to exile you from it, but want to live with you in it. On the contrary, they need to blend with you; they need your blood. Even if it seemed to you until now that the Jews separate themselves, there is no doubt that in the future they will adopt your customs and speak your language. More than that: they have already begun to assimilate and, if many of them immigrate to this land, it will be like Switzerland—that is to say, bilingual: the Jews already speak Hebrew and Arabic, and no doubt the Arabs will learn the Hebrew language through mutual contact and common interest. The more perceptive Jews would like to mix with you and to meet with you socially, but one thing still stands in the way, and this is the place of the woman: the Jews want their wives to come to meetings, while the Muslims do not allow their wives to come. But time will solve this problem."

I said to him: "If you ask the Arabs: 'By what right do you occupy this land?'— they would say: 'This is a natural part of the lands of Arabia.' True, it was not the birthplace of Arab culture, but it had a part in it; here is the mosque and here is the religious school—ancient structures that testify that the land is Arab and Islamic; the Arabs settled in the land in very ancient times. And if this land is the birthplace of your spirituality and the homeland of your chronicles, then for Arabs there is another claim that is irreproachable: that they filled it with their language and their culture. Your claim died in the course of time and our claim is alive and well."

Chapter 4

The Emergence of Israel

World War I completely shattered the existing political map of the Middle East. The Ottoman Empire was gone, and in its place British and French Mandates ruled over much of its former territory. In accord with their proclaimed support for a Jewish "national home" in Palestine (the Balfour Declaration of November 1917), the British were mandated to help establish this home — but also to further the competing goal of preparing the (largely Arab) population for self-government—in the new Mandate of Palestine. The history of the Mandate was largely the story of the clash between these two responsibilities.

Within the Jewish community more militant voices appeared, organized as "Revisionist Zionism" under the leadership of Vladimir (Ze'ev) Jabotinsky. Jabotinsky argued that Arabs would accept the reality of a Jewish state in Palestine only when confronted by an "iron wall" (Reading 15). When the British proposed partitioning Palestine between an Arab state and a Jewish state, the Revisionists opposed the acceptance of this partition by the dominant Jewish leadership.

When the British referred the problem to the new United Nations in 1947, Arabs in Palestine as well as in neighboring Arab states likewise opposed the partition model. As expressed by the Lebanese foreign minister, they made the case for Palestine remaining undivided, with its Arab majority (Reading 16). Nevertheless the United Nations Special Committee on Palestine recommended partition, which led to the declaration of the Jewish state—Israel—when Great Britain ended the Mandate and withdrew. The significance of the first Jewish state in 2,000 years is expressed in the recollections of Golda Meir, later foreign minister and prime minister of Israel (Reading 17).

The war that followed Israel's Declaration of Independence brought in Arab states that had previously played marginal roles in the conflict. But Arab armies performed poorly, a fact that motivated young Arab army officers, such as Egypt's Gamal Abdul Nasser, to blame their own corrupt governments—and, in Egypt's case, eventually to seize power. Nasser's memoirs of his experience in the 1948 war (Reading 18) are thus a backdrop to revolution. But the period of Nasser's rule in Egypt was marked by two other major wars—in 1956 and 1967—in which Israel emerged victorious. The calculations that led to the 1967 war, in particular, are still debated by historians. Egyptian thinking is represented by an unusually frank statement, made by Nasser himself on the eve of the war (Reading 19), while a Central Intelligence Agency (CIA) memorandum (Reading 20), classified at the time, tried to make sense of Egyptian (and Soviet) moves in the crisis.

Further online resources:

Husayn-McMahon correspondence on future borders, 1915: http://www1.udel.edu/ History-old/figal/Hist104/assets/pdf/readings/13mcmahonhussein.pdf, http://www. mideastweb.org/mcmahon.htm (see also the relevant subdirectories at fmep.org and zionism-israel.com).

League of Nations Mandate for Palestine, 1922: http://avalon.law.yale.edu/20th_ century/palmanda.asp.

Peel Commission Report, 1937: http://www.jewishvirtuallibrary.org/text-of-the-peel-commission-report; https://www.britannica.com/event/Peel-Commission.

British White Paper, 1939: http://avalon.law.yale.edu/20th_century/brwh1939. asp, https://ecf.org.il/issues/issue/955, http://www.alliedpowersholocaust.org/wp-content/uploads/2015/03/1939-May-White-Paper.pdf (see also the relevant subdirectories at fmep.org, mideastweb.org, zionism-israel.com).

United Nations Partition Plan for Palestine, General Assembly Resolution 181, 1947: https://unispal.un.org/DPA/DPR/unispal.nsf/0/7F0AF2BD897689B785256C330061 D253 (see also https://www.britannica.com/topic/United-Nations-Resolution-181.

Declaration of Independence of State of Israel, 1948: https://www.knesset. gov.il/docs/eng/megilat_eng.htm, https://www.jta.org/1948/05/16/archive/full-text-of-israels-proclamation-of-independence-issued-in-tel-aviv.

United Nations General Assembly Resolution 194, 1948: https://unispal.un.org/DPA/ DPR/unispal.nsf/0/C758572B78D1CD0085256BCF0077E51A, http://www.un.org/ documents/ga/res/3/ares3.htm.

Major Knesset Debates, 1948–1981: jcpa.org/article/major-knesset-debates-1948–1981.

Second Arab Summit Conference, 1964: http://www.mideastweb.org/arabsummit 1964.htm.

Gamal Abdul Nasser Archives: nasser.org/home/main.aspx?lang=en.

15. "The Iron Wall"

*Vladimir Jabotinsky**

EDITOR'S NOTE *Vladimir Jabotinsky (1880–1940) was a Russian-born Zionist leader who founded Revisionist Zionism, taking a more militant position on territorial issues and relations with the Arabs. During World War I Jabotinsky worked diligently to form Jewish units within the British army. Settled in Palestine after the war, he pushed the development of military forces and in 1923 broke with mainstream Zionism, founding a Revisionist Zionist movement of his own. During the same year he published a widely circulated article titled "The Iron Wall," setting out his views on the unlikelihood of agreement with Arabs and consequently the need to build strong military forces. But at the same time Jabotinsky believed that Arabs could enjoy equal rights in a Jewish state once they accepted their status as a minority, following their inability to breach "the iron wall."*

It is an excellent rule to begin an article with the most important point, but this time I find it necessary to begin with an introduction, and, moreover, with a personal introduction.

I am reputed to be an enemy of the Arabs, who wants to have them ejected from Palestine, and so forth. It is not true.

Emotionally, my attitude to the Arabs is the same as to all other nations— polite indifference. Politically, my attitude is determined by two principles. First of all, I consider it utterly impossible to eject the Arabs from Palestine. There will always be two nations in Palestine—which is good enough for me, provided the Jews become the majority. And secondly, I belong to the group that once drew up the Helsingfors Programme, the programme of national rights for all nationalities living in the same state. In drawing up that programme, we had in mind not only the Jews but all nations everywhere, and its basis is equality of rights.

I am prepared to take an oath binding ourselves and our descendants that we shall never do anything contrary to the principle of equal rights, and that we shall never try to eject anyone. This seems to me a fairly peaceful credo.

But it is quite another question whether it is always possible to realise a peaceful aim by peaceful means. For the answer to this question does not

---

* Vladimir Jabotinsky, "O Zheleznoi Stene" ["The Iron Wall"], *Rassvyet*, November 4, 1923; translation at http://www.jewishvirtuallibrary.org/quot-the-iron-wall-quot.

depend on our attitude to the Arabs, but entirely on the attitude of the Arabs to us and to Zionism.

Now, after this introduction, we may proceed to the subject.

Voluntary agreement not possible

There can be no voluntary agreement between ourselves and the Palestine Arabs. Not now, nor in the prospective future. I say this with such conviction, not because I want to hurt the moderate Zionists. I do not believe that they will be hurt. Except for those who were born blind, they realised long ago that it is utterly impossible to obtain the voluntary consent of the Palestine Arabs for converting "Palestine" from an Arab country into a country with a Jewish majority.

My readers have a general idea of the history of colonisation in other countries. I suggest that they consider all the precedents with which they are acquainted, and see whether there is one solitary instance of any colonisation being carried on with the consent of the native population. There is no such precedent.

The native populations, civilised or uncivilised, have always stubbornly resisted the colonists, irrespective of whether they were civilised or savage.

And it made no difference whatever whether the colonists behaved decently or not. The companions of Cortez and Pizzaro, or (as some people will remind us) our own ancestors under Joshua Ben Nun, behaved like brigands; but the Pilgrim Fathers, the first real pioneers of North America, were people of the highest morality, who did not want to do harm to anyone, least of all to the Red Indians, and they honestly believed that there was room enough in the prairies both for the Paleface and for the Redskin. Yet the native population fought with the same ferocity against the good colonists as against the bad.

Every native population, civilised or not, regards its lands as its national home, of which it is the sole master, and it wants to retain that mastery always; it will refuse to admit not only new masters but even new partners or collaborators. [...]

The iron wall

We cannot offer any adequate compensation to the Palestinian Arabs in return for Palestine. And therefore there is no likelihood of any voluntary agreement being reached. So that all those who regard such an agreement as a condition *sine qua non* for Zionism may as well say "non" and withdraw from Zionism.

Zionist colonisation must either stop or else proceed regardless of the native population. Which means that it can proceed and develop only under the protection of a power that is independent of the native population—behind an iron wall, which the native population cannot breach.

That is our Arab policy; not what we should be, but what it actually is, whether we admit it or not. What need [is there], otherwise, of the Balfour Declaration? Or of the Mandate? Their value to us is that [an] outside power has undertaken to create in the country such conditions of administration and security that, if the native population should desire to hinder our work, they will find it impossible.

And we are, all of us without any exception, demanding day after day that this outside power should carry out this task vigorously and with determination.

In this matter there is no difference between our 'militarists' and our 'vegetarians'. Except that the first prefer that the iron wall should consist of Jewish soldiers, and the others are content that they should be British.

We all demand that there should be an iron wall. Yet we keep spoiling our own case by talking about 'agreement', which means telling the mandatory government that the important thing is not the iron wall, but discussions. Empty rhetoric of this kind is dangerous. And that is why it is not only a pleasure but a duty to discredit it and to demonstrate that it is both fantastic and dishonest.

Zionism moral and just

Two brief remarks:

In the first place, if anyone objects that this point of view is immoral, I answer: it is not true: either Zionism is moral and just, or it is immoral and unjust. But that is a question that we should have settled before we became Zionists. Actually we have settled that question, and in the affirmative.

We hold that Zionism is moral and just. And since it is moral and just, justice must be done, no matter whether Joseph or Simon or Ivan or Achmet agree with it or not.

There is no other morality.

Eventual agreement

In the second place, this does not mean that there cannot be any agreement with the Palestine Arabs. What is impossible is a voluntary agreement. As long as the Arabs feel that there is the least hope of getting rid of us, they will refuse to give up this hope in return for either kind words or for bread and butter, because they are not a rabble, but a living people. And when a living people yields in matters of such a vital character it is only when there is no longer any hope of getting rid of us, because they can make no breach in the iron wall.

Not till then will they drop their extremist leaders, whose watchword is 'Never!'. And the leadership will pass to the moderate groups, who will approach us with a proposal that we should both agree to mutual concessions. Then we may expect them to discuss honestly practical questions, such as a guarantee against Arab displacement, or equal rights for Arab citizen[s], or Arab national integrity.

And when that happens, I am convinced that we Jews will be found ready to give them satisfactory guarantees, so that both peoples can live together in peace, like good neighbours.

But the only way to obtain such an agreement is the iron wall, which is to say a strong power in Palestine that is not amenable to any Arab pressure. In other words, the only way to reach an agreement in the future is to abandon all idea of seeking an agreement at present.

16. "The Arab Case for Palestine" (Testimony before UNSCOP, July 22, 1947)

*Hamid Frangieh**

EDITOR'S NOTE *Hamid Frangieh (1907–1981) was a Lebanese politician and diplomat, from a prominent Maronite Christian family, who served as foreign minister during 1945–1949. When the British government referred the issue of the Palestine Mandate to the United Nations in early 1947, the UN General Assembly established the United Nations Special Committee on Palestine (UNSCOP) to consider the future of the Mandate. When UNSCOP held hearings in Palestine, most Arab representatives refused to cooperate. Meeting briefly in Beirut, the committee did hear testimony from representatives of Arab states. Frangieh's testimony presented here expressed the consensus adopted by the Arab League at the time.*

Mr Chairman, Members of the Committee,

The governments of the Arab states, though convinced that there is only one solution for the Palestinian problem, namely cessation of the Mandate and independence for Palestine, and that any investigation of so obvious a question has become unnecessary, nevertheless warmly welcomed the invitation of your Committee, as representative of the highest international authority the world has yet known.

The governments of the Arab states are persuaded that the Committee, desirous of establishing the conditions necessary for international cooperation, as the result of its investigation will adopt recommendations in conformity with the principles of self-determination and independence consecrated by the United Nations Charter.

The governments of the Arab states do not intend to enumerate in this Memorandum all the arguments in support of the Palestine case. They will confine themselves to drawing the Committee's attention to two main points:

1 Palestine's right to self-determination;
2 the need to maintain peace in the Middle East.

---

* Abridged testimony of Hamid Frangieh before the Special Committee on Palestine: Verbatim Record of the Thirty-Eighth Meeting, Beirut, Lebanon, July 22, 1947, United Nations General Assembly A/AC.13/PV. 38. https://unispal.un.org/DPA/DPR/unispal.nsf/c17b3a9d4bfb04c985257b28006e4ea6/9559f15d11159a028525776c0071fe0b?OpenDocument.

Palestine's right to self-determination

When the Balfour Declaration was issued, envisaging the establishment of a Jewish national home and opening the way for Zionist immigration, the Arabs formed 93 per cent of the population of Palestine. The Declaration, which cannot in any case be considered valid as regards Arab Palestine, ignored Palestine's right to self-determination both at the time it was issued and afterwards. Later, attempts were even made to silence the Arabs and bring them to an attitude of resignation. Far from stifling their claims, these attempts had the effect of strengthening their desire for liberation and their faith in the justice of their cause.

Their struggle for independence and for the safeguarding of their rights started at the beginning of this century with the natural awakening of the Arab peoples and the movement against Ottoman domination. They took part in this liberation movement and spared no effort or sacrifice. Together with the rest of the Arabs, they rose against the Turks, fighting alongside the Allies on all the battlefields of the Middle East, in the Hedjaz, Palestine, Syria, Lebanon, and Iraq.

As partners of the victorious Allies in 1918, they were entitled to enjoy the freedom for which the Allies had fought. But that freedom, to which they aspired and for which they had fought, was denied them for reasons irrelevant to their case. Abruptly confronted by Zionist ambitions and Allied promises to satisfy them, the Arabs of Palestine were forced to turn their struggle against the Ottoman Empire into one against their own Allies.

The Allies renounced the promises they had made to the Arabs at the beginning of their struggle for independence, imposing a mandate system which is nothing less than colonization. And the strictest of the mandates was the one applied to Palestine.

In spite of the promises made in the course of hostilities, the mandate system imposed upon all the Arab countries which had formed part of the old Ottoman Empire was applied at the same time, in all its severity, to Palestine. Whereas, by the texts of the Mandates for the Lebanon, Syria and Iraq, the mandatory power was under obligation to assist the mandated state and lead it towards independence, the principle of which had been recognized by Article 22 of the League of Nations Covenant, the text of the Mandate for Palestine provided for the establishment of a Jewish national home and opened the door to immigration and the settlement of foreign Jews in Palestine.

The Mandate thereby distorted the normal development of Arab Palestine and deflected the natural course of its history. In the attempt to recover their lost freedom and independence, the Palestinian Arabs found themselves compelled not only to throw off the yoke of foreign control but also to struggle against the inroads of a foreign population whose ultimate aim was to relegate them to a secondary position in their own country.

While the people of Iraq were casting off the heavy burden of the Mandate and Syria and the Lebanon [were] freeing themselves from foreign occupation and gaining full independence and sovereignty, the situation in Palestine became steadily worse. Wave upon wave of Zionist immigrants streamed into the Holy Land. National liberation became nothing more than a mirage.

The origin of Palestine's troubles is to be found in two documents, which are null and valueless, although it is upon them that Zionist claims are based: the Balfour Declaration and the Mandate.

In the first of these documents, the British government undertook to facilitate the establishment of a Jewish National Home, thereby violating the principle of self-determination and the rules of international law. At the time when the undertaking was given, Great Britain had no legal relations with Palestine, which then formed part of the Ottoman Empire. [...]

To sum up, the right to self-determination to which the Arab people of Palestine are entitled and which they should be able to exercise has been continually violated and is still violated today. It is nonetheless a natural, absolute, inalienable right, which neither force nor *fait accompli* can remove; and it consecrates the Arab claims and condemns Zionist ambitions.

The governments of the Arab states, looking towards the democratic principles on which the United Nations was founded as the best defence and surest guarantee of that right, demand the full application of those principles in Palestine. They are convinced that the Special Committee would not envisage a solution violating that right or the principles of the United Nations.

Threats to peace in the Middle East

The attitude of the Arab governments and peoples to Zionism is based, secondly, upon their anxiety to maintain peace in the Middle East.

Peace there is threatened by the expansionist aims and terrorist methods of Zionism.

1 At the outset the Zionist movement was content merely to look to Palestine for a refuge. Then it demanded a National Home. Having obtained that, it sought to extend its domain and create a kind of state within the Palestinian state, with its own institutions and finances, its own economy and its own army. Now the Zionists are planning to establish a Jewish state on Palestinian territory, a state which will take in the whole of Palestine. And even before achieving that, they are already seeking to spread further at the expense of the neighbouring Arab states. [...]

2 Zionism, however, does not content itself with mere propaganda in favour of the fulfilment of its expansionist projects at the expense of the Arab countries, Its plan involves recourse to terrorism, both in Palestine and in other countries. It is known that a secret army has been formed with a view to creating an atmosphere of tension and unrest by making attempts on the lives of representatives of the governing authority and by destroying public buildings. [...]

3 No state could tolerate mass immigration such as that to which Palestine is subjected. Immigration restrictions are established in all countries to protect the best interests of the country and the rights of the inhabitants. [...]

4 The Jewish state which the Zionists are endeavouring to establish in Palestine is not, moreover, a viable state either from the political or from the economic point of view. The Arab states could not, in fact, tolerate the creation of a state composed of foreign elements from so many parts, each with its own mentality, its insatiable desires, for the fulfilment of which they deliberately use violent and destructive means such as those we have mentioned. Against a state established by violence, the Arab states will be obliged to use violence; that is a legitimate right of self-defence. [...]

Concluding remarks

The governments of the Arab states firmly hope that the Committee will bear these considerations in mind and endeavour to propose such a solution as may put an end to the present unrest and ensure the triumph of justice and the establishment of peace. They feel sure that this solution could only be inspired by the democratic principles on which the United Nations is founded.

The first of these principles establishes respect for the independence of the peoples and their right of self-determination. [...]

The governments of the Arab states could not bring this statement to a close without again expressing the hope that your Committee, taking into consideration the views we have expressed herein, will adopt the only just solution to the problem, namely recognition of the sovereign independence of Palestine and immediate discontinuation of immigration, which threatens to change the face of the country. For any solution which does not take into account the atmosphere of Palestine—that is, the attitude of the peoples and of the governments of the Arab states—would be doomed to certain failure. Moreover, it would only increase the dangers which now exist and hold dire threats for the future.

17. "We Have Our State"

*Golda Meir**

EDITOR'S NOTE *Golda Meir (1898–1978) was born in Ukraine, immigrated to the United States at the age of eight, and moved to Palestine in 1921. She rose through the ranks of the Labor Zionists and, by the time the Mandate ended, was a key figure in the Israeli government that was emerging under the leadership of David Ben-Gurion. Her autobiography, from which this account is taken, records the drama and excitement felt by veteran Zionists when the Jewish state was proclaimed, despite the immediate threats to its existence.*

Within two days the final decision had to be taken. Should a Jewish state be proclaimed or not? [...] So Ben-Gurion called in two men: Yigael Yadin, who was the Haganah's [Defense Force's] chief of operations, and Yisrael Galili, who was its *de facto* commander-in-chief. The answers were virtually identical—and terrifying. We could be sure of only two things, they said: The British would pull out, and the Arabs would invade. And then? They were both silent. But after a minute Yadin said: "The best we can tell you is that we have a fifty-fifty chance. We are as likely to win as we are to be defeated."

So it was on that bright note that the final decision was made. On Friday, May 14, 1948 [...] the Jewish state would come into being, its population numbering 650,000, its chance of surviving its birth depending on whether or not the *yishuv* [Jewish community] could possibly meet the assault of five regular Arab armies actively aided by Palestine's 1,000,000 Arabs. [...]

[On May 14,] at exactly 4 p.m., the ceremony began. Ben-Gurion, wearing a dark suit and tie, stood up and rapped a gavel. According to the plan, this was to be the signal for the orchestra, tucked away in a second floor gallery, to play "Hatikvah." But something went wrong, and there was no music. Spontaneously, we rose to our feet and sang our national anthem. Then Ben-Gurion cleared his throat and said quietly, "I shall now read the Scroll of Independence." It took him only a quarter of an hour to read the entire proclamation. He read it slowly and very clearly, and I remember his voice changing and rising a little as he came to the eleventh paragraph:

---

* Excerpts from Golda Meir, *My Life* (New York: G. P. Putnam's Sons, 1975), pp. 221–228.

Accordingly we, the members of the National Council, representing the Jewish people in the Land of Israel and the Zionist movement, have assembled on the day of the termination of the British Mandate for Palestine, and, by virtue of our natural and historic right and of the resolution of the General Assembly of the United Nations, do hereby proclaim the establishment of a Jewish state in the Land of Israel—the State of Israel.

The State of Israel! My eyes filled with tears, and my hands shook. We had done it. We had brought the Jewish state into existence—and I, Golda Mabovitch Meyerson, had lived to see the day. Whatever happened now, whatever price any of us would have to pay for it, we had re-created the Jewish national home. The long exile was over. From this day on we would no longer live on sufferance in the land of our forefathers. Now we were a nation like other nations, master—for the first time in twenty centuries—of our own destiny. The dream had come true—too late to save those who had perished in the Holocaust, but not too late for the generations to come. Almost exactly fifty years ago, at the close of the First Zionist Congress in Basel, Theodor Herzl had written in his diary: "At Basel, I founded the Jewish state. If I were to say this today, I would be greeted with laughter. In five years perhaps, and certainly in fifty, everyone will see it." And so it had come to pass.

As Ben-Gurion read, I thought again about my children and the children that they would have, how different their lives would be from mine and how different my own life would be from what it had been in the past, and I thought about my colleagues in besieged Jerusalem, gathered in the offices of the Jewish Agency, listening to the ceremony through static on the radio, while I, by sheer accident, was in the museum itself. It seemed to me that no Jew on earth had ever been more privileged than I was that Friday afternoon.

Then, as though a signal had been given, we rose to our feet, crying and clapping, while Ben-Gurion, his voice breaking for the only time, read: "The State of Israel will be open to Jewish immigration and the ingathering of exiles." This was the very heart of the proclamation, the reason for the state and the point of it all. I remember sobbing out loud when I heard those words spoken in that hot, packed little hall. But Ben-Gurion just rapped his gavel again for order and went on reading:

Even amid the violent attacks launched against us for months past, we call upon the sons of the Arab people dwelling in Israel to keep the peace and to play their part in building the state on the basis of full and equal citizenship and due representation in all its institutions, provisional and permanent.

And:

We extend the hand of peace and good neighborliness to all the states around us and to their peoples, and we call upon them to cooperate in mutual helpfulness with the independent Jewish nation in its land. The State of Israel is prepared to make its contribution in a concerted effort for the advancement of the entire Middle East.

When he finished reading the 979 Hebrew words of the proclamation, he asked us to stand and "adopt the scroll establishing the Jewish state," so once again we rose to our feet. Then, something quite unscheduled and very moving happened. All of a sudden Rabbi Fishman-Maimon stood up and, in a trembling voice, pronounced the traditional Hebrew prayer of thanksgiving. "Blessed be Thou, O Lord our God, King of the Universe, who has kept us alive and made us endure and brought us to this day. Amen." It was a prayer that I had heard often, but it had never held such meaning for me as it did that day. [...]

All I recall about my actual signing of the proclamation is that I was crying openly, not able even to wipe the tears from my face, and I remember that as [Moshe] Sharett held the scroll in the place for me, a man called David Zvi Pincus, who belonged to the religious Mizrachi Party, came over to try and calm me. "Why do you weep so much, Golda?" he asked me.

"Because it breaks my heart to think of all those who should have been here today and are not," I replied, but I still couldn't stop crying. [...]

After the Palestine Philharmonic Orchestra played "Hatikvah," Ben-Gurion rapped his gavel for the third time. "The State of Israel is established. This meeting is ended." We all shook hands and embraced each other. The ceremony was over. Israel was a reality.

18. "Memoirs of the First Palestine War"

Gamal Abdul Nasser*

EDITOR'S NOTE *Gamal Abdul Nasser (1918–1970), later to become president of Egypt and the dominant face of Arab nationalism, was a staff officer in the Egyptian army during the 1948–1949 war over the creation of Israel. In 1952 the Free Officers Movement that he headed seized power in Cairo and sent Egyptian ruler King Farouk into exile. Three years later Nasser published an account of his experience in the 1948–1949 war, an experience that left him deeply disillusioned with the existing regime and deeply commit-ted to restoring the prestige and honor of Egypt as a frontline combatant in the conflict with Israel.*

On May 16 I left my house carrying my kit and leaving behind on a table the morning paper. The front page of the paper carried the first official communi-qué of the then Ministry of Defence announcing the beginning of military operations in Palestine. I was seized by a strange feeling as I raced down the steps, thinking: "So I am on my way to the front." [...]

The Egyptian army at the time was made up of nine battalions. Only three of these were anywhere near the frontier when the order was given to enter Palestine, and a fourth was on the way. We kept asking ourselves questions. Why hadn't a larger number of battalions been concentrated near the frontier since we had decided to enter the war? Why had the reserves not been called up and formed into new battalions that could be sent to the front when the need arose? Why did the first communiqué describe the Palestine operations as merely a punitive expedition against the Zionist "gangs"? Soon enough, however, our sense of elation would fill in these gaps to form a solid, continu-ous front. [...]

As staff officer of the 6th Battalion, I soon began more than anybody else to realize the bewilderment and incompetence which characterized our High Command. A hundred factors clashed within me, and I did not know how to express my feelings. Perhaps the clearest description of our predicament was given by a private. He expressed it in his simple, colloquial language, not

* Excerpts from Gamal Abdul Nasser, "Nasser's Memoirs of the First Palestine War," translated by Walid Khalidi, *Journal of Palestine Studies* 2.2 (1973): 3–32; the Arabic original was published by the Egyptian weekly *Akher Sa'a* in the spring of 1955.

knowing that I could hear him and unaware that his simple words summed up our position.

Orders had been received by our battalion to move camp to another site that lay about three kilometers away. I myself could think of no reason for this move, and, what is worse, I did not think that the High Command had any reason for it either. My doubts were to be presently confirmed; for, three hours after we had received the first order and just as we had settled down in our new camp, fresh orders reached us to move to the station and entrain for Gaza. As we began to strike the tents we had just erected, a sergeant came up to a private who was still pitching one of the tents and ordered him to take it down. The private looked uncomprehendingly at the sergeant. When new orders had arrived to move to the station, he began to take down a tent which he had taken down in the morning in one place and had begun to erect at noon in another; now he was being ordered to take down the same tent again before he had finished erecting it and, as he was doing all this, he kept repeating: "Shame, shame on us." He said this in the drawn-out, sarcastic intonation of the Egyptian countryside, and when I heard him I felt that the doubts about the competence and determination of the High Command which had already assailed me had also found their way to the men, and that this private's words were a simple expression of these doubts. [...]

As I followed these movements, which the Cairo papers announced before they had actually been carried out by our troops in the field, I almost lost my self-control. I could make no sense out of any of these movements. The chief interest of our High Command, as it appeared, was to occupy the largest extent of territory possible. But the only result of this was that the four battalions were dispersed at the end of long lines of communication. They became so scattered that their main concern was to defend themselves and protect their lines of communication. Our High Command no longer had a reserve to use against the enemy. The commander of what had been a fighting force became virtually a commander with no troops to command, or at best a commander of a string of outposts scattered over a wide front. I could see that we had lost all power of initiative which of our own free will we had surrendered to the enemy.

All this that I could visualize from where I was at Gaza was also clear to the officers and men in the forward trenches and had its corrosive effect on their morale. Every soldier felt the lack of arms, but what was more significant was that he felt the lack of proper planning. Everyone felt that our CO [commanding officer] had no effective control over his forces and that he acted according to the pressure of factors of which the actual requirements of the front had perhaps the least bearing on his calculations. The feeling of the men and officers was that, in their isolated, widely scattered positions, they were at the mercy of the enemy. They felt that they formed sitting targets to a highly mobile enemy. [...]

At about this time I attended a conference at Brigade HQ [headquarters]. I still remember that, as I sat at the conference table, my whole being was filled with the thought that conviction was utterly lacking in the plans that were being drawn up. It occurred to me that I was sitting in front of a stage. All those standing on the stage had perfected their roles and were exerting themselves in playing them. But everyone on the stage knew that it was just a role that he was playing and that this would come to an end, after which he would revert to his original personality. [...]

Presently events were to take a sharp, unexpected turn. And I must here be absolutely frank and confess, though six years have elapsed since then, that I found myself in a situation where for the first time I raised my voice in the field against an order given to me by my superiors.

The day was July 9. We were sitting at lunch in our mess at Battalion HQ. A sergeant walked in and delivered to me a sealed envelope which was addressed to me as staff officer of the battalion. Still eating, I opened the envelope. As my eyes ran along the lines of the message, I felt the food stick in my throat. The note comprised the following two lines:

1. The 6th Battalion will hand over its positions to the 5th Battalion, which is on its way from Gaza.
2. The 6th Battalion will occupy the town of Julis in the early morning of July 10.

The expression on my face must have betrayed my feelings; for the other officers suddenly stopped eating and stared in my direction. When I informed them of the contents of the message, their reaction was no different from mine.

Once again, we were facing a battle for which we had made no preparation. We had no information about the enemy at Julis. How strong was the enemy at Julis? What were his fortifications like? What other units of ours were in the neighbourhood? What roles were assigned to them? We had no time to study our objective, as we had done in the case of Sawafir. I started to protest but I knew that it was pointless to do so. [...]

I started eagerly to go through the messages sent by the companies from their scattered positions all over the battlefield. One message read: "Arrived at objective. Awaiting new orders." Another: "Have run out of ammunition." A third: "Objective reached. Send stretchers." What made matters worse was that these messages had arrived quite some time before. I wondered what had happened to the companies that sent them. How had they faced the situation by themselves, without getting any response from their HQ? I tried to do what I could. I wanted in particular to get in touch with our forces west of Julis but could get no reply from them. But I soon understood what was happening when a dispatch rider arrived to say that the CO had given his orders to the forces in the west to withdraw and wanted me to withdraw the force attacking from the south.

How was I to withdraw the force in the south? The CO had already withdrawn the force that diverted the enemy's attention from the south without giving me or our forces any prior warning. I began to see in clear outline the catastrophe that was hovering over our heads. What made me feel more strongly about matters was that the force delivering the main attack from the west had actually been carrying out its task successfully. I decided at this point to do what I had long contemplated but shrank from doing. I bypassed my immediate superior—the CO of the battalion—and got in touch with the CO of the brigade, to whom I fully explained the situation. Our object had now become not so much to occupy Julis but rather to make desperate efforts to pull our forces out of the trap into which they were about to fall. [...]

I returned to my battalion in a state of revolt against everything. I was in revolt against the fact that it was by sheer accident that we had escaped catastrophe. I was in revolt against the valuable information contained in aerial photographs, which our air force had taken of the very objective that we were to attack, but which were lying about at General HQ with no one thinking of sending them along to us. I was in revolt against the smooth, closely shaven chins and the smart and comfortable offices at General HQ, where no one had any idea what the fighting men in the trenches felt or how much they suffered from orders sent out at random. But my state of revolt was pointless. It would have been more profitable for me to spare my nerves for the new battle that we were presently to receive orders to prepare ourselves for.

The new battle was typical of the battles that our men had so far taken part in. It was a battle decided on a map. Somebody at HQ looked at a coloured map and felt—with perhaps every reason—that such and such a place was of supreme importance. He thereupon placed his finger on it and sent us orders to occupy it. But he did not send, with the orders, anything that could help us in our task.

Frankly I did not consider the orders that reached us from HQ operational orders in the true sense of the word. I preferred to call them "scraps of paper" and I do not think that I was far wrong in my designation.

19. "War Is Inevitable: Why?"

*Gamal Abdul Nasser**

EDITOR'S NOTE *As President of Egypt, Nasser frequently expressed the view that confrontation with Israel was inevitable and that Egypt would launch a campaign to reverse the results of the 1948–1949 war when preparations were completed and the time was right. In May 1967, Egypt moved its forces toward Israel, expelled the United Nations Emergency Force installed there as a peacekeeping body after the 1956 Suez War, and reimposed a blockade of Israel's southern port that had triggered the earlier confrontation. Had Nasser reached the conclusion that the time was right? Speaking on May 26, he portrayed the moves as part of a deliberately planned program aimed at the destruction of Israel and the restoration of Arab Palestine. Other observers, however, doubted that the confrontation had been planned in advance and conjectured that Nasser had simply been swept along in the momentum of events.*

Thank you for this initiative. You have provided me with an opportunity to see you. I have actually heard your speeches and resolutions; there is nothing to add during this meeting to what you have already said. You, the Arab workers' federations, represent the biggest force in the Arab world.

We can achieve much by Arab action, which is a main part of our battle. We must develop and build our countries to face the challenge of our enemies. The Arab world now is very different from what it was ten days ago. Israel is also different from what it was ten days ago. Despair has never found its way into Arab hearts and never will. The Arabs insist on their rights and are determined to regain the rights of the Palestinian people. The Arabs must accomplish this set intention and this aim. The first elements of this aim appeared in the test of Syria and Egypt in facing the Israeli threat. I believe that this test was a major starting point and basis from which to achieve complete cohesion in the Arab world. What we see today in the masses of the Arab people everywhere is their desire to fight. The Arab people want to regain the rights of the people of Palestine.

For several years, many people have raised doubts about our intentions towards Palestine. But talk is easy and action is difficult, very difficult. We

* Gamal Abdul Nasser, Speech to Arab Trade Unionists, May 26, 1967; translation available at http://www.jewishvirtuallibrary.org/statement-by-president-nasser-to-arab-trade-unionists-may-1967.

emerged wounded from the 1956 battle. Britain, Israel and France attacked us then. We sustained heavy losses in 1956. Later, union was achieved. The 1961 secession occurred when we had only just got completely together and had barely begun to stand firmly on our feet.

Later the Yemeni revolution broke out. We considered it our duty to rescue our brothers, simply because of the principles and ideals which we advocated and still advocate.

We were waiting for the day when we would be fully prepared and confident of being able to adopt strong measures if we were to enter the battle with Israel. I say nothing aimlessly. One day two years ago, I stood up to say that we had no plan to liberate Palestine and that revolutionary action was our only course to liberate Palestine. I spoke at the summit conferences. The summit conferences were meant to prepare the Arab states to defend themselves.

Recently we felt that we are strong enough, that, if we were to enter a battle with Israel, with God's help, we could triumph. On this basis we decided to take actual steps.

A great deal has been said in the past about the UN Emergency Force (UNEF). Many people blamed us for UNEF's presence. We were not strong enough. Should we have listened to them, or rather built and trained our army while UNEF still existed? I said once that we could tell UNEF to leave within half an hour. Once we were fully prepared we could ask UNEF to leave. And this is what actually happened.

The same thing happened with regard to Sharm el-Sheikh. We were attacked on this score by some Arabs. Taking Sharm el-Sheikh meant confrontation with Israel. Taking such action also meant that we were ready to enter a general war with Israel. It was not a separate operation. Therefore we had to take this fact into consideration when moving to Sharm el-Sheikh. The present operation was mounted on this basis.

Actually I was authorized by the [Arab Socialist Union's] Supreme Executive Committee to implement this plan at the right time. The right time came when Syria was threatened with aggression. We sent reconnaissance aircraft over Israel. Not a single brigade was stationed opposite us on the Israeli side of the border. All Israeli brigades were confronting Syria. All but four brigades have now moved south to confront Egypt. Those four are still on the border with Syria. We are confident that once we have entered the battle we will triumph, God willing.

With regard to military plans, there is complete coordination of military action between us and Syria. We will operate as one army fighting a single battle for the sake of a common objective—the objective of the Arab nation.

The problem today is not just Israel, but also those behind it. If Israel embarks on an aggression against Syria or Egypt, the battle against Israel will be general and not confined to one spot on the Syrian or Egyptian borders. The battle will be a general one, and our basic objective will be to destroy Israel. I probably could not have said such things five, or even three years ago. If I had said such things and had been unable to carry them out, my words would have been empty and worthless.

Today, some eleven years after 1956, I say such things because I am confident. I know what we have here in Egypt and what Syria has. I also know about other states: Iraq, for instance, has sent its troops to Syria; Algeria will send troops; Kuwait also will send troops. They will send armoured and infantry units. This is Arab power. This is the true resurrection of the Arab nation, which at one time was probably in despair.

Today people must know the reality of the Arab world. What is Israel? Israel today is the United States. The United States is the chief defender of Israel. As for Britain, I consider it America's lackey. Britain does not have an independent policy. Wilson always follows Johnson's steps and says what he wants him to say. All western countries take Israel's view.

The Gulf of Aqaba was a closed waterway prior to 1956. We used to search British, US, French and all other ships. After the tripartite aggression—and we all know the tripartite plot—we left the area to UNEF, which came here under a UN resolution to make possible the withdrawal of Britain, France and Israel. The Israelis say they opened the maritime route. I say they told lies and believed their own lies. We withdrew because the British and the French attacked us. This battle was never between us and Israel alone.

I have recently been with the armed forces. All the armed forces are ready for a battle face to face between the Arabs and Israel. Those behind Israel are also welcome.

We must know and learn a big lesson today. We must actually see that, in its hypocrisy and in its talks with the Arabs, the United States sides with Israel 100 per cent and is partial in favour of Israel. Why is Britain biased towards Israel? The West is on Israel's side. General de Gaulle's personality caused him to remain impartial on this question and not to toe the US or the British line; France therefore did not take sides with Israel.

The Soviet Union's attitude was great and splendid. It supported the Arabs and the Arab nation. It went to the extent of stating that, together with the Arabs and the Arab nation, it would resist any interference or aggression.

Today every Arab knows foes and friends. If we do not learn who our enemies and our friends are, Israel will always be able to benefit from this behaviour. It is clear that the United States is an enemy of the Arabs because it is completely biased in favour of Israel. It is also clear that Britain is an enemy of the Arabs because it, too, is completely biased in favour of Israel. On this basis we must treat our enemies and those who side with our enemies as actual enemies.

We can accord them such treatment. In fact we are not states without status. We are states of status occupying an important place in the world. Our states have thousands of years of civilization behind them—7,000 years of civilization. Indeed, we can do much; we can expose the hypocrisy—the hypocrisy of our enemies if they try to persuade us that they wish to serve our interest. The United States seeks to serve only Israel's interests. Britain also seeks to serve only Israel's interests.

The question is not one of international law. Why all this uproar because of the closure of the Gulf of Aqaba? When Eshkol and Rabin threatened Syria, nobody spoke about peace or threats to peace. They actually hate the progressive regime in Syria. The United States, Britain, and any nation which is the friend of the United States and Britain do not favour the national progressive regime in Syria. Israel, of course, shares their feelings. Israel is an ally of the United States and Britain. When Israel threatened Syria, they kept quiet and accepted what it said. But when we exercise one of our legitimate rights, as we always do, they turn the world upside down and speak about threats to peace and about a crisis in the Middle East. They fabricate these matters and threaten us with war.

We shall not relinquish our rights. We shall not concede our right in the Gulf of Aqaba. Today the people of Egypt, the Syrian army, and the Egyptian army comprise one front. We want the entire front surrounding Israel to become one front. We want this. [...] We want the front to become one united front around Israel. We will not relinquish the rights of the people of Palestine, as I have said before. I was told at the time that I might have to wait seventy years. During the Crusaders' occupation, the Arabs waited seventy years before a suitable opportunity arose and they drove away the Crusaders. Some people commented that Abdel Nasser said we should shelve the Palestinian question for seventy years, but I say that, as a people with an ancient civilization, as an Arab people, we are determined that the Palestine question will not be liquidated or forgotten. The whole question, then, is the proper time to achieve our aims. We are preparing ourselves constantly.

You are the hope of the Arab nation and its vanguard. As workers, you are actually building the Arab nation. The quicker we build, the quicker we will be able to achieve our aim. I thank you for your visit and wish you every success. Please convey my greetings and best wishes to the Arab workers in every Arab country.

20. Memorandum, May 26, 1967

Central Intelligence Agency*

EDITOR'S NOTE *Interpretation of Egyptian and Soviet actions in the 1967 crisis was a major concern for US policymakers. On the same day when Gamal Abdul Nasser presented his explanation of Egypt's thinking (Reading 19), intelligence officials in Washington circulated the memorandum presented here, with their own estimates of the Egyptian moves and the likely responses. These estimates agreed to some extent with Nasser's projection of a likely war, but they took a somewhat different view of the outcome. They also lend some support to later appraisals that this was not a war that any of the parties necessarily had planned or intended at the outset.*

SUBJECT: **The Middle Eastern Crisis**

1 The first thing that calls for explanation in the present crisis is why Nasser chose at this moment to abandon his long-standing reluctance to risk military confrontation with Israel.

(a) At the immediate moment Nasser was probably prompted to initiate these maneuvers by Israeli threats against Syria. He probably felt that he had to identify himself with Arab nationalist interests and that some action on his part would refurbish his image in the Arab world. These views, however, are probably insufficient to explain all the events that have occurred.

(b) He probably had decided (though he stated the contrary not long ago) that his armed forces were improved to the point where they could successfully stand off an Israeli offensive, even though they might be unable to defeat Israel decisively. Accordingly, he may have felt that, if he could get his army properly deployed in the Sinai Peninsula and elsewhere, the chances of war would be acceptable.

(c) It is possible that the Soviets encouraged him in these views. We do not believe that the whole operation is a Soviet plan, or even that the Soviets

---

* Memorandum from the Central Intelligence Agency's Board of National Estimates to Director of Central Intelligence Richard Helms, May 26, 1967: Lyndon Johnson Library, National Security File, Country File, Middle East Crisis, vol. 2. Secret.

urged him to his present course of action, but their attitude must have been sufficiently permissive so that he knew he could count on political and logistic support from them in the course of the crisis. The interests of the Soviet Union itself would obviously be served by successes for Nasser at the expense of Israel and the United States.

(d) The US preoccupation with Vietnam and the bad blood occasioned thereby between the United States and the Soviet Union probably had some important influence on the nature of Nasser's decision, as well as [on] its timing.

(e) There may have been some element of desperation in Nasser's attitude arising from the parlous condition of the Egyptian economy, the worsening of relations with the United States, a belief that some sort of US–Israeli plot against him existed, and perhaps a fatalistic conclusion that a showdown with Israel must come sooner or later, and might best be provoked before Israel acquired nuclear weapons.

(f) He may also have concluded, from a tactical point of view, that he could gamble on US influence and perhaps [on] some Israeli indecisiveness to prevent an Israeli offensive at the early and most vulnerable stages of his deployments.

2 The movement of UAR troops seems to have gone smoothly and expertly. Yet there must have been, in this as in other crises, a large element of accident in the actual course of events. For example, Nasser probably did not expect such a speedy departure of UN forces from Sharm el Sheikh, giving him [sic] opportunity for a quick seizure of the position and an announced closing of the Strait. He has thus far managed the crisis, from his point of view, with great skill and success.

3 Clearly Nasser has won the first round. It is possible that he may seek a military showdown with Israel, designed to settle the whole problem once and for all. This seems to us highly unlikely. We still do not believe that Nasser considers his forces (together with those of other Arab states) capable of carrying such a campaign to a successful conclusion. And in our opinion they are not so capable. Moreover, we believe that the Soviets would almost certainly advise Nasser against a military effort of this magnitude, perhaps with strong insistence.

4 The most likely course seems to be for Nasser to hold to his present winnings as long as he can, and in as full measure as he can. As of the moment he has vastly enhanced his own prestige in Egypt and throughout the Arab world, diminished the standing of Israel, and, at least for the moment, administered a serious setback to the United States. Moreover, by simply standing where he is, he places the Israelis in an extremely difficult position. He keeps the crisis at high pitch, and as long as this continues the

Israelis must remain mobilized. This they cannot do for long without adverse effects upon their economy.

5   The Israelis face dismaying choices. Surprised and shaken by Nasser's action, they failed to take the instant military counteraction which might have been most effective. If they attack now, they will face far more formidable opposition than in the rapid campaign of 1956. We believe that they would still be able to drive the Egyptians away from the entrance to the Strait of Tiran, but it would certainly cost them heavy losses of men and materiel. We are not sure that they have sufficient stockpiles of ammunition and equipment for a war lasting more than three or four weeks, and it is possible that they would not embark upon a major campaign without prior assurances from the United States of adequate resupply.

6   But the alternative for the Israelis is perilous. To acquiesce in the permanent closing of the Strait of Tiran would constitute an economic and political setback from which no early recovery would be foreseeable. The Israelis would expect, correctly we believe, that the Arabs over the long run would be encouraged to undertake new and still more dangerous harassments. We are inclined to believe that, unless the United States and other major powers take whatever steps are necessary to reopen the Strait, the Israelis will feel compelled to go to war.

7   In this event they might choose to begin hostilities by attacking Syria and wait for the Egyptians to respond. If the Egyptians did not, Nasser would lose much of what he has gained. If they did, they would lose the advantage of their defensive positions.

8   The Soviets are unlikely to take vigorous steps to calm down the crisis so long as it continues to produce deleterious effects upon Israel (and the United States) and advantages for Nasser. Nevertheless, they may be apprehensive about the future course of events. They may not have known in advance about the closing of the Strait. We do not believe that they desire a Middle Eastern war, or that they have planned with Nasser the destruction of Israel at this juncture. They will probably oppose by diplomatic and propagandistic means any efforts by the United States and the western powers to open the Strait. But, if we assume an attempt by the western powers to open the Strait by military force, we do not think that the Soviets would use their own armed forces in opposition.

9   One almost certain objective of the Soviets is to see the United States more firmly and publicly identified with Israel. This would have the obvious effect of making the entire Arab world—including, in an ambivalent way, even the more conservative states—convinced that the United States is irrevocably committed to their common enemy. It would further weaken the US position in the area, threaten US oil interests, and strengthen the

Soviet position as friend and protector of all Arabs against their imperialist foes. This Soviet aim has already been realized in considerable degree. Moreover, the Soviets must be glad to see US attention diverted from Vietnam, but it does not seem likely that they think the Middle Eastern crisis will appreciably affect US military capabilities or intentions in Southeast Asia.

10   One important question is what the Soviets would do if the Israelis attacked the United Arab Republic and waged a successful campaign. Such an event would be a grave setback for Nasser and, by extension, for the Soviet Union itself. Nevertheless, we do not believe that the Soviets would intervene in the conflict with their own combat forces. They could, of course, use their bomber and missile forces against Israel, but they would be very unlikely to do so, though they might threaten it. They do not have the capability of introducing lesser kinds of forces (ground troops, or volunteers) in this area with sufficient speed to be decisive, and we do not think they would try to do so. They would be cautious about the risk of armed confrontation with US forces. And they would probably count upon the political intervention of great powers, including themselves, to stop the fighting before Nasser had suffered too much damage.

11   The position of other Arab countries than the United Arab Republic is, at this stage of crisis, ancillary and comparatively unimportant. Conceivably Syria might touch off larger hostilities by attacking Israel in force, but we believe that both Nasser and the Soviet Union would be opposed to such action. If war broke out, Syrian forces would engage, other Arab states would send help, but it would not matter very much. The crisis in its present acute intensity is essentially one between Israel and the United Arab Republic, the United States and the United Arab Republic, and (to a more moderate degree) between the United States and the Soviet Union. The course of events will depend upon the action and reactions of these powers.

For the Board of National Estimates:
Sherman Kent, Chairman

Chapter 5

The Reemergence of the Palestinians

The 1967 war, as seen by Palestinians, demonstrated that Arab states could neither defeat Israel nor reverse the results of the 1948–1949 war. Accordingly, over the next two decades Palestinian leaders and organizations reclaimed their position as frontline actors in the conflict. The crux of this development was the rise of the Palestine Liberation Organization (PLO), as it became a dominant voice for Palestinians rather than, as before, a vehicle serving the interests of Arab states.

The intense emotions aroused by Israeli rule, even before 1967, are reflected in a poem from that period by Mahmoud Darwish (Reading 21). The rise of Palestinian armed movements to reclaim a central role opposite Israel was marked by PLO Chairman Yasir Arafat's address to the United Nations General Assembly in November 1974 (Reading 22). Arafat's speech still embodied the original Palestinian demand for a Palestinian state in place of Israel (the "1948 file"), and only secondarily the aim of ending the Israeli occupation of territories conquered in 1967 (the "1967 file"). But, as attention shifted to the "1967 file," a possible solution took center stage: Israeli withdrawal from the territories occupied in 1967, in return for an end to the conflict—or land for peace. The implication was that Palestinians would set aside the "1948 file" and accept the existence of Israel along pre-1967 lines.

As Palestinians moved in, some Arab states were pulling back. Egypt, in particular, focused more intensely on reclaiming the territory lost to Israel in 1967 (the Sinai peninsula). This disengagement produced the first peace treaty in the history of the conflict: the 1979 treaty between Israel and Egypt. The thinking that led Egypt to conclude a separate peace is expressed here by the Egyptian president who negotiated the agreement, Anwar Sadat (Reading 23). The same process as seen on the Israeli side is represented by the minister of defense at the time, Ezer Weizman (Reading 24).

So this period was characterized by seemingly contradictory trends. On one hand, there was the steady drumbeat of violence: the 1973 war, the 1982 Lebanon War and its aftermath, the Palestinian Intifada ("uprising") beginning in 1985, and the proliferation of attacks on civilian targets ("terrorism" in the eyes of those targeted). But at the same time Palestinian leaders were moving toward the "land for peace" (or "two-state") solution, which culminated in their acceptance of UN resolutions on this model and in the declaration of a Palestinian state. This process is described by one of its agents, Mahmoud Abbas, who was at the time in charge of negotiations for the PLO (Reading 25).

Further online resources:

Khartoum Resolutions (Arab summit), 1967: http://www.mideastweb.org/khartoum. htm, http://www.mfa.gov.il/mfa/foreignpolicy/peace/guide/pages/the%20khartoum% 20resolutions.aspx.

Palestinian National Charter, 1968: http://www.acpr.org.il/publications/books/38-Zero-plo_charter.pdf, http://avalon.law.yale.edu/20th_century/plocov.asp.

Palestine National Council Resolution, 1974: http://www.mideastweb.org/plo1974. htm.

Camp David Framework Agreements, 1978: http://avalon.law.yale.edu/20th_century/ campdav.asp, http://mfa.gov.il/MFA/ForeignPolicy/MFADocuments/Yearbook3/ Pages/192%20The%20Camp%20David%20agreements-%20annexes-%20 exchange%20o.aspx.

Kahan Commission Report, 1983: http://www.mfa.gov.il/mfa/foreignpolicy/mfadoc-uments/yearbook6/pages/104%20report%20of%20the%20commission%20of%20 inquiry%20into%20the%20e.aspx.

Hamas Charter, 1988: http://avalon.law.yale.edu/20th_century/hamas.asp, http:// www.palestine-studies.org/sites/default/files/jps-articles/2538093.pdf, http://www. acpr.org.il/resources/hamascharter.html.

Palestinian Declaration of Independence, 1988: http://www.mideastweb.org/ plc1988.htm, www.palestinelink.nl/pdf/declaration-of-independence.pdf.

Al-Jazeera account of the rise of the PLO, 2009: http://www.aljazeera.com/pro-grammes/plohistoryofrevolution/2009/07/200974133438561995.html.

21. "Identity Card"

*Mahmoud Darwish**

EDITOR'S NOTE *Mahmoud Darwish (1941–2008) is often considered the national Palestinian poet. He grew up in Israel and left in 1970, by which time he was established as a literary figure and activist. Given the importance of poetry in Arab culture, it has naturally served as a vehicle for political protest and the expression of nationalist sentiments. The poem here was written in 1964 and caused controversy later on, when broadcast over Israeli radio.*

Write down!
I am an Arab
And my identity card number is fifty thousand
I have eight children
And the ninth will come after a summer
Will you be angry?

Write down!
I am an Arab
Employed with fellow workers at a quarry
I have eight children
I get them bread
Garments and books
from the rocks
I do not supplicate charity at your doors
Nor do I belittle myself at the footsteps of your chamber
So will you be angry?

Write down!
I am an Arab
I have a name without a title
Patient in a country
Where people are enraged
My roots
Were entrenched before the birth of time

---

* Available at http://www.barghouti.com/poets/darwish/bitaqa.asp.

And before the opening of the eras
Before the pines, and the olive trees
And before the grass grew

My father [...] descends from the
family of the plow
Not from a privileged class
And my grandfather [...] was a farmer
Neither well bred, nor well born!
Teaches me the pride of the sun
Before teaching me how to read
And my house is like a watchman's hut
Made of branches and cane
Are you satisfied with my status?
I have a name without a title!

Write down!
I am an Arab
You have stolen the orchards of my ancestors
And the land which I cultivated
Along with my children
And you left nothing for us
Except for these rocks [...]
So will the state take them
As it has been said?!

Therefore!
Write down on the top of the first page:
I do not hate people
Nor do I encroach
But if I become hungry
The usurper's flesh will be my food
Beware...
Beware...
Of my hunger
And my anger!

22. "An Olive Branch and a Gun"

Yasir Arafat*

EDITOR'S NOTE *Yasir Arafat (1929–2004) emerged after the 1967 war as the dominant figure in the reassertion of Palestinian centrality in the conflict with Israel. Arafat was co-founder of Fatah, the Palestine Liberation Movement, in the late 1950s. In 1968 Fatah took over the PLO, initially founded by Arab states in 1964 as an umbrella organization for all Palestinian movements. Redirected to reflect Palestinian priorities, by late 1974 the PLO managed to achieve recognition from the Arab states as the only legitimate representative of the Palestinian people and to secure an invitation for Chairman Arafat to address the UN General Assembly. In his UN speech, Arafat combined the call for Israeli withdrawal from territories occupied in 1967 with the longstanding Palestinian goal of replacing Israel with a democratic and predominantly Arab Palestinian state.*

Mr. President,

I thank you for having invited the PLO to participate in this plenary session of the United Nations General Assembly. I am grateful to all those representatives of states of the United Nations who contributed to the decision to introduce the question of Palestine as a separate item on the agenda of this Assembly. That decision made possible the Assembly's resolution inviting us to address it on the question of Palestine. [...]

In addressing the General Assembly today, our people proclaims its faith in the future, unencumbered either by past tragedies or by present limitations. If, as we discuss the present, we enlist the past in our service, we do so only to light up our journey into the future alongside other movements of national liberation. If we return now to the historical roots of our cause, we do so because present at this very moment in our midst are those who, while they occupy our homes, as their cattle graze in our pastures, and as their hands pluck the fruit of our trees, claim at the same time that we are disembodied spirits, fictions without presence, without traditions or future. We speak of our roots also because until recently some people have regarded—and continued to regard—our problem as merely a problem of refugees. They have portrayed the

---

* Abridgement of Yasir Arafat, Address to the United Nations General Assembly, 29th Session, Official Records, A/PV.2282, November 13, 1974.

Middle East question as little more than a border dispute between the Arab States and the Zionist entity. They have imagined that our people claims rights not rightfully its own and fights neither with logic nor with valid motive, with a simple wish only to disturb the peace and to terrorize wantonly. [...]

In any event, as our discussion of the question of Palestine focuses upon historical roots, [it does] so because we believe that any question now exercising the world's concern must be viewed radically, in the true root sense of that word, if a real solution is ever to be grasped. We propose this radical approach as an antidote to an approach to international issues that obscures historical origins behind ignorance, denial, and a slavish obeisance to the present.

The roots of the Palestinian question reach back into the closing years of the nineteenth century, in other words, to that period we call the era of colonialism and settlement as we know it today. This is precisely the period during which Zionism as a scheme was born; its aim was the conquest of Palestine by European immigrants, just as settlers colonized, and indeed raided, most of Africa. This is the period during which, pouring forth out of the west, colonialism spread into the furthest reaches of Africa, Asia, and Latin America, building colonies, everywhere cruelly exploiting, oppressing, plundering the peoples of those three continents. This period persists into the present. Marked evidence of its totally reprehensible presence can be readily perceived in the racism practiced both in South Africa and in Palestine. [...]

The Jewish invasion of Palestine began in 1881. Before the first large wave of immigrants started arriving, Palestine had a population of half a million; most of the population was either Muslim or Christian, and only 20,000 were Jewish. Every segment of the population enjoyed the religious tolerance characteristic of our civilization.

Palestine was then a verdant land, inhabited mainly by an Arab people in the course of building its life and dynamically enriching its indigenous culture.

Between 1882 and 1917 the Zionist movement settled approximately 50,000 European Jews in our homeland. To do that, it resorted to trickery and deceit in order to implant them in our midst. Its success in getting Britain to issue the Balfour Declaration once again demonstrated the alliance between Zionism and imperialism. Furthermore, by promising to the Zionist movement what was not its to give, Britain showed how oppressive was the rule of imperialism. As it was constituted then, the League of Nations abandoned our Arab people, and Wilson's pledges and promises came to naught. In the guise of a Mandate, British imperialism was cruelly and directly imposed upon us. The Mandate issued by the League of Nations was to enable the Zionist invaders to consolidate their gains in our homeland.

Over a period of 30 years after the Balfour Declaration, the Zionist movement, together with its colonial ally, succeeded in bringing about the immigration of more European Jews and the usurpation of the lands of the Arabs of Palestine. Thus, in 1947, the Jewish population of Palestine was approximately 600,000, owning less than 6 percent of the fertile lands of Palestine, while the Arab population of Palestine numbered approximately 1,250,000.

As a result of the collision between the mandatory power and the Zionist movement and with the support of some countries, this General Assembly early in its history approved a recommendation to partition our Palestinian homeland. This took place in an atmosphere poisoned with questionable actions and strong pressure. The General Assembly partitioned what it had no right to divide—an indivisible homeland. When we rejected that decision, our position corresponded to that of the natural mother who refused to permit King Solomon to cut her son into two when the unnatural mother claimed the child for herself and agreed to his dismemberment. Furthermore, even though the partition resolution granted the colonialist settlers 54 percent of the land of Palestine, their dissatisfaction with the decision prompted them to wage a war of terror against the civilian Arab population. They occupied 81 percent of the total area of Palestine, uprooting a million Arabs. Thus they occupied 524 Arab towns and villages, of which they destroyed 385, completely obliterating them in the process. Having done so, they built their own settlements and colonies on the ruins of our farms and our groves. The roots of the Palestine question lie here. Its causes do not stem from any conflict between two religions or two nationalisms. Neither is it a border conflict between neighboring states. It is the cause of people deprived of its homeland, dispersed and uprooted, and living mostly in exile and in refugee camps.

With support from imperialist and colonialist powers, the Zionist entity managed to get itself accepted as a member of the United Nations. It further succeeded in getting the Palestine question deleted from the agenda of the United Nations and in deceiving world public opinion by presenting our cause as a problem of refugees in need either of charity from do-gooders or of settlement in a land not theirs.

Not satisfied with all this, the racist entity, founded on the imperialist–colonialist concept, turned itself into a base of imperialism and into an arsenal of weapons. This enabled it to assume its role of subjugating the Arab people and of committing aggression against them, in order to satisfy its ambitions for further expansion on Palestinian and other Arab lands. In addition to the many instances of aggression committed by this entity against the Arab states, it has launched two large-scale wars, in 1956 and 1967, thus endangering world peace and security.

As a result of Zionist aggression in June 1967, the enemy occupied Egyptian Sinai as far as the Suez Canal. The enemy occupied Syria's Golan Heights, in addition to all Palestinian land west of the Jordan. All these developments have led to the creation in our area of what has come to be known as the "Middle East problem." The situation has been rendered more serious by the enemy's persistence in maintaining its unlawful occupation and in further consolidating it, thus establishing a beachhead for world imperialism's thrust against our Arab nation. All Security Council decisions and appeals to world public opinion for withdrawal from the lands occupied in June 1967 have been ignored. Despite all the peaceful efforts at the international level, the enemy has not been deterred from its expansionist policy. The only alternative open before our Arab nations, chiefly Egypt and Syria, was to expend exhaustive efforts in preparing forcefully to resist that barbarous armed invasion—and this in order to liberate Arab lands and to restore the rights of the Palestinian people, after all other peaceful means had failed.

Under these circumstances, the fourth war broke out in October 1973, bringing home to the Zionist enemy the bankruptcy of its policy of occupation and expansion and its reliance on the concept of military might. Despite all this, the leaders of the Zionist entity are far from having learned any lesson from their experience. They are making preparations for the fifth war, resorting once more to the language of military superiority, aggression, terrorism, subjugation—and, finally, always to war in their dealings with the Arabs. [...]

For the past 30 years, our people have had to struggle against British occupation and Zionist invasion, both of which had one intention, namely the usurpation of our land. Six major revolts and tens of popular uprisings were staged to foil these attempts, so that our homeland might remain ours. Over 30,000 martyrs, the equivalent in comparative terms of 6 million Americans, died in the process.

When the majority of the Palestinian people was uprooted from its homeland in 1948, the Palestinian struggle for self-determination continued under the most difficult conditions. We tried every possible means to continue our political struggle to attain our national rights, but to no avail. Meanwhile we had to struggle for sheer existence. Even in exile we educated our children. This was all a part of trying to survive. [...]

It is through our popular armed struggle that our political leadership and our national institutions finally crystallized and a national liberation movement, comprising all the Palestinian factions, organizations, and capabilities, materialized in the PLO.

Through our militant Palestine national liberation movement, our people's struggle matured and grew enough to accommodate political and social struggle in addition to armed struggle. The PLO was a major factor in creating a new Palestinian individual, qualified to shape the future of our Palestine, not merely content with mobilizing the Palestinians for the challenges of the present. [...]

The PLO represents the Palestinian people, legitimately and uniquely. Because of this, the PLO expresses the wishes and hopes of its people. Because of this, too, it brings these very wishes and hopes before you, urging you not to shirk the momentous historic responsibility toward our just cause.

For many years now our people has been exposed to the ravages of war, destruction, and dispersion. It has paid in the blood of its sons that which cannot ever be compensated. It has borne the burdens of occupation, dispersion, eviction, and terror more uninterruptedly than any other people. And yet all this has made our people neither vindictive nor vengeful. Nor has it caused us to resort to the racism of our enemies. Nor have we lost the true method by which friend and foe are distinguished.

For we deplore all those crimes committed against the Jews; we also deplore all the real discrimination suffered by them because of their faith.

I am a rebel and freedom is my cause. I know well that many of you present here today once stood in exactly the same resistance position as I now occupy and from which I must fight. You once had to convert dreams into reality by your struggle. Therefore you must now share my dream. I think this is exactly why I can ask you now to help, as, together, we bring out our dream into a bright reality, our common dream for a peaceful future in Palestine's sacred land. [...]

Why therefore should I not dream and hope? For is not revolution the making real of dreams and hopes? So let us work together that my dream may be fulfilled, that I may return with my people out of exile, there in Palestine, to live with this Jewish freedom fighter and his partners, with this Arab priest and his brothers, in one democratic state where Christian, Jew, and Muslim live in justice, equality, and fraternity.

Is this not a noble dream, worthy of my struggle alongside all lovers of freedom everywhere? For the most admirable dimension of this dream is that it is Palestinian, a dream from the land of peace, the land of martyrdom and heroism, and the land of history, too.

Let us remember that the Jews of Europe and the United States have been known to lead the struggles for secularism and the separation of church and state. They have also been known to fight against discrimination on religious grounds. How can they then refuse this humane paradigm for the Holy Land? How then can they continue to support the most fanatic, discriminatory, and closed of nations in its policy?

In my formal capacity as chairman of the PLO and leader of the Palestinian revolution I proclaim before you that, when we speak of our common hopes for the Palestine of tomorrow, we include in our perspective all Jews now living in Palestine who choose to live with us there in peace and without discrimination.

In my formal capacity as chairman of the PLO and leader of the Palestinian revolution I call upon Jews to turn away one by one from the illusory promises made to them by Zionist ideology and Israeli leadership. They are offering Jews perpetual bloodshed, endless war, and continuous thralldom.

We invite them to emerge from their moral isolation into a more open realm of free choice, far from their present leadership's efforts to implant in them a Masada complex.

We offer them the most generous solution, that we might live together in a framework of just peace in our democratic Palestine.

In my formal capacity as Chairman of the PLO I announce here that we do not wish one drop of either Arab or Jewish blood to be shed; neither do we delight in the continuation of killing, which would end once a just peace based on our people's rights, hopes, and aspirations has been finally established.

In my formal capacity as Chairman of the PLO and leader of the Palestinian revolution I appeal to you to accompany our people in its struggle to attain its right to self-determination. This right is consecrated in the United Nations Charter and has been repeatedly confirmed in resolutions adopted by this august body since the drafting of the Charter. I appeal to you, further, to aid our people's return to its homeland from an involuntary exile imposed upon it by force of arms, by tyranny, by oppression, so that we may regain our property and our land and thereafter live in our national homeland, free and sovereign, enjoying all the privileges of nationhood. Only then can we pour all our resources into the mainstream of human civilization. Only then can Palestinian creativity be concentrated on the service of humanity. Only then will our Jerusalem resume its historic role as a peaceful shrine for all religions.

I appeal to you to enable our people to establish national independent sovereignty over its own land.

Today I have come bearing an olive branch and a freedom fighter's gun. Do not let the olive branch fall from my hand. I repeat: do not let the olive branch fall from my hand.

War flares up in Palestine, and yet it is in Palestine that peace will be born.

23. "The Road to Peace"

*Anwar Sadat**

EDITOR'S NOTE *Anwar Sadat (1918–1981) succeeded Gamal Abdul Nasser as president of Egypt upon Nasser's death in 1970. During the decade that followed, he made two unexpected moves on the Arab–Israeli front. Together with Syria, he launched a war against Israel in 1973, showing that Egypt still had military options and sparking renewed efforts to negotiate a settlement. When peace talks stagnated, he initiated in 1977 a historic visit to Israel, which led to the 1979 Egypt–Israel peace treaty. For this Sadat shared a Nobel Peace Prize; but in 1981 he was assassinated by radical Islamists. The selection presented here from his autobiography describes his historic initiative and was written after that event but before a final agreement had been reached.*

One last thing remains to be said to the American people: We are ready for peace. We want it and welcome it. I have been extending a hand to peace since my 1971 [Peace] Initiative and up to this very moment. How earnestly I want Israel to do the same was made only too evident to the entire world by the historic trip I took to Jerusalem in November 1977. [...]

I realized that we were about to be caught up in a terrible, vicious circle, precisely like the one we'd lived through over the last thirty years. *And the root cause was none other than that very psychological barrier I have referred to.* It was because of that barrier that Israel was objecting, at a preliminary stage of the Peace Process, to formalities and procedural points—even down to the most insignificant features such as a comma or a period, a word added or deleted here or there in a proposed text. [...]

By a "psychological barrier" I mean that huge wall of suspicion, fear, hate, and misunderstanding that has for so long existed between Israel and the Arabs. It made each side simply unwilling to believe the other, and quite unprepared psychologically to accept anything transmitted through the USA (if channeled through other parties, a message from one side to the other would be viewed with even greater suspicion). I have therefore tended to compare that barrier to the Australian Great Barrier Reef—which is so dangerous to navigation in the southern hemisphere. And, if the apparent barrier goes back only

---

* Excerpts from Anwar El-Sadat, *In Search of Identity: An Autobiography* (New York: Harper & Row, 1978), pp. 301–312.

thirty years, it really has far deeper roots in history. For if, as Begin alleges, the question has a religious dimension for the Israelis, it certainly has such a dimension for us. So I decided to look at the situation from a new angle and to embark on a fresh study that took all the dimensions into consideration. [...]

What was it, then, that I needed to change? We had been accustomed (and a whole generation had been brought up) to regard Israel as taboo—as an entity whose emotional associations simply prevented anyone from approaching it. The situation went from bad to worse as the cumulative effect of things said and done over the years rendered any change difficult, if it didn't actually preclude that possibility for both the Arabs and the Israelis. So I concluded that any possible change should occur to the *substance* of that attitude itself. If indeed we wanted to get to grips with the substance of the dispute—with the basis of the problem—in order to establish a durable peace, I reasoned, we ought to find a completely new approach that would bypass all formalities and procedural technicalities by pulling down the barrier of mutual mistrust. Only thus, I decided, could we hope to break out of the vicious circle and avert the blind alley of the past. [...]

This earliest version of the Initiative began consequently to give place to another—a visit I would personally pay to Jerusalem to perform the Bairam prayers at al-Aqsa Mosque, in fulfillment of my claim that I was ready to go to the end of the world to achieve peace. I had said that I would be willing to go anywhere in search of peace. Could I now exclude Israel? I have always meant what I said and stood responsible for my words. I therefore decided to go right to the Knesset, the political body representing the Israeli people, in order to submit to them the complete facts of the situation, and to confront them with the choice they would have to make if they really wanted to live in peace in this part of the world. I wanted to put the ball in their court.

This modified version of the Initiative soon crystallized and grew quite acceptable to me. I decided to declare it in my speech at the opening of the new session of the People's Assembly. I did so, stressing my willingness to go to the end of the world, not excluding Israel, in order to avoid the unnecessary wounding, not to mention killing, of a single soldier. I stressed that I meant exactly what I said, and that I was willing to go to the Knesset if the trip would help achieve our objectives. Everybody was present—the government ministers and so on, as well as Yasir Arafat. The immediate reaction was quite funny. Some imagined it was a slip of the tongue, or an effusion unbacked by proper thought. Some people still believe that politicians say things they don't mean—which I could never do. [...]

It was at this point that my foreign minister felt himself unequal to the Initiative. When we were preparing to go to Syria, he had said he couldn't come along because, he was unwell. "All right," I said to the Vice-President; "he could come along with me to Israel." The Vice-President explained that it wasn't like that at all, and that the minister objected to the entire Initiative. "Fair enough," I said. "I can't ask anybody to do something against his wishes." I subsequently accepted his resignation.

My plane took off from Abu Suwayr airfield in the Canal region and, in less than forty minutes, landed at Lod airport. I was in Israel. Disbelief prevailed and people were practically stunned. The minute I stepped out of the plane, I found myself face to face with Mrs. Golda Meir, who had cut short her US visit in order to see me on arrival. We exchanged greetings. I saw Dayan next—recognizing the man against whom I had fought the 1973 battle. Then Abba Eban, and General Ariel Sharon, who had led the famous counterattack. "If you attempt to cross to the West Bank again," I told him, "I'll put you in jail!" "Oh, no!" he said, "I'm Minister of Culture now!" [...]

In the afternoon I went to the Knesset. I made my speech, which was followed by speeches from Premier Begin and Opposition leader Peres. The Knesset session was over. In spite of the great emotional and physical fatigue, I felt very happy indeed. And I learned that my daughter had given birth to a girl at eight o'clock that very morning, while I had been praying at al-Aqsa Mosque. The fatigue—indeed, the immense exhaustion—wasn't due to overwork or to the hectic time I had spent since I arrived (in meetings, talks, etc.) but to extremely deep mental concentration. It was this that made me feel so tired. My mind was highly alert and my concentration almost unprecedented, for the simple reason that I regarded my mission in Israel as truly sacred. Though confident of my people's support, I was willing, if the least sign of rejection became apparent, to go back and submit my resignation to our People's Assembly.

My confidence was vindicated. On my return nearly 5 million Cairenes were out to welcome me, staging an unprecedented demonstration of support. Everybody was anxious for my safety. Believing that my Initiative had been more risky than brave, their thanksgiving was quite genuine; indeed, they were still stunned and unable to express their joy. I was naturally very happy at this, but felt that it meant I had been entrusted with the binding task of bringing my mission to a successful conclusion. I had been, as it were, ordered to continue to serve my people until the object of the Initiative had been achieved. [...]

But what of the outcome? Did my plan come off?

I had reckoned that my Jerusalem trip would break the vicious circle within which we had been caught up for years. On this my calculations proved accurate enough. For, just as my people's reception was remarkable, even stunning, so too the Israeli people— women, children, and old men—showed a remarkable and equally stunning response. Even the Israeli special forces and paratroopers who were there to guard me actually danced for joy. They saluted me, though I had fought against them in 1973 and inflicted unprecedented losses on them.

Why? It was, I believe, because they respect men who fight and, perhaps even more importantly, because they respect a man who after his victory can stand up and say: "Right. Let the October War put an end to all wars! And now let us sit down together like civilized men around the negotiating table to discuss what you want—security—instead of resorting to force."

I returned from Israel having agreed on two basic points: first, that the October War would be our last war; and, second, that we should discuss around the negotiating table the question of security both for them and for us. I took this result to our People's Assembly and, having recounted all that had transpired, put it down for their consideration. I was happy to get almost unanimous endorsement (with only two or three members, out of 360, objecting). As a result, my immediate plan, to spend a few days in the Canal region for a rest, was modified. I decided instead to convene the Cairo Conference, with a view to maintaining the peace momentum and paving the way for the Geneva Conference.

What the situation will be like when this book is published, in a few months' time, I don't know. What I do know is that I will stand by my Peace Initiative, whatever happens; and that I will waste no chance whatsoever of ensuring that the problem of peace in the Middle East receives a radical and civilized solution. Let me reiterate here the point that I made to the Israeli Knesset: that I am not after a bilateral agreement on Sinai (which couldn't solve the problem), but seek a wider peace, based on justice to all concerned. I will work in future—until this book is out, and after—for the establishment of a just peace in our region, which includes the restoration of the Arab territories occupied in 1967, and the solution of the Palestinian problem through the establishment of a national Palestinian state, or—to use Carter's term—homeland.

My major target is to put an end to the crisis in the Middle East by solving the Palestinian problem and by effecting a withdrawal from the Arab land occupied in 1967. I shall always be guided by the principle of just peace and am willing to make any effort, and any sacrifice necessary, however long the process may take. If it turns out to be a question of one side trying to impose its will on the other, let me affirm that, just as I stated my willingness to go to the end of the world to achieve peace, so I would be willing to fight to the end of the world for the same target.

24. "The 1978 Negotiations at Camp David"

Ezer Weizman*

EDITOR'S NOTE *Ezer Weizman (1924–2005) was a former commander of the Israeli Air Force who served in the Likud-led government of Menahem Begin as minister of defense from 1977 to 1980. In this capacity he played a key role in the negotiations that followed Sadat's 1977 visit to Israel and culminated in an agreement reached at Camp David, the US presidential retreat, in September 1978. Over time Weizman's views became more dovish and he later held various posts in Labor governments, finally serving as the seventh president of Israel. This selection from his autobiography recounts the critical last phase of the Camp David talks.*

With the conference apparently headed for a final rupture, [US President Jimmy] Carter and [Israeli Prime Minister Menahem] Begin held their last private meeting.

It was the breakthrough. Informed by President Carter of Sadat's concession and under unprecedented pressure, Begin reversed the whole course of events with a dramatic declaration. "If what is holding up peace are the Sinai settlements," he told the president of the United States, "I shall submit the matter to the decision of the Knesset and honor whatever the Knesset decides. I shall even recommend that, on this important and sensitive issue, party discipline shall not be enforced in the voting. That is all I can do. Nothing more."

In the course of that talk, Begin understood that he had to decide—then and there—whether he preferred the airfields or peace. In choosing the latter, he surrendered the former. He also agreed to include in the framework agreement a term never previously accepted by Israel, "recognition of the legitimate rights of the Palestinian people," although his consent did not include recognition of the Palestinians' rights to establish an independent state within the boundaries of the land of Israel.

Begin, who had only recently explained the danger involved in using terms like "legitimate rights," now denied to us that what he had agreed to jeopardized Israel.

* Excerpts from Ezer Weizman, *The Battle for Peace* (New York: Bantam Books, 1981), pp. 372–377.

"What is the ultimate importance of the term 'legitimate rights'?" he asked, promptly answering his own question: "The origin of the word is in the Latin *lex*, denoting 'law.' With the development of language, this turned into the English word 'legitimate.' What is the meaning of 'legitimate right'? If it is a right—that means it is legitimate. Can a right be illegitimate?"

By such verbal acrobatics Begin managed to come to terms with reality.

Sunday morning—the last day of the summit conference—found us exhausted and battered, but satisfied. There was a sense of historic achievement, of "All's well that ends well."

Then it suddenly transpired that Carter had promised Sadat a letter in which the United States would declare that it viewed east Jerusalem as occupied territory, just like the rest of the territory Israel had been holding since 1967.

"If that's the case," Begin said grimly, "we can pack our bags and go home without another word."

If the talks were to fail at the very moment when success was finally possible, no issue was better chosen than Jerusalem. Every Jew the world over would justify Israel's obduracy.

The problem was resolved by a letter stating that the US position on Jerusalem remained as defined by the American delegation to the UN General Assembly in June 1967, when the United States had called for international supervision of the holy places while refusing to recognize Israel's annexation of east Jerusalem. [...]

However, a few secondary issues remained to be resolved. It emerged that the agreement also required Israel to demilitarize a zone along our borders, albeit a small one.

All the same, it was hard for Israel to concede this point. We wanted to enlarge the force we would be permitted to station within this zone. I went to talk with Sadat to see if I could win his consent.

"How many battalions do you want?" Sadat demanded.

"Three battalions of our border guard," I replied.

"All right, Ezer," Sadat said grandly. "For you—four battalions. Ever since the October war, I have no more complexes."

The Camp David Conference did not produce a complete peace agreement. Instead, there were two framework agreements that the two sides were required to complete within three months. The agreements laid down lines for future developments; however, it was evident right from the outset that many issues had been left open—deliberately.

One agreement provided the framework for an Israeli–Egyptian peace treaty. It was the easier and simpler of the two. Israel gave up the whole of the Sinai, including the settlements and airfields. The United States lent its assistance by a verbal undertaking to construct two airfields inside Israel to replace those we were abandoning in the Sinai, promising to complete them before the time came for our withdrawal.

The United States was abandoning its umpire role. It would continue to supervise; however, unlike [in] the previous arrangements, neither side could remove the UN observers without the consent of the other and without the unanimous agreement of the Security Council. With the exception of combat planes and antiaircraft missiles, the Sinai would not be demilitarized as Israel had once desired; however, a wide buffer zone would be created between the two armies.

The second agreement was a framework for an overall Middle East peace settlement. While it dealt with peace between Israel and all the Arab states, including Egypt, it was mainly directed at the West Bank and the Gaza Strip. In it, Egypt recognized Israel's need for security guarantees with regard to those areas, while Israel undertook to grant full autonomy to their inhabitants.

In the framework of this agreement, Israel consented to the inclusion of terms and concepts she had never previously accepted: negotiations to include Palestinian representatives, not restricted to the inhabitants of those areas; solution of the Palestinian problem "in all its aspects." The agreement specified that a solution must acknowledge the legitimate rights of the Palestinian people and their just demands. Both sides agreed that autonomy would apply for no more than a five-year interim period. However, Israel reserved a veto over a number of central points of particular sensitivity, as well as the right to demand full sovereignty in the future.

In this second agreement—even more than in the first—most of the issues were left open to later negotiations. The two sides parted well aware that they could scarcely hope to reach agreement on some points, such as the status of Jerusalem, Israeli settlement in the occupied territories, and the argument over "abrogation" or "withdrawal" of the Israeli military government.

Some of my colleagues were still dubious about the agreement, and I tried to reassure them. "An agreement," I said, "is like a Jewish marriage contract. You don't look at it, you put it away in the closet. If things go wrong with the marriage, you get it out and study it—but by then, it's too late, and heaven help you if you need it!"

Israel and Egypt attended the Camp David Conference because they were unable to refuse the invitation from the president of the United States. In view of the minimal goals set by the sides— concluding the conference without suffering any harm in their vital interests—the conference's success in working out a framework agreement came as a surprise. The success evidently stemmed from the desire to reach agreement, which outweighed the desire of each side to protect its own private interests, and from the role played by the United States in the deliberations.

The greatest achievement of the Camp David Conference lay in reaching an agreement, with all the implications of that achievement: breaking the psychological barrier between the Israeli people and the Arab world; eliminating the taboo imposed on Israel thirty years ago by restoring the Arab–Israeli conflict to the conventional terms of international disputes. At the same time, the road to the stabilization of a permanent peace in the region is still long.

Study of the two framework agreements reveals clear distinctions: while the bilateral agreement with Egypt is clear, the framework agreement about the future of Judea and Samaria and Gaza is marked by its deliberately vague formulations. While there is no conditional link between the two agreements, the mere fact of their simultaneous signing constitutes a kind of conditional link. It would be naive to imagine that progress could be made in implementing Israeli–Egyptian peace without some progress in Judea, Samaria, and Gaza. President Sadat continues to point out that he has not signed a separate agreement or relinquished a single Arab national objective with regard to Israel.

In the immediate future, the key to any further progress is in the hands of King Hussein, whose commitment to the peace process would affect the outcome of the negotiations, and particularly developments in the occupied territories, as the agreements go into effect during the interim period and subsequently. On the other hand, without Hussein's commitment, it is doubtful whether Israel can implement the autonomy plan unaided. Hussein seems to be in no hurry to give an affirmative answer; if he does, he will probably attempt to squeeze out the maximum number of concessions—in advance.

The dangers facing the first agreement hinge on Sadat. In the whole Camp David mosaic, Sadat constitutes the key link whose fracture would lead to the disintegration of the entire chain. However, Sadat does not seem overly vulnerable. There is no prospect of popular unrest, revolution, or coup attempts against Sadat in consequence of the agreements. The Egyptian army and its commanders seem likely to remain loyal.

Two risks do remain: an assassination attempt and Sadat's state of health.

Inter-Arab pressures against him are probably not going to threaten the Camp David accord. Sadat's most important backing comes from the Saudis. Even if they are not overjoyed with the agreements, they will probably not enter into an overt confrontation with him. On the other hand, Syria's interests draw her in the opposite direction, although her room for maneuver in trying to foil the agreements is not great. Syria was greatly surprised by the agreements, having long believed that Sadat's initiative was doomed to failure. Syria could choose the military option against Israel, but such a move would not likely undermine the Israeli–Egyptian agreement. On the contrary, there is the danger that Israel would see herself as being at greater liberty than she is now in her actions against Syria. In view of this, the Syrians may be expected to undertake anti-Egyptian moves while trying to draw Hussein to their side.

With all that, I do not rule out the possibility of Syria joining in the political process, particularly if Jordan decides to take part in the negotiations.

The agreement has placed the PLO in a dilemma. On the one hand, they naturally want to foil this development; on the other, they're afraid of being left out in the cold. The result will probably be increased terrorist action—against Israel, against individual candidates for membership of the autonomy council, against Egypt, and perhaps even against Sadat in person. A less likely possibility is that they'll go for a daring political gambit, with a PLO initiative toward a direct understanding between Israel and the PLO.

In any event, the Israeli–Egyptian agreement is difficult for the Arab world to swallow—because of the very fact of Sadat's signing an agreement with Israel and putting an end to the boycott against us.

Outside Camp David, a storm was raging.

I looked at Begin. "I suggest we go and pay a visit to Sadat," I said. The prime minister thought it over for a moment or two. Then he phoned Sadat's lodge. The Egyptian president answered. Begin congratulated him on the agreement, adding that he would like to come and visit.

"With the greatest of pleasure," Sadat replied.

When Begin entered Sadat's lodge, he shook the Egyptian president's hand with great warmth. It was their first meeting since their joint outing to Gettysburg, ten days previously, at the early stages of the conference.

Later, Sadat paid a return visit to Begin's cabin.

I filled up glasses with wine for everyone, including Sadat—forgetting in my excitement that, as a devout Muslim, he does not drink alcohol.

"I'm not a heathen like you!" he rebuked me. "I drink fruit juice!"

Standing there, holding our glasses of wine or fruit juice, we drank to one another's health. "*L'chaim!*"

Later we all flew by helicopter to Washington for the closing celebration. When the ceremony ended at the White House, it was late at night in Washington—early morning in Israel. I dialed the familiar Israeli number. My wife answered.

"Re'uma," I said, "it's peace."

25. "The Road to Oslo"

Mahmoud Abbas*

EDITOR'S NOTE *Mahmoud Abbas (1935–), also known as Abu Mazen, was born in what is now Israel and became a refugee during the 1948–1949 war. He was among the founding members of Fatah (the Palestine Liberation Movement) in the late 1950s, under the leadership of Yasir Arafat. After the 1967 war Fatah gained control of the PLO, which had been founded by Arab states in 1964. Abbas was a key figure in the rise of the PLO and in the reassertion of the Palestinian role in the conflict, working closely with Arafat. During the 1970s and 1980s, as he recounts here, contact between the two sides began to develop and the possibility of negotiation was explored.*

In 1948 Israel occupied part of our land and displaced part of our people. Then in 1967 it occupied the remainder of this land and displaced another part of our people. All the Palestinian people had become either displaced or under occupation. Israel also occupied a part of Syria's Golan Heights and all of Egypt's Sinai. Thus all we knew of Israel was the manifestations of its power and omnipotence. Beyond that we were kept in the dark about the Israeli people. The slogan 'Know Thine Enemy' was reiterated everywhere, but was not acted upon. The Arab masses therefore lived in a state of ignorance, deliberately barred from knowing their enemy. At times we feared and dreaded him, sometimes to the point of terror, at other times we underestimated him to the point of apathy. It was considered reprehensible for a Palestinian or an Arab to be caught following the news of Israeli society or reading a book about Israel. To acquaint oneself with this society's secrets, its lifestyle, the way it thinks and behaves was the only way of discovering its weaknesses and its strengths; but this was denied us.

The first principle of a successful military campaign requires the commander to reconnoitre the ground and understand the enemy before an attack is mounted. In political terms, governments send out envoys, spies and intelligence officers to foreign countries to observe at close quarters the nature of the people and the composition of the society in order to take the appropriate

---

* Excerpts from Mahmoud Abbas, *Through Secret Channels* (Reading: Garnet Publishing, 1995), pp. 12–18.

action. As for us in the Arab world, the simple act of seeking knowledge about one's opponent used to provoke accusations of disloyalty and doubts about one's patriotism. We, the ordinary Arab people, believed that our superiors—the leaders, civil servants, intelligence officers and diplomats—were fully equipped with knowledge and information, but to our surprise we discovered that these people were quite ignorant about the enemy they were confronting with their fingers on the trigger. And they fought four wars against it.

In early 1970, after I had assumed responsibility for mobilization and organization within the Fatah movement, I found nothing with which to indoctrinate our cadres apart from a few books about revolutionary experiments that had preceded ours, such as those of Vietnam, China, Algeria, and Guevara's Cuba. As for the Zionist experiment, from Herzl to the establishment of the Jewish state and beyond, we knew little more than a few simple headings devoid of any detail. One day I read an item in a local newspaper reporting that Jews from Arab countries now made up more than half of Israel's population. The report aroused my curiosity. How did the Arab states supply Israel with half its population? What was the relationship between them and the occidental Jews in Israel? There were other questions too that I could not answer, and thus a programme of reading and research into the intricacies and hidden aspects of Israeli society became necessary. Between 1970 and 1977 I published two books about Jewish emigration from the Arab states and the West, and about Israel's relations with the United States and the proponents of peace in its society. I also raised two slogans during this period. The first demanded that Arab states should seek to repatriate Jews who had emigrated or had been evicted; Egypt, Iraq, Libya, Tunisia, Morocco and Yemen responded by issuing either a statement or a governmental decision permitting the return of Jews. The second slogan called for contacts with Israeli factions so as to initiate a dialogue for the attainment of peace. [...]

Our efforts pointed in two directions. First, all pro-peace Israeli factions grouped under the banner of the Peace Now movement. These factions have many different ideas and vary in their understanding of the peace process, but they are united by the general concept of 'peace' without defining the exact meaning of the word. Second, oriental Jews of Andalusian descent who had previously lived in Arab countries as well as in Turkey and Bulgaria. They differ from Ashkenazi Jews in custom, tradition and belief, and form two-thirds of Israel's population. The circumstances of their arrival in Israel were often shrouded in mystery, and they lived, and many of them still do, at the bottom of the social ladder. Their status in the new society was largely due to their background, but possibly also to faulty planning by earlier Israeli settlers, who were mostly Ashkenazi. The oriental Jews were more violent and cruel towards the Arabs, because they wanted to integrate themselves with the ruling elite;

to prove themselves more Zionist than the Ashkenazis, they tended towards extremism. Consequently they sided with the Herut movement, which led the Israeli opposition against Labour in 1977. When the Likud coalition of Herut and its allies assumed power in Israel, the oriental Jews believed they had realized their dreams and goals, which they thought the Labour Party had obstructed for thirty years.

After 1977 we held dozens of meetings and attended dozens of conferences, which grouped Israelis of all leanings, whether from Peace Now or oriental Jews, with whom we tried to build bridges of peace linking Palestinians and Israelis. We were not dissuaded from our line by statements branding them enemies of the Arabs and the Palestinians, even though we knew they supported the extreme right. Through our meetings with them we got the feeling that they were prepared, as far as their influence and energies would allow, to act as a go-between for Palestinians and Israelis, Arabs and Jews. But the disinformation of the media and the propaganda of the Israeli Right often nullified the benefits of meetings that did take place, especially after the Knesset's decision of 6 August 1986 banning contacts with the PLO under penalty of imprisonment.

It is impossible for the Israelis to live forever in the Middle East without meeting their neighbours and for Israel to remain an alien state in the heart of the Arab world. I do not believe that it is in the interest of Israelis to live by the words of Moshe Arens, the former Likud defence minister, who was born in America and emigrated to Israel to join Likud, where he proudly proclaimed, 'I know more about weeds in Alaska than I do about Arabs'. The Israelis used to complain to the world that the Palestinians in particular and the Arabs in general refused to accept the hand that was stretched to them in peace, because they wanted to destroy Israel and throw the Jews into the sea. At the same time, the Israelis never tired of declaring their acceptance of international legality as a basis for a political solution, convinced that the Arabs were not prepared to do the same. Thus our initiatives after 1977 embarrassed the Israelis and prompted them to invent reasons for not responding to us. They would not talk with terrorists, saboteurs and murderers, they would say. [...]

Moreover, there was the immense contribution of the six years of uprising, the Intifada, which had claimed and maimed thousands of children, women and men as its victims. The end of the Cold War and its consequences, the breakup of the socialist camp and the trauma caused by the Gulf War also played their part in the political windmill. The extensive networks of contacts which the PLO had set up with local Israeli and international Jewish factions, which were (or became) champions of peace, played an important role in the transformation and convergence of Israeli public opinion; they did so by emphasizing that coexistence was possible and the achievement of peace was no longer impossible. As we honour our fallen heroes, we honour the heroes of peace.

The PLO must be given credit too, for it paved the way to peace in the Middle East. Prompted by the strength and momentum of the Palestinian uprising, it decided at the nineteenth session of the PNC in 1988 to accept Security Council Resolutions 242 and 338, which the world had designated the basis for settling the region's conflict.

Chapter 6
The First Pass at Peace

The Palestinian Intifada ("Uprising") that began in late 1987 was part of the process of reducing the conflict to its two core parties. It also contributed to the emergence of majority support for a two-state solution among both Palestinians and Israelis, as it became more evident to both that there was no purely military solution to their confrontation. In this regard, the end of the Cold War and of broad Soviet support to radical parties in the Arab world was also an underlying factor.

Palestinians saw the Intifada not only as an expression of opposition to the Israeli occupation of the West Bank and Gaza but also as an assertion of their own independence and control over their destiny. The immediate grievances that sparked the uprising are outlined in an important statement authored by Sari Nusseibeh, a leading Palestinian intellectual (Reading 26). But at the same time Nusseibeh calls for an international peace conference that will establish a Palestinian state, implicitly alongside rather than in place of Israel.

On the Israeli side, similar factors were pushing toward the search for a diplomatic solution. The 1992 election returned a Labor-led government to power, under Yitzhak Rabin, and several channels were explored. The most notable at the time were the negotiating forums established after a peace conference in Madrid in October, 1991. But what proved most important were informal secret contacts developed with the help of Norway—hence the name of the Oslo peace process. This led to a dramatic announcement of mutual recognition and a joint Declaration of Principles, from Israel and from the Palestine Liberation Organization (PLO), on September 13, 1993. This event is seen from both sides: by Deputy Foreign Minister Yossi Beilin for Israel (Reading 27) and by chief negotiator Mahmoud Abbas for the PLO (Reading 28).

The Oslo peace process produced further agreements during the 1990s and created a Palestinian Authority that ruled over Gaza and over most of the Arab residents of the West Bank. But the attempt to reach some understanding on the basic issues of the conflict—the "final status" issues—collapsed in the first two full-scale negotiations between the authorities recognized on both sides, at Camp David in July 2000 and at Taba in January 2001. Ehud Barak, Israel's prime minister at the time, indicts the Palestinian leadership—and Yasir Arafat in particular—in a widely noted interview published after the event (Reading

29). Among the many responses defending the PLO's role at Camp David and expressing broad censure of Barak's part in its failure was a critique by Robert Malley (a US participant in the talks) and by British academician Hussein Agha (Reading 30).

Further online resources:

Exchange of letters between Yitzhak Rabin and Yasser Arafat (mutual recognition), 1993: http://www.jewishvirtuallibrary.org/israel-palestinian-letters-of-mutual-recognition-september-1993, https://ecf.org.il/issues/issue/15, http://jcpa-lecape.org/wp-content/uploads/2017/10/Reconnaissance-mutuelle-Israel-OLP.pdf, http://www.mfa.gov.il/mfa/foreignpolicy/peace/guide/pages/israel-plo%20recognition%20-%20exchange%20of%20letters%20betwe.
Oslo Declaration of Principles, 1993: http://avalon.law.yale.edu/20th_century/isrplo.asp.
Oslo Interim Agreement, 1995: http://www.jewishvirtuallibrary.org/Israeli–Palestinian-interim-agreement.
Oslo Accords, key documents: pbs.org/wgbh/pages/frontline/shows/oslo/negotiations.
Letter of Assurance from PA Chairman Yasser Arafat, 1998 (changes in PLO Charter), 1998: http://www.mideastweb.org/peacechild/plocharter_letter_1996.htm, http://www.jewishvirtuallibrary.org/arafat-letter-of-assurance-affirming-changes-in-the-plo-charter-january-1998.
Wye River Memorandum, 1998: http://avalon.law.yale.edu/21st_century/wyeriv.asp, https://www.gpo.gov/fdsys/pkg/WCPD-1998-11-02/pdf/WCPD-1998-11-02-Pg2104.pdf, http://mfa.gov.il/MFA/ForeignPolicy/Peace/Guide/Pages/The%20Wye%20River%20Memorandum.aspx.
Clinton Bridging Proposals, 2000: http://www.mideastweb.org/clintonproposal.htm.
Moratinos Non-Paper (summary Camp David/Taba talks), 2001: https://ecf.org.il/issues/issue/190.

26. "The Palestinians' Fourteen Demands"

*Sari Nusseibeh**

EDITOR'S NOTE Sari Nusseibeh (1949–) comes from a prominent Jerusalem family, long active in Palestinian Arab politics. Nusseibeh studied philosophy at Oxford and at Harvard, earning a doctorate in Islamic thought. When the First Palestinian Intifada broke out in December, 1987, he was professor of philosophy at Birzeit University, in the West Bank, and one of the leading intellectual figures in the Palestinian community. Shortly thereafter he formulated the document below, also known as the Palestinian Declaration of Principles, which expresses grievances and motivations behind the uprising. Nusseibeh's call for an end to Israeli occupation policies and practices, to which Palestinians objected, was seen as a prelude to an international peace conference where the PLO would represent Palestinians and where a just and lasting settlement, presumably on a two-state basis, would be achieved.

During the past few weeks the occupied territories have witnessed a popular uprising against Israel's occupation and its oppressive measures. This uprising has so far resulted in the martyrdom of tens of our people, the wounding of hundreds more, and the imprisonment of thousands of unarmed civilians.

This uprising has come to further affirm our people's unbreakable commitment to its national aspirations. These aspirations include our people's firm national rights of self-determination and of the establishment of an independent state on our national soil under the leadership of the PLO, as our sole legitimate representative.

The uprising also comes as further proof of our indefatigable spirit and our rejection of the sense of despair which has begun to creep to the minds of some Arab leaders, who claim that the uprising is the result of despair.

The conclusion to be drawn from this uprising is that the present state of affairs in the Palestinian occupied territories is unnatural and that Israeli occupation cannot continue forever. Real peace cannot be achieved except through the recognition of Palestinian national rights, including the right of

---

* Presented at a press conference in Jerusalem on January 14, 1988, in the name of "Palestinian Nationalist Institutions and Personalities from the West Bank and Gaza." Published in *Journal of Palestine Studies* 17.3 (1988): 63–65.

self-determination and the establishment of an independent Palestinian state on Palestinian national soil. Should these rights not be recognized, then the continuation of Israeli occupation will lead to further violence and bloodshed, and the further deepening of hatred. The opportunity for achieving peace will also move farther away.

The only way to extricate ourselves from this scenario is through the convening of an international conference, with the participation of all concerned parties—including the PLO, the sole legitimate representative of the Palestinian people, as an equal partner, as well as the five permanent members of the Security Council, under the supervision of the two superpowers.

On this basis we call upon the Israeli authorities to comply with the following list of demands as a means to prepare the atmosphere for the convening of the suggested international peace conference, which conference will ensure a just and lasting settlement of the Palestinian problem in all its aspects, bringing about the realization of the inalienable national rights of the Palestinian people, peace and stability for the peoples of the region, and an end to violence and bloodshed:

1 To abide by the Fourth Geneva Convention and all other international agreements pertaining to the protection of civilians, their properties and rights under a state of military occupation; to declare the Emergency Regulations of the British Mandate null and void, and to stop applying the iron fist policy.

2 The immediate compliance with Security Council resolutions 605 and 607, which call upon Israel to abide by the Geneva Convention of 1949 and [by] the Declaration of Human Rights, and which further call for the achievement of a just and lasting settlement of the Arab–Israeli conflict.

3 The release of all prisoners who were arrested during the recent uprising, and foremost among them our children; also the rescinding of all proceedings and indictments against them.

4 The cancellation of the policy of expulsion and allowing all exiled Palestinians, including the four sent yesterday into exile, to return to their homes and families. Also the release of all administrative detainees and the cancellation of the hundreds of house arrest orders. In this connection, special mention must be made of the several hundreds of applications for family reunions, which we call upon the authorities to accept forthwith.

5 The immediate lifting of the siege of all Palestinian refugee camps in the West Bank and Gaza and the withdrawal of the Israeli army from all population centers.

6 Carrying out a formal inquiry into the behavior of soldiers and settlers in the West Bank and Gaza as well as inside jails and detention camps, and

taking due punitive measures against all those convicted of having unduly caused death or bodily harm to unarmed civilians.

7 A cessation of all settlement activities and land confiscation and the release of lands already confiscated, especially in the Gaza Strip; also putting an end to the harassments and provocations of the Arab population by settlers in the West Bank and Gaza as well as in the Old City of Jerusalem—in particular the curtailment of the provocative activities, in the Old City of Jerusalem, by Sharon and the ultra-religious settlers of Shuvu Banim and Ateret Cohanim.

8 Refraining from any act which might impinge on the Muslim and Christian holy sites or which might introduce changes to the status quo in the city of Jerusalem.

9 The cancellation of the VAT and all other direct Israeli taxes, which are imposed on Palestinian residents in Jerusalem, in the rest of the West Bank, and in Gaza; and putting an end to the harassments caused to Palestinian business and tradesmen.

10 The cancellation of all restrictions on political freedoms, including restrictions on meetings and conventions; also making provisions for free municipal elections under the supervision of a neutral authority.

11 The immediate release of all monies deducted from the wages of laborers from the territories who worked and still work inside the green line, which amount to several hundreds of millions of dollars. These accumulated deductions, with interest, must be returned to their rightful owners through the agency of nationalist institutions headed by the workers' unions.

12 The removal of all restrictions on building permits and licenses for industrial projects and artesian wells, as well as on agricultural development programs in the occupied territories. Also rescinding all measures taken to deprive the territories of their water resources.

13. Terminating the policy of discrimination practiced against industrial and agricultural produce from the occupied territories either by removing the restrictions on the transfer of goods to within the green line or by placing comparable trade restrictions on the transfer of Israeli goods into the territories.

14 Removing the restrictions on political contacts between inhabitants of the occupied territories and the PLO, in such a way as to allow for the participation of Palestinians from the territories in the proceedings of the Palestine National Council, in order to ensure a direct input into the decision-making processes of the Palestinian nation by the Palestinians under occupation.

27. "The Oslo Accord"

Yossi Beilin*

EDITOR'S NOTE *Yossi Beilin (1948–) was deputy foreign minister in the Israeli government established after the 1992 election by Prime Minister Yitzhak Rabin and Foreign Minister Shimon Peres. In this capacity he was a key figure in the initiation of informal contacts with the PLO, which led to the surprise announcement, in September 1993, of mutual recognition between Israel and the PLO and of agreement between them on a Declaration of Principles that would guide the negotiation of a final settlement of the conflict. In this selection Beilin recounts the culmination of this secret negotiation in a dramatic ceremony on the While House lawn in Washington.*

On the flight to the United States the atmosphere was relaxed enough. We sat in the central cabin, dozing or chatting—the Rabins, Motta and Rita Gur, Peres and I. Rabin went through his speech. Peres went through his. But when we arrived in Washington it turned out that the negotiating was not yet over. The morning before the ceremony was due to take place, we had an urgent call from Dr Ahmed Tibi at the hotel where the Palestinians were staying, asking to meet us. When he arrived, he explained that Arafat was packing his bags and about to leave, having discovered that, according to the preamble, the agreement was to be signed by the Palestinian delegation and not by the PLO. Apparently we didn't acknowledge that we were dealing with the PLO.

All were furious at the prospect of yet more tiresome arguments, at this, the very last moment. Rabin was livid. He wanted to leave the wording as it was, but in the end a compromise was reached: this was to be a declaration of principles signed jointly by a PLO team (although the expression 'Palestinian delegation' remained, in brackets) and by the government of Israel. Thus the negotiations which had begun on 20 January were concluded on the morning of 13 September 1993. [...]

In the course of the ceremony I sat, watching the three First Ladies, watching Peres and Abu Mazen [Mahmoud Abbas], and finally the three leaders—Clinton, Rabin and Arafat—and for the first time in my life I had to pinch myself to be sure this was real. If I hadn't turned up for that meeting at the Tandoori sixteen

* Excerpts from Yossi Beilin, *Touching Peace: From the Oslo Accord to a Final Agreement*, trans. Philip Simpson (London: Weidenfeld & Nicolson, 1999), pp. 129–135.

months before, would this have happened anyway? Was the need for secret talks with the PLO so self-evident that the same result would have transpired sooner or later, whoever the participants might have been? How much should be attributed to chance and how much to the natural momentum of political development?

After the ceremony the Israeli team was invited to meet President Clinton. Antony Lake, the president's national security adviser, whom I had met a number of times, introduced me to him. 'Now this one's over, got any more negotiations in mind?' Clinton joked, not realising just how far from a joke this was. Then, in more serious mood, he asked what was expected of him. I told him there was no alternative to the provision of American economic aid to the Palestinians, but negotiations with the Palestinians and the Jordanians we could handle ourselves. [...]

The rest of the day passed at dizzying speed. In the afternoon, in Peres's suite, we met with the PLO delegation to the Oslo talks, accompanied by Abu Mazen. I had never seen any of these people before, but they seemed to regard me as an old acquaintance. 'The man who started it all is the last to be met', Abu Ala said to me. He wasn't quite the way I had pictured him in my imagination, in spite of Yair's detailed description.

This was an amicable conversation. There was nothing pressing on the agenda, no more compromises to be fought over. For a moment I felt as if I was in the army again, at the end of basic training when the sergeants stop being monsters and turn into human beings, staging stretcher races or clowning around on the assault course. The agreement was supposed to come into force within a month, and in the meantime it would be up to us to present it to our parliamentary institutions. We exchanged our assessments of the reception to be expected, for ourselves and for the Palestinians. We all hoped that the shock waves from this extraordinary and positive event would also move Israeli and Palestinian public opinion, that people on both sides would realise a new page was being turned and that this was an agreement not to be judged on a narrow, partisan basis. We assured one another we would continue to meet, although it wasn't clear how and under what circumstances; nor were we sure with whom we would be negotiating over the interim settlement and Gaza and Jericho. Would all these people, living comfortably in Tunis, really be prepared to shift their domicile to the slums of Gaza?

This, incidentally, was a question often repeated in the countless television interviews I gave that day between meetings. 'Will Mr Arafat be permitted to live in Jericho?' 'Will the PLO close its headquarters in Tunis and transfer it to Gaza?' My answers were evasive—not the kind of answers I like giving. The truth is that, at that stage, I simply didn't know how quickly things would develop, or if Arafat's arrival in the territories could be regarded as imminent. In spite of the handshake, and although Arafat had ceased to be a concept and became a human being, I too still had difficulty imagining him as a neighbour. [...]

At home we got an enthusiastic welcome from senior Labour Party members—and from others too. This extraordinary combination of firm and radical leadership by Rabin, exemplary co-operation between the two veteran rivals, Rabin and Peres, an achievement to make the world clap its hands, the silence of opponents, reluctant to spoil the party—all this was immensely gratifying to Labour activists. As for me, I went home happy but exhausted and collapsed on a mountain of Rosh Hashanah newspaper supplements. The year 5754 was getting off to an auspicious start.

What was the breakthrough in Oslo? In fact it was twofold: there was the historic mutual recognition between Israel and the PLO; but this was made possible only by the other breakthrough, separation between interim and permanent settlement and the implementation of some interim measures on the ground even before elections to the Palestinian self-governing Council. For years, the Palestinians had been saying—whenever asked to consider the five-year interim period—that they would agree to an interim period before the permanent settlement only if the terms of the permanent settlement were guaranteed to them from the start. They had demands of their own: a Palestinian state with the 1967 borders and Jerusalem as its capital, eradication of the Jewish settlements and repatriation of Palestinian refugees. Israel, they conceded, would of course have other positions. So there should be negotiation to determine the principles of the permanent settlement, and then the Palestinians would agree to an interim period, knowing in advance how it would end.

Israel would not agree to this demand, having insisted—since 1978—that the interim period should be fixed without either side having any preconceptions as to the form of the permanent settlement; the interim period would in itself influence the content of the permanent settlement, as well as providing the two sides with useful experience of collaboration. In Washington the Palestinians had rejected this concept; in Oslo they accepted it, in that they agreed—at variance with their positions in Washington—that Jerusalem, the settlements and Israel's military security zones would be left outside the scope of autonomy.

Something else also happened in Oslo. Since the start of negotiations over autonomy with Egypt, it had been understood that the period of self-rule would begin only after elections to the Palestinian Council. When it emerged in Washington just how hard it was going to be to reach agreement on procedures for the election—international supervision, voting rights of East Jerusalem's Arabs, the number of deputies to be elected, the question whether this was to be a legislative or [an] executive body—and when it seemed that negotiations over electoral issues might continue indefinitely, the idea was raised of transferring powers to the Palestinians before the elections, including the establishment of a Palestinian police force. Even in Oslo the central questions of electoral procedure were not solved, leading us to wonder whether the Palestinians were as interested in elections as they claimed, but we created a scenario in which the interim settlement was no longer dependent on elections; so that, whether elections were held or not, negotiations on the permanent settlement had to begin no later than two years after the implementation of 'Gaza–Jericho'. The moment that elections ceased to be a condition for determining the permanent settlement, negotiating on them, which began at a later stage, actually became much easier.

The story of the Oslo track is a story of historical paradoxes. The discussions that were supposed to be absolutely secret, to be revealed to the world only with the opening of the archives, long after peace had become a fact, did—it is true—maintain their secrecy for a period of eight months; but, once agreement was reached, not only were they exposed, they became known to every television viewer and newspaper reader in the world—and entered the language of political terminology. When someone says he is putting his trust in 'Oslo', no one imagines he is referring to the Norwegian capital. [...]

But Oslo also created prodigious expectations on account of the very image of the signing on 13 September. [...] Before the signing of the 1979 agreement between Sadat and Begin, the two leaders had met several times over the previous ten months. Before the signing of the 1994 agreement between Rabin and King Hussein, they themselves and their representatives had been meeting for decades. The agreement between Israel and the PLO was signed at the very first encounter between Arafat and Rabin and the handshake, in reality just the handshake of recognition, was interpreted as the handshake of peacemaking.

As of this moment, at the time that these lines are being written, we have *not made* peace with the PLO; it certainly didn't happen in September 1993, when we had yet to finalise the Gaza–Jericho deal and the interim agreement. The Oslo Accord was an initial agreement on principles, which paved the way for the introduction of the interim settlement but deferred all the sensitive issues to the negotiations on the permanent settlement. The event of 13 September had such an impact, and was so dramatic, that it was taken by the world, as well as by Israeli and Palestinian public opinion, to mean much more than just the beginning of the beginning. Many were under the impression that a peace treaty had been signed. Expectations of it were similar to those of a peace treaty, but this was an agreement incapable of meeting these expectations, especially when it was forced to face the test of violence. 'If there is peace, why can violence not be overcome?' was a question asked on both sides, and it was hard to be satisfied with the reply that in fact there was no peace yet.

28. "The Oslo Accord"

Mahmoud Abbas*

EDITOR'S NOTE Mahmoud Abbas (see Reading 25) was chief negotiator for the PLO under Yasir Arafat, during the period of the Oslo peace process. His account of the signing of the 1993 Declaration of Principles thus reflects an official Palestinian perspective on this process, just as Yossi Beilin (Reading 27) represents that of the Israeli government at the time. Abbas's account, published while the peace process was still ascendant, conveys a sense of both achievement in restoring the Palestinian role at the center of the conflict and uneasiness about the risks taken and the issues left unresolved.

On Sunday, 12 September 1993, our delegation left Tunis on board the private jet of His Majesty King Hassan II of Morocco, which he had put at the disposal of the Palestinian leadership. I kept to myself for most of the ten-and-a-half-hour flight, reviewing what we had accomplished over thirty years of struggle and nearly half a century of estrangement and refuge in exile. Was this the trip back home? Or was it the journey signing the surrender of a major part of our homeland? Why was I heading for a place where I would be signing an agreement which might not offer me a home or a place of residence? Would what we were about to do open the gates of a future for us or shut them? Had we forfeited the people's rights or preserved them?

It was a heavy burden and a great responsibility. The risks could well outweigh the benefits. How would our people react at home and in the diaspora? Who would be in favour and who would oppose? And what would history say about us? Can the ten hours of flying time from Tunis to Washington summarize the journey of homelessness that has lasted decades? Can we forget those whose blood has nourished the soil of the homeland? Can we, at the gates of an historic accomplishment, forget the generations of martyrs who have made this achievement possible? The recent history of Palestine was like a train that has travelled through all weather and across all terrains, its passengers boarding and alighting, but pressing ahead to its destination. It was like a ship tossing on a dark raging sea, hoping to come at last to a safe harbour. [...]

---

* Excerpts from Mahmoud Abbas, *Through Secret Channels* (Reading: Garnet Publishing, 1995), pp. 1–9.

There were many questions on my mind during the flight to Washington. I examined the faces around me, and saw others in my mind's eye, but I always came back to myself; for, while everyone else, present or absent, could declare themselves innocent, it was I who would stand before the world to sign an agreement with the Israelis and take the responsibility.

In the end I concluded two things: first, that I was engaged in an historic undertaking and was presenting our people with a great achievement, and, second, that reckless actions and a backward-looking mentality on either side would wreck this achievement. Thus I was prey to two contradictory feelings: on the one hand there was a sense of achievement, on the other there was fear about its realization in the future. [...]

The Palestine Liberation Organization and its leadership had moved very swiftly from being a terrorist organization (according to the American Administration) to one worthy of the White House's interest. I was reminded of the moment at which the United States had begun a dialogue with the PLO after the Palestine National Council (PNC) had decided to set in motion the peace drive. [...] I reviewed those days as I stood on a podium at the White House, to the left of the Secretary of State Warren Christopher. President Bill Clinton stood one step away. The president congratulated us, as did his wife, Vice-President Al Gore and his wife, then former Presidents Jimmy Carter and George Bush, some senior State Department officials and the guest of honour, the Norwegian Foreign Minister Johan Joergen Holst, the man who had overseen the secret Oslo negotiations so superbly. We stood under the blazing sun for an hour and a half. The heat of the moment quite outweighed the heat of the sun. As I stood on the White House lawn in the bright light, I felt that our people too had assumed their place in the sun, a people whose right of existence had been ignored. Thousands of eyes, hundreds of cameras and millions of people were anxiously watching these scenes and this small podium on which a new page in the history of the region and maybe of the world was being made.

After finishing my speech, and in the absence of pre-planned protocol arrangements, I had to shake President Clinton's hand, but I also went and shook hands with Yitzhak Rabin, Andrei Kozyrev, the Russian foreign minister, and Shimon Peres. This gesture was welcomed by the audience, who applauded vigorously, though handshaking is contrary to protocol. People told me afterwards about many things that I did not notice myself then; they said, for example, that President Clinton had positioned my chair as I sat down to sign. Perhaps the emotion and the heat of the moment were to blame for my blankness.

A few days before, no Israeli official would have dared to come face to face with members of the PLO, and some months before that Israeli citizens had been banned from mentioning the PLO, let alone having contact with its officials. [...]

All these images were rushing through my mind on board the plane to Washington. It was as though I was trying to condense the long period of hardship and struggle into the brief hours before we were due to arrive in Washington to begin a new chapter in this long and still unfinished saga. I did not think that signing would end everything, but saw it rather as a beginning for many things, particularly since the accord did not settle many issues and did not clarify many points that still required continuous hard work.

My memory sailed far back in time, to the days when I had devoted my time to following up developments in Israeli society and had been keen to meet any Israelis willing to meet me. I suffered much criticism from the people closest to me in Fatah. They were often sarcastic, asking: 'Can you change Israeli society through these simpletons you are meeting? What effect does this handful of people from the lowliest echelons of Israeli society have?' [...]

Israeli society has progressed. These contacts were not the only reason behind this progress. There were many other reasons, particularly the continued struggle of the Palestinian people and the Intifada, the uprising of the 'children of the stones'. But through these contacts the message of this struggle was delivered to the Israelis: Your obstinacy is to no avail, we must sit round the table. Here is our voice calling out to you; listen to the voice of reason, look to the future of your children. [...]

And thus we are back to the present. Hours after the signing in Washington DC, I met Shimon Peres at his quarters. I had not requested such a meeting, but our delegation had telephoned, wanting to discuss amending the names of the two signatories to the agreement, and his secretary thought I wanted to meet Peres. I had no objection to a meeting with Peres now that the accord had been concluded. Indeed I had had no qualms about meeting him previously, especially since the media had reported that we had met more than once, and he had never tried to deny any of these reports.

But today, after the signing, we were meeting in public, in front of the media, for forty minutes. His delegation, which had run the Oslo negotiations, and our delegation, as well as Yasser Abd Rabbo, the chief Palestinian interlocutor with the United States, were in attendance. Observing that the two teams were having a warm exchange, a sign of a friendly relationship and shared memories, Peres turned to me and said: 'It seems that we two are the only strangers in this session.' Peres tried to be objective and practical when speaking about the future. He expressed a desire for the economic development of the occupied territories, and told me that he had asked the Europeans to prepare an economic development programme for the territories during his previous European tour. I tried to study this personality whom I knew only through the press, messengers, the Oslo negotiations and dozens of special reports to which I had access. I was comparing my image of him with the real man in front of me.

The real picture was no different from the one that I had sketched in my imagination. I noticed that he was a diplomat with a clear vision of the future and a desire for peace. [...]

Peres's deputy, Yossi Beilin, took part in the meeting. We talked in a relaxed manner, dropping all reserve and ignoring protocol. The other thing that drew my attention was that he looked like a young man in his twenties, although he was really in his forties. He has a presence in the Labour Party and was one of a few who had maintained a good relationship with Peres and did not side with Rabin, as many others did. [...]

In Washington DC, it was as though there had been an instant transformation. Everything had moved from one extreme to the other, with various American figures coming in droves to meet us, and with the media hailing the PLO's constructive attitude and its fine efforts to achieve peace. Jews and Arabs, enemies before that day, 13 September 1993, suddenly were organizing joint receptions, receiving congratulations and good wishes, poised to erase decades of enmity.

Between the signing of the Declaration of Principles and our departure, everywhere we went we were met with welcoming smiles and requests for autographs, until we felt like film stars. But, as we were leaving Washington DC, the joy of the occasion began to fade and to be replaced by the anxieties about the future.

29. "Collapse at Camp David" (Interview with Ehud Barak)

*Benny Morris**

EDITOR'S NOTE *Ehud Barak (1942–) was prime minister of Israel from 1999 to 2001, having previously served as chief of staff in the Israeli army. During his tenure as prime minister he played a key role in the first intensive negotiations between recognized leaders of the two sides over the basic issues of the conflict. This culminated in the Camp David summit of July 2000, which broke up with no agreement and with much acrimony regarding the blame for its failure. Two years later Barak expressed his views on Camp David more fully in a frank interview with the Israeli historian Benny Morris of the Ben-Gurion University of the Negev.*

Barak today portrays Arafat's behavior at Camp David as a "performance" geared to exacting from the Israelis as many concessions as possible without ever seriously intending to reach a peace settlement or sign an "end to the conflict." "He did not negotiate in good faith, indeed, he did not negotiate at all. He just kept saying 'no' to every offer, never making any counterproposals of his own," he says. Barak continuously shifts between charging Arafat with "lacking the character or will" to make a historic compromise (as did the late Egyptian President Anwar Sadat in 1977–1979, when he made peace with Israel) and accusing him of secretly planning Israel's demise while he strings along a succession of Israeli and Western leaders and, on the way, hoodwinks "naive journalists." [...] According to Barak,

> What they [Arafat and his colleagues] want is a Palestinian state in all of Palestine. What we see as self-evident, [the need for] two states for two peoples, they reject. Israel is too strong at the moment to defeat, so they formally recognize it. But their game plan is to establish a Palestinian state while always leaving an opening for further "legitimate" demands down the road. For now, they are willing to agree to a temporary truce à la Hudnat Huday-

* Excerpts from Benny Morris, "Camp David and After: An Exchange, 1: An Interview with Ehud Barak," *New York Review of Books*, June 13, 2002, pp. 41–45.

biyah.[1] They will exploit the tolerance and democracy of Israel first to turn it into "a state for all its citizens," as demanded by the extreme nationalist wing of Israel's Arabs and extremist left-wing Jewish Israelis. Then they will push for a binational state; and then demography and attrition will lead to a state with a Muslim majority and a Jewish minority. This would not necessarily involve kicking out all the Jews. But it would mean the destruction of Israel as a Jewish state. This, I believe, is their vision. They may not talk about it often, openly, but this is their vision. Arafat sees himself as a reborn Saladin—the Kurdish Muslim general who defeated the Crusaders in the twelfth century—and Israel as just another, ephemeral crusader state.

Barak believes that Arafat sees the Palestinian refugees of 1948 and their descendants, numbering close to four million, as the main demographic–political tool for subverting the Jewish state.

Arafat, says Barak, believes that Israel "has no right to exist, and he seeks its demise." Barak buttresses this by arguing that Arafat "does not recognize the existence of a Jewish people or nation, only a Jewish religion, because it is mentioned in the Koran and because he remembers seeing, as a kid, Jews praying at the Wailing Wall." This, Barak believes, underlay Arafat's insistence at Camp David (and since) that the Palestinians have sole sovereignty over the Temple Mount compound (Haram al-Sharif—the noble sanctuary) in the southeastern corner of Jerusalem's Old City. Arafat denies that any Jewish temple has ever stood there—and this is a microcosm of his denial of the Jews' historical connection and claim to the Land of Israel/Palestine. [...]

Regarding the core of the Israeli–American proposals, the "revisionists" have charged that Israel offered the Palestinians not a continuous state but a collection of "bantustans" or "cantons." "This is one of the most embarrassing lies to have emerged from Camp David," says Barak.

I ask myself why is he [Arafat] lying. To put it simply, any proposal that offers 92 percent of the West Bank cannot, almost by definition, break up the territory into noncontiguous cantons. The West Bank and the Gaza Strip are separate, but that cannot be helped [in a peace agreement, they would be joined by a bridge].

But in the West Bank, Barak says, the Palestinians were promised a continuous piece of sovereign territory except for a razor-thin Israeli wedge running from Jerusalem through from Maale Adumim to the Jordan River. Here Palestin-

---

[1] A temporary truce that the Prophet Muhammad concluded with the leaders of Mecca during 628–629 and that he subsequently unilaterally violated.

ian territorial continuity would have been assured by a tunnel or bridge: "The Palestinians said that I [and Clinton] presented our proposals as a diktat, take it or leave it. This is a lie. Everything proposed was open to continued negotiations. They could have raised counterproposals. But they never did."

Barak explains Arafat's "lie" about "bantustans" as stemming from his fear that, "when reasonable Palestinian citizens would come to know the real content of Clinton's proposal and map, showing what 92 percent of the West Bank means, they would have said: 'Mr. Chairman, why didn't you take it?'"

In one other important way, the "revisionist" articles are misleading: they focused on Camp David (July 2000) while almost completely ignoring the follow-up (and more generous) Clinton proposals (endorsed by Israel) of December 2000 and the Palestinian–Israeli talks at Taba in January 2001. The "revisionists," Barak implies, completely ignored the shift—under the prodding of the Intifada—in the Israeli (and American) positions between July and the end of 2000. By December and January, Israel had agreed to Washington's proposal that it withdraw from about 95 percent of the West Bank with substantial territorial compensation for the Palestinians from Israel proper, and that the Arab neighborhoods of Jerusalem would become sovereign Palestinian territory. The Israelis also agreed to an international force at least temporarily controlling the Jordan River line between the West Bank and the kingdom of Jordan instead of the IDF [Israel Defense Forces]. (But on the refugee issue, which Barak sees as "existential," Israel had continued to stand firm: "We cannot allow even one refugee back on the basis of the 'right of return,'" says Barak. "And we cannot accept historical responsibility for the creation of the problem.")

Barak seems to hold out no chance of success for Israeli–Palestinian negotiations, should they somehow resume, so long as Arafat and like-minded leaders are at the helm on the Arab side. He seems to think in terms of generations and hesitantly predicts that only "eighty years" after 1948 will the Palestinians be historically ready for a compromise. By then, most of the generation that experienced the catastrophe of 1948 at first hand will have died; there will be "very few 'salmons' around who still want to return to their birthplaces to die." (Barak speaks of a "salmon syndrome" among the Palestinians—and says that Israel, to a degree, was willing to accommodate it, through the family reunion scheme, allowing elderly refugees to return to be with their families before they die.) He points to the model of the Soviet Union, which collapsed roughly after eighty years, after the generation that had lived through the revolution had died. He seems to be saying that revolutionary movements' zealotry and dogmatism die down after the passage of three generations and, in the case of the Palestinians, the disappearance of the generation of the *nakba*, or catastrophe, of 1948 will facilitate compromise.

How does Barak see the Middle East in a hundred years' time? Would it contain a Jewish state? Unlike Arafat, Barak believes it will, "and it will be strong and prosperous. I really think this. Our connection to the Land of Israelis is not like the Crusaders' [...] Israel fits into the Zeitgeist of our era. It is true that there are demographic threats to its existence. That is why a separation from the Palestinians is a compelling imperative. Without such a separation [into two states] there is no future for the Zionist dream."

30. "Collapse at Camp David"

Robert Malley and Hussein Agha*

EDITOR'S NOTE *Robert Malley (1963–) was special assistant to the president for Arab–Israeli affairs at the time of the 2000 Camp David summit; at the end of the Clinton administration in 2001 he became Middle East and North Africa program director at the International Crisis Group. Hussein Agha was a senior associate member of St. Antony's College, Oxford. The article presented here was a response to Ehud Barak's explanation of the failure of Camp David (previous reading); it appeared two years after the event and drew on Malley's experience as a participant in the talks.*

The various interpretations of what happened at Camp David and its aftermath continue to draw exceptional attention both in Israel and in the United States.

Ehud Barak's interview with Benny Morris makes it clear why that is the case: Barak's assessment that the talks failed because Yasser Arafat cannot make peace with Israel and that his answer to Israel's unprecedented offer was to resort to terrorist violence has become central to the argument that Israel is in a fight for its survival against those who deny its very right to exist. So much of what is said and done today derives from and is justified by that crude appraisal. First, Arafat and the rest of the Palestinian leaders must be supplanted before a meaningful peace process can resume, since they are the ones who rejected the offer. Second, the Palestinians' use of violence has nothing to do with ending the occupation, since they walked away from the possibility of reaching that goal at the negotiating table not long ago. And finally, Israel must crush the Palestinians—"badly beat them" in the words of the current prime minister—if an agreement is ever to be reached.

The one-sided account that was set in motion in the wake of Camp David has had devastating effects—on Israeli public opinion as well as on US foreign policy. That was clear enough a year ago; it has become far clearer since. Rectifying it does not mean, to quote Barak, engaging in "Palestinian propaganda." Rather, it means taking a close look at what actually occurred.

Barak's central thesis is that the current Palestinian leadership wants "a Palestinian state in all of Palestine. What we see as self-evident, two states for

---

* Excerpts from Robert Malley and Hussein Agha, "A Reply to Ehud Barak," *New York Review of Books*, June 13, 2002, pp. 46–49.

two peoples, they reject." Arafat, he concludes, seeks Israel's "demise." Barak has made that claim repeatedly, both here and elsewhere, and indeed it forms the crux of his argument. His claim therefore should be taken up, issue by issue.

On the question of the boundaries of the future state, the Palestinian position, formally adopted as early as 1988 and frequently reiterated by Palestinian negotiators throughout the talks, was for a Palestinian state based on the June 4, 1967 borders, living alongside Israel. At Camp David (at which one of the present writers was a member of the US administration's team), Arafat's negotiators accepted the notion of Israeli annexation of West Bank territory to accommodate settlements, though they insisted on a one-for-one swap of land "of equal size and value." The Palestinians argued that the annexed territory should neither affect the contiguity of their own land nor lead to the incorporation of Palestinians into Israel.

The ideas put forward by President Clinton at Camp David fell well short of those demands. In order to accommodate Israeli settlements, he proposed a deal by which Israel would annex 9 percent of the West Bank in exchange for turning over to the Palestinians parts of pre-1967 Israel equivalent to 1 percent of the West Bank. This proposal would have entailed the incorporation of tens of thousands of additional Palestinians into Israeli territory near the annexed settlements; and it would have meant that territory annexed by Israel would encroach deep inside the Palestinian state. In his December 23, 2000 proposals—called "parameters" by all parties—Clinton suggested an Israeli annexation of between 4 and 6 percent of the West Bank in exchange for a land swap of between 1 and 3 percent. The following month in Taba, the Palestinians put their own map on the table which showed roughly 3.1 percent of the West Bank under Israeli sovereignty, with an equivalent land swap in areas abutting the West Bank and Gaza.

On Jerusalem, the Palestinians accepted at Camp David the principle of Israeli sovereignty over the Wailing Wall, the Jewish Quarter of the Old City, and Jewish neighborhoods of East Jerusalem—neighborhoods that were not part of Israel before the 1967 Six-Day War—though the Palestinians clung to the view that all of Arab East Jerusalem should be Palestinian.

In contrast to the issues of territory and Jerusalem, there is no Palestinian position on how the refugee question should be dealt with as a practical matter. Rather, the Palestinians presented a set of principles. First, they insisted on the need to recognize the refugees' right of return, lest the agreement lose all legitimacy with the vast refugee constituency—roughly half the entire Palestinian population. Second, they acknowledged that Israel's demographic interests had to be recognized and taken into account. Barak draws from this the conclusion that the refugees are the "main demographic–political tool for subverting the Jewish state." The Palestinian leadership's insistence on a right of return demonstrates, in his account, that their conception of a two-state solution is one state for the Palestinians in Palestine and another in Israel. But the facts suggest that the Palestinians are trying (to date, unsuccessfully) to reconcile these two competing imperatives—the demographic imperative and the right of return. Indeed, in one of his last pre-Camp David meetings with Clinton, Arafat asked him to "give [him] a reasonable deal [on the refugee question] and then see how to present it as not betraying the right of return."

Some of the Palestinian negotiators proposed annual caps on the number of returnees (though at numbers far higher than their Israeli counterparts could accept); others wanted to create incentives for refugees to settle elsewhere and disincentives for them to return to the 1948 land. But all acknowledged that there could not be an unlimited, "massive" return of Palestinian refugees to Israel. The suggestion made by some that the Camp David summit broke down over the Palestinians' demand for a right of return simply is untrue: the issue was barely discussed between the two sides and President Clinton's ideas mentioned it only in passing. (In an op-ed piece in *The New York Times* this February Arafat called for "creative solutions to the right of return while respecting Israel's demographic concerns.") [...]

The question is whether, as Barak claims, the Palestinian position was tantamount to a denial of Israel's right to exist and to seeking its destruction. The facts do not validate that claim. True, the Palestinians rejected the version of the two-state solution that was put to them. But it could also be said that Israel rejected the unprecedented two-state solution put to them by the Palestinians from Camp David onward, including the following provisions: a state of Israel incorporating some land captured in 1967 and including a very large majority of its settlers; the largest Jewish Jerusalem in the city's history; preservation of Israel's demographic balance between Jews and Arabs; security guaranteed by a US-led international presence. [...]

The interpretation of what happened before, during, and after Camp David —and why—is far too important and has shown itself to have far too many implications to allow it to become subject to political caricature or posturing by either side. The story of Barak is of a man with a judicious insight—the need to aim for a comprehensive settlement—that tragically was not realized. The Camp David process was the victim of failings on the Palestinian side; but it was also, and importantly, the victim of failings on Israel's (and the United States') part as well. By refusing to recognize this, Barak continues to obscure the debate and [to] elude fundamental questions about where the quest for peace ought to go now.

One of those questions is whether there is not, in fact, a deal that would be acceptable to both sides, respectful of their core interests, and achievable through far greater involvement (and pressure) by the international community. Such a deal, we suggest, would include a sovereign, nonmilitarized Palestinian state with borders based on the 1967 lines, with an equal exchange of land to accommodate demographic realities, and with contiguous territory on the West Bank. Jewish neighborhoods of Jerusalem would be the capital of Israel and Arab neighborhoods would be the capital of Palestine. Palestinians would rule over the Haram al-Sharif (Temple Mount), Israelis would rule over the Kotel (Wailing Wall), with strict, internationally backed guarantees regarding excavation. A strong international force could provide security and monitor implementation of the agreement. A solution to the problem of the refugees would recognize their desire to return while preserving Israel's demographic balance—for example by allowing unrestricted return to that part of 1948 land that would then be included in the land swap and fall under Palestinian sovereignty.

Barak closes his interview with the thought that Israel will remain a strong, prosperous, and Jewish state in the next century. In order to achieve that goal, there are far better and more useful things that Barak could do than the self-justifying attempt to blame Arafat and his associates for all that has gone awry.

Chapter 7

The Fourth Stage

The failure of peace talks at Camp David and Taba in 2000–2001 was accompanied by the Second Intifada, which pushed both sides into more hawkish postures. More fundamentally, the conflict during this period entered a new stage with new actors, "fuzzy" wars instead of the conventional battles of the past, and an expanded role of religious extremism. All three elements combined in the rise of Hamas, a militant Islamist movement that had been founded during the First Intifada. As reflected in its "covenant," which was issued at the time, Hamas rejected all forms of coexistence or compromise with the Jewish state, basing its position on religious ideology more than on Arab or Palestinian nationalism (Reading 31).

During the Second Intifada there were more Palestinian attacks on Israeli targets than during the First Intifada. Aside from Hamas, other new Palestinian leaders emerged, in particular Marwan Barghouti, associated with the military wing of Fatah, whose call for use of "all means" was expressed in an early interview (Reading 32). In response, the government of Israel took care to document Palestinian violence in the Intifada (Reading 33). Public reaction can be measured by the overwhelming victory of the hawkish Ariel Sharon over Ehud Barak in the prime ministerial elections of February 2001. Sharon initiated a number of harsh measures against the uprising and refused all negotiations while the violence continued. Moving unilaterally, in August 2005 he evacuated Israeli military forces and settlers from the Gaza strip. But shortly thereafter, in January 2006, Hamas won a majority in Palestinian legislative elections, and in June 2007 it actually took physical control of the Gaza strip, leaving the Palestinian Authority in control only of the West Bank.

Nevertheless efforts to renew negotiations continued, leading to the Annapolis Conference of November 2007, which in turn led to talks between the governments of Israeli Prime Minister Ehud Olmert (who had succeeded Sharon upon his incapacitating illness) and Palestinian President Mahmoud Abbas (who had succeeded Arafat upon his death). These negotiations, the second full-scale effort to resolve basic issues, led to a final Israeli offer that was later revealed by a leak on the Palestinian side (Reading 34) and by Olmert's reaction to the leak (Reading 35).

This second failure to bridge the gap was followed by one of the new, "sub-conventional" wars, which was fought between Israel and Hamas forces in Gaza, in December 2008–January 2009. At about the same time, Israeli elections returned Likud leader Benjamin Netanyahu to power with a center-right coalition, but with growing pressure to find a way to renew the peace process. Accordingly, Netanyahu gave a widely noted speech (Reading 36), offering a two-state model for resolving the conflict—the first time for a Likud-led government to do this. The offer came, however, with strict conditions tied to acceptance of an independent Palestinian state alongside Israel.

Further online resources:

Arab Peace Initiative, 2002: https://www.theguardian.com/world/2002/mar/28/israel7, http://jcpa.org/text/Arab-Peace-Initiative.pdf.
President George W. Bush, Road Map for Palestinian–Israel Settlement, 2002: http://mideastweb.org/quartetrm3.htm, http://www.un.org/News/dh/mideast/roadmap 122002.pdf, https://2001–2009.state.gov/r/pa/ei/rls/22520.htm.
Ariel Sharon's Disengagement Plan, 2004: http://www.mideastweb.org/disengagement.htm.
The Future Vision of the Palestinian Arabs in Israel, 2006: https://www.adalah.org/uploads/oldfiles/newsletter/eng/dec06/tasawor-mostaqbali.pdf.
Human Rights in Palestine and Other Occupied Arab Territories: Report of the United Nations Fact Finding Mission on the Gaza Conflict (Goldstone Report), 2009: https://www.un.org/ruleoflaw/blog/document/human-rights-in-palestine-and-other-occupied-arab-territories-report-of-the-united-nations-fact-finding-mission-on-the-gaza-conflict.
Initial Response to Report of the Fact Finding Mission on the Gaza Conflict (Israeli Response to Goldstone Report), 2009: http://mfa.gov.il/MFA/PressRoom/2009/Pages/Initial-response-goldstone-report-24-Sep-2009.aspx.
Richard Goldstone, "Reconsidering the Goldstone Report on Israel and War Crimes," 2011: https://www.washingtonpost.com/opinions/reconsidering-the-goldstone-report-on-israel-and-war-crimes/2011/04/01/AFg111JC_story.html?noredirect=on&utm_term=.be6a84d151b0.
Hamas Charter, 2017: http://www.middleeasteye.net/news/hamas-charter-16377 94876 (see also the website hamas.ps).

31. Hamas Covenant (1988)*

EDITOR'S NOTE *The Islamic Resistance Movement (known by its Arabic initials as "Hamas") was founded in Gaza in 1987 during the First Intifada, as a branch of the Muslim Brotherhood, a fundamentalist movement founded in Egypt by Hassan al-Banna in 1928. Hamas operated, however, as an independent organization devoted to the complete liberation of Palestine and with an unyielding opposition to compromise, as seen in its founding document presented here. Though never renounced, this Covenant was superseded in 2017 by another, which—like the Palestine Liberation Organization (PLO) in 1974—accepted the transitional goal of a Palestinian state in the West Bank and Gaza as a stage in the complete liberation of Palestine (see online references).*

"Israel will exist and will continue to exist until Islam will obliterate it, just as it obliterated others before it" (The Martyr, Imam Hassan al-Banna, of blessed memory). [...]

The Islamic Resistance Movement: The Movement's program is Islam. From it, it draws its ideas, ways of thinking and understanding of the universe, life, and man. It resorts to it for judgment in all its conduct, and it is inspired by it for guidance of its steps. [...]

The Islamic Resistance Movement is a distinguished Palestinian movement, whose allegiance is to God, and whose way of life is Islam. It strives to raise the banner of God over every inch of Palestine, for under the wing of Islam followers of all religions can coexist in security and safety where their lives, possessions and rights are concerned. [...]

The Islamic Resistance Movement is one of the links in the chain of the struggle against the Zionist invaders. It goes back to 1939, to the emergence of the martyr Izz al-Din al Qassem and his brethren the fighters, members of Moslem Brotherhood. It goes on to reach out and become one with another chain[, which] includes the struggle of the Palestinians and Moslem Brotherhood in the 1948 war and the Jihad operations of the Moslem Brotherhood in 1968 and after.

---

* Excerpts from Covenant of the Islamic Resistance Movement (Hamas), August 18, 1988, available at http://avalon.law.yale.edu/20th_century/hamas.asp.

Moreover, if the links have been distant from each other and if obstacles, placed by those who are the lackeys of Zionism in the way of the fighters, obstructed the continuation of the struggle, the Islamic Resistance Movement aspires to the realization of God's promise, no matter how long that should take. The Prophet, God bless him and grant him salvation, has said:

The Day of Judgment will not come about until Moslems fight the Jews (killing the Jews), when the Jew will hide behind stones and trees. The stones and trees will say O Moslems, O Abdulla, there is a Jew behind me, come and kill him. [...]

The Islamic Resistance Movement believes that the land of Palestine is an Islamic Waqf [Trust] consecrated for future Moslem generations until Judgment Day. It, or any part of it, should not be squandered: it, or any part of it, should not be given up. [...] There is no solution for the Palestinian question except through Jihad. Initiatives, proposals and international conferences are all a waste of time and vain endeavors. [...]

For a long time, the enemies have been planning, skillfully and with precision, for the achievement of what they have attained. They took into consideration the causes affecting the current of events. They strived to amass great and substantive material wealth, which they devoted to the realization of their dream. With their money, they took control of the world media, news agencies, the press, publishing houses, broadcasting stations, and others. With their money they stirred revolutions in various parts of the world, with the purpose of achieving their interests and reaping the fruit therein. They were behind the French Revolution, the communist revolution, and most of the revolutions we heard and hear about, here and there. With their money they formed secret societies, such as Freemasons, Rotary clubs, the Lions, and others, in different parts of the world, for the purpose of sabotaging societies and achieving Zionist interests. With their money they were able to control imperialistic countries and instigate them to colonize many countries in order to enable them to exploit their resources and spread corruption there.

You may speak as much as you want about regional and world wars. They were behind World War I, when they were able to destroy the Islamic caliphate, making financial gains and controlling resources. They obtained the Balfour Declaration, formed the League of Nations through which they could rule the world. They were behind World War II, through which they made huge financial gains by trading in armaments and paved the way for the establishment of their state. It was they who instigated the replacement of the League of Nations with the United Nations and the Security Council, to enable them [sic] to rule the world. [...]

World Zionism, together with imperialistic powers, try through a studied plan and an intelligent strategy to remove one Arab state after another from the circle of struggle against Zionism, in order to have it finally face the Palestinian people only. Egypt was, to a great extent, removed from the circle of the struggle, through the treacherous Camp David Agreement. They are trying to draw other Arab countries into similar agreements and to bring them outside the circle of struggle.

The Islamic Resistance Movement calls on Arab and Islamic nations to take up the line of serious and persevering action to prevent the success of this horrendous plan, to warn the people of the danger emanating from leaving the circle of struggle against Zionism. Today it is Palestine, tomorrow it will be one country or another. The Zionist plan is limitless. After Palestine, the Zionists aspire to expand from the Nile to the Euphrates. When they will have digested the region they overtook, they will aspire to further expansion, and so on. Their plan is embodied in *The Protocols of the Elders of Zion*, and their present conduct is the best proof of what we are saying.

Leaving the circle of struggle with Zionism is high treason, and cursed be he who does that. [...] There is no way out except by concentrating all powers and energies to face this Nazi, vicious Tatar invasion. The alternative is loss of one's country, the dispersion of citizens, the spread of vice on earth, and the destruction of religious values. Let every person know that he is responsible before God, for "the doer of the slightest good deed is rewarded in like, and the doer of the slightest evil deed is also rewarded in like." [...]

Expansionists have more than once put their eye on Palestine, which they attacked with their armies to fulfill their designs on it. Thus it was that the Crusaders came with their armies, bringing with them their creed and carrying their cross. They were able to defeat the Moslems for a while, but the Moslems were able to retrieve the land only when they stood under the wing of their religious banner, united their word, hallowed the name of God, and surged out fighting under the leadership of Salah ed-Din al-Ayyubi. They fought for almost twenty years and at the end the Crusaders were defeated and Palestine was liberated. [...]

This is the only way to liberate Palestine. There is no doubt about the testimony of history. It is one of the laws of the universe and one of the rules of existence. Nothing can overcome iron except iron. Their false, futile creed can only be defeated by the righteous Islamic creed. A creed could not be fought except by a creed, and in the last analysis victory is for the just, for justice is certainly victorious. [...]

The Islamic Resistance Movement views seriously the defeat of the Crusaders at the hands of Salah ed-Din al-Ayyubi and the rescuing of Palestine from their hands, as well as the defeat of the Tatars at Ein Galot, breaking their power at the hands of Qataz and Al-Dhaher Bivers and saving the Arab world from the Tatar onslaught, which aimed at the destruction of every meaning of human civilization. The Movement draws lessons and examples from all this. The present Zionist onslaught has also been preceded by crusading raids from the West and [by] other Tatar raids from the East. Just as the Moslems faced those raids and planned fighting and defeating them, they should be able to confront the Zionist invasion and defeat it. This is indeed no problem for the Almighty God, provided that the intentions are pure, [that] the determination is true, and that Moslems have benefited from past experiences, rid themselves of the effects of ideological invasion, and followed the customs of their ancestors. [...]

While paving its way, the Islamic Resistance Movement emphasizes time and again, to all the sons of our people, to the Arab and Islamic nations, that it does not seek personal fame, material gain, or social prominence. It does not aim to compete against any one from among our people, or take his place. Nothing of the sort at all. It will not act against any of the sons of Moslems or those who are peaceful toward it from among non-Moslems, be they here or anywhere else. It will only serve as a support for all groupings and organizations operating against the Zionist enemy and its lackeys.

The Islamic Resistance Movement adopts Islam as its way of life. Islam is its creed and religion. Whoever takes Islam as his way of life, be it an organization, a grouping, a country, or any other body, the Islamic Resistance Movement considers itself as their soldiers and nothing more.

We ask God to show us the right course, to make us an example to others, and to judge between us and our people with truth. "O Lord, do thou judge between us and our nation with truth; for thou art the best judge" (Al Araf, Verse 89).

The last of our prayers will be praise to God, the Master of the Universe.

32. "The Second Intifada" (Interview with Marwan Barghouti)

*Toufic Haddad**

EDITOR'S NOTE *Marwan Barghouti (1959–) is a leading Palestinian political figure, formerly secretary-general of the Fatah movement in the West Bank. During the Second Intifada, beginning in late 2000, he was identified as the leader of the Tanzim, a paramilitary wing of Fatah. Arrested by Israel in 2002, he was convicted of five murders and sentenced to life imprisonment. From prison he has continued to wield great influence on the Palestinian political scene. The following interview took place in the early days of the Intifada, before his arrest.*

One enters the Fateh Central Headquarters building in El Bireh (near Ramallah) hardly expecting it to be so dilapidated. Its dingy stairs cause one to ponder the suggestions of Israeli media pundits who figure this top-floor apartment to be one of the central headquarters of current events in the Intifada. It has taken no fewer than eight telephone calls advising "to call back later," before the promise of a half-hour interview with Marwan Barghouti is finally granted. The "close aide" (read: bodyguard) who confirms this information does so over a telephone connection that is so clearly tapped that one can virtually hear the convergence of several intelligence gathering agencies fighting for their ears at the speaker.

As the secretary-general of Fateh in the West Bank and the man identified as the political spokesman for the Fateh paramilitary grouping Tantheem, Marwan Barghouti remains somewhat of a mystery. How much of a genuine challenge to the current Palestinian political regime and how much power he actually commands is not quite known. It is, however, clear that one can hardly ignore his presence on the political map in the wake of recent events.

Three young men walk into the office helping a fourth, who limps in on crutches. They look at the foreign journalists waiting in line for their turn to see Barghouti and begin to speak in Arabic among themselves:

---

* From Tikva Honig-Parnass and Toufic Haddad, *Between the Lines: Israel, the Palestinians, and the US War on Terror* (Chicago: Haymarket Books, 2007), pp. 65–69.

"I'm thinking about going to the press about this if things aren't resolved." When I ask what the problem is and what they are doing here, one of them explains: "We are from a village outside Ramallah [in Area C, under full Israeli control]. Over three weeks ago there were clashes with the [Israeli] army, and our friend here [the one on crutches] got shot. We carried him through the valley to get him to the main road so we could get him some medical attention. We suspected the army already wanted us, and indeed soon after we came to Ramallah we heard that they had raided our homes and beat our family members to see if they knew where we were. We are now stranded in Ramallah without a place to stay, without money, and we don't even know whether we will be able to return to our village. Every time we go to the PA [Palestine Authority] for help, they tell us to 'go talk to so and so,' or they simply lie and say that 'things are in process.' We decided to turn here. They say Barghouti can help."

Barghouti keeps himself tucked away in a secluded part of the office, sitting in front of a massive picture of the Dome of the Rock and gradually taking in the long line of each day's visitors. Assistants are constantly whispering things in his ear, handing him mobile phones, or changing the satellite television station so that he can time himself better when doing a live interview. His answers to most questions are well-versed sound bites that speak to the person in the street. In fact, it is difficult to get Barghouti to switch out of sound-bite mode, and even more difficult to get him to concentrate on one thing at a time. Amid constant interruptions, this interview was carried out in an effort to gain insight into what Marwan Barghouti is all about.

Q: *What are* the goals of the Intifada?

A: The goal of the Intifada is to put an end to the Israeli occupation. This is a very clear goal, and there is consensus on that to mean independence.

[...] The Intifada will not stop until there is an end to the occupation of the entire Occupied Territories and the establishment of an independent Palestinian state on 1967 borders.

Q: *What is your strategy for achieving this goal?*

A: To continue the Intifada, meaning resistance [to] the occupation by all means. It is the shortest way to achieve independence and to make the Israeli occupation pay a high price. Eventually Israeli public opinion will change its mind. This is our strategy: to fight.

Q: Do you feel the Palestinian people *are* prepared *for* this?

A: Yes, absolutely. The leadership is not prepared, but the people are prepared.

Q: In what *way* do you find the leadership not prepared?

A: I don't think they put enough efforts, abilities, and power into this Intifada.

Q: *What* do you think should be the *balance* between negotiations and diplomacy on the one hand and the Intifada on the other?

A: We are not against negotiations in general because we do believe that, at some point, we will reach the stage where we will have to negotiate. But we do not believe in negotiations on the same basis as they have been operating for the last seven years.

I think this Intifada asked to change the rules of the game, and it did this. First of all, everyone has to understand and recognize the condition that in order for the negotiations to be a success, there is a need for the continuation of the Intifada and the resistance. There will not be any fruit of these negotiations unless this Intifada continues. Second, there is a need to again put UN resolutions on the table and not to get caught up in meaningless details [in negotiations] about this street here and that corner there. As far as I am concerned, all we have to talk about is the timetable for the implementation of the UN resolutions. Finally, we have to change the sponsorship of the talks. We should not leave the Americans alone [as "facilitators" of negotiations]: they are not fair, they are not honest.

Q: Yet the PA went directly *back* to negotiations [in Taba in January 2001] on the basis of the exact same conditions that existed before.

A: Unfortunately. They are wasting a historical opportunity to correct the direction of negotiations. Still, however, we feel that the chance is still there [to change the rules].

Q: *What* does that *say* about the ability of the PA to represent the people?

A: I think every leadership has to deal with the people's opinion. And in general, throughout the Arab world, leaders ignore their public's opinion. In this, the PA is a little better than the Arab regimes, but not by much. [...] It [the PA] tried to achieve independence, and it failed. Now the Intifada has broken out. I believe it has to change its mind and play by a new set of rules. Unfortunately, it has not done this till now. Partially, it deals with the Intifada and its demands, but it is not enough. We will judge a final agreement by whether it fulfills Palestinian national aspirations or not and will consider any agreement that violates Palestinian red lines as an illegitimate agreement.

Q: In this light, *how* important is democratization of the Palestinian *national* movement in achieving national aims?

A: I think a very important relation links the two. Since the Oslo agreement, and when I took up my position as secretary-general of Fateh in the West Bank in 1994, we started the process of democratizing our institutions [Fateh]. During the first twenty-seven years of Israeli occupation, most of our activities were underground and secret, so the process of democratization could only come after Oslo.[1] We have so far succeeded in convening 172 local conferences, rep-

---

[1] When the Israeli army withdrew from the major Palestinian cities.

resenting more than 120,000 Fateh members throughout the West Bank. For the first time, these people elected their own leaders as well as their local committees. This was an effort toward hosting a national conference that we plan on having. Unfortunately, the Central Committee and leadership of Fateh are not satisfied with this idea, because it would mean that new leaders from a new generation will come to power.

I believe democratization is part of our struggle for independence and must be used as a means to strengthen our organizations. All political factions must begin this process, though I acknowledge that this is still not enough.

Q: Do you feel it is time for general elections to be held to get a more representative national leadership?

A: Right now I think it would be technically difficult to have elections. One month ago, though, we did call for an Intifada government. This means allowing all Palestinian factions that are united (and this is the first time they are all working together on the ground) to have representatives that will formally adopt the Intifada as the policy of the government. This is a good solution until we are somehow able to have general elections, which we will of course support.

Q: *What was* the response from the PA to your calls for an Intifada government?

A: It criticized and refused this, but the people have welcomed the idea.

Q: This seems to be the situation that *we are always in*?

A: Yes, it's stalemate.

33. The Intifada: Israel Government White Paper*

EDITOR'S NOTE *In response to the outbreak of the Second Intifada in late September 2000, the Israeli government gathered evidence for what it considered to be violations of the agreements reached with the PLO and the Palestinian Authority (PA) in the course of the Oslo peace process. Protest centered on accusations that PA and Fatah personnel (such as Marwan Barghouti) were involved in violent actions against Israeli targets. Following are excerpts from the White Paper released two months after the onset of the Intifada.*

Why were formal commitments important in the post-1993 peace process?

In September 1993, the PLO, as an organization, became a signatory to the Declaration of Principles and Israel's negotiating partner. This meant that, on a broad set of issues, formal commitments were needed to try and ensure, as much as possible, that the PLO leadership had clearly broken with past positions, practices, and patterns of bad faith, which had marked its conduct as a coalition of *fedayee* (i.e. terrorist) organizations.

At various points in their history, the PLO and its constituent organizations were committed to a strategy of eliminating Israel as a state. (This strategy was embodied, at the time, in the Palestinian National Covenant.) They were implicated in:

- extensive terrorist activity;
- breach of agreements and understandings reached with host Arab states;
- abuse and misgovernment in the zones which their "state within a state" controlled in Lebanon.

It is against this background that Israel felt obliged to demand formal commitments on some of the most basic and presumably obvious aspects of the process. Such commitments were indeed obtained; but, more often than not,

---

* Excerpts from Israel Government White Paper regarding Palestinian non-compliance with their commitments and agreements, November 20, 2000, available at http://mfa.gov.il/MFA/ForeignPolicy/MFADocuments/Yearbook13/Pages/200%20%20Israel%20Government%20 White%20Paper%20regarding%20Pales.aspx.

they were interpreted in a slippery way, particularly as regards the key issues of security, the use of violence, and the prevention of terrorism.

Against the mounting evidence of bad faith, as detailed below, Israel—and other parties engaged in the negotiations—kept alive the hope for a stable peace, based on the assumption that the process, and its momentum, would modify Arafat's stance on compliance and on the question of violence as an option. This hope has now been shattered. [...]

Specific aspects of non-compliance

The issues listed below are by no means exhaustive. They do, however, prove that the rationale for non-compliance, as presented above, actually led to a repeated pattern of abuse, misconduct, and outright violence on the part of the PA.

In this respect, the current crisis does mark a watershed. It has been preceded by previous "eruptions," including the tunnel crisis of September 1996 and the short-lived Nakba [Day] events in May 2000. Nevertheless, nothing in previous PA practice resembles the collapse of all existing commitments and the systematic creation—day by day, week by week—of an atmosphere of raw emotions, fear, and hatred in pursuit of a general Palestinian and pan-Arab mobilization.

All of this is not only in breach of the clearly stated commitments offered at the beginning of the Oslo process, but also in obvious, at times blatant, rejection of the understandings reached at the recent Sharm e-Sheikh Summit. The overwhelming pattern of disregard for both written and informal understandings (overt or otherwise), and in particular the use of an illegally armed militia—answerable to Arafat—in a low-intensity conflict masked as "popular protest" or in an Intifada, all confirm that, from a Palestinian point of view, the new dynamics of the "struggle"—and of the call for Arab and international intervention—take precedence over *pacta sunt servanda*.[1]

Beyond the current state of warfare, Palestinian non-compliance encompasses broad aspects of everyday practice, from school texts to car theft. Some (not all) of these are discussed here.

Direct use of violence

Clearly, the most obvious breach of the Palestinian commitments involves the direct participation of its armed forces—the Palestinian "police" (in effect, Arafat's regular army) and the various security organs—in armed clashes with the IDF [Israel Defense Forces] or in attacks on Israeli citizens.

---

[1] The principle "agreements must be respected."

The pattern evident in the current crisis had already been established in 1996, when Palestinian policemen played a major role in the extensive clashes that left 15 Israeli soldiers dead; in effect, they acted as a fighting force—even in places where only hours earlier some of them participated in the joint patrols with the IDF, according to the Interim Agreement.

In the recent crisis, the role of the regular Palestinian forces has been somewhat more ambiguous, in line with Arafat's interest in keeping his hand half-hidden and [in] using mainly his militia forces—the Fatah *tanzim* (cadres)—in the firefights and attacks on Israeli targets. Local police commanders were in fact given orders, at times, to re-establish law and order and restore the calm—but their actions often indicated that they felt (or rather realized) that such instructions do not fit in with Arafat's broader support for the struggle and were therefore half-hearted in carrying them out.

In many cases, Palestinian policemen took an active part in the fighting, in an organized fashion or as individuals, and there is no evidence (now or on previous occasions) of disciplinary action being taken against those who did so. There is evidence, moreover, as to the complicity of preventive security operatives—particularly in the Gaza strip—in armed attacks on the IDF and on Israelis.

Perhaps the most serious event for which the Palestinian police bears a major share of responsibility in the recent crisis was the lynching of two Israeli reserve soldiers in Ramallah on October 12, 2000. It was indeed a mob which killed them and mutilated their bodies, but it had been the Palestinian policemen who captured them, brought them into the police headquarters at the center of town, and then put up only a half-hearted effort to prevent the attack. So far, the PA did nothing to punish those responsible. [...]

The shattered assumptions: What does this all add up to?

The very nature of the Oslo [peace] process assumed that, over time, if not overnight, a new reality of bilateral relations would be created on the ground, with an open prospect [of] Palestinian sovereignty in sight. This would lead Arafat away from the option of violence and "struggle" (which he and others in the PA continued to articulate). This has not happened. [...]

The root causes

What has led Arafat and the PA leadership to opt for violence and incitement as an instrument of policy? A consistent pattern of behavior over several weeks, with a clearly defined set of goals ("internationalization" of the conflict) and with the means (televised Palestinian sacrifice and suffering) apparently well tailored to achieve them, cannot be simply dismissed as a passing aberration or a "caprice." Within the limits of what modern political science calls "bounded rationality," Arafat's gamble is risky, but not irrational.

Still, to understand the root causes for this choice—or rather the Palestinian refusal to choose, once and for all, the path of peace—it is necessary to point out, albeit briefly, some of the recurrent themes in Arafat's political conduct over the years.

Arafat's strategy of avoiding choices

Throughout his tenure as a leader of the Fatah movement and of the PLO, Arafat attached particular importance to the principle of maintaining *Istiqlal al-Qarrar*, that is, his ability to avoid becoming anyone's "agent" (and there were many in the Palestinian arena identified as working for some Arab or foreign interests).

A key element in his ability to do so, at least until a major crisis forced a choice or a decision on him, was the constant maneuver between the poles of any regional or international system in which he worked—Egypt and its rivals in the Arab world, the Cold War protagonists, the Syrians and their enemies in Lebanon.

In recent years, this pattern of "fence-sitting" and indecision evolved around two polarities:

- Playing the United States (with which he established a dialogue in December 1988) against Iraq (which he came to see as a heroic Arab counter-balance to US power). To some extent, this tactic is still at work. While speaking favorably of Clinton (as distinct from the US Congress) at the Emergency Arab Summit in Cairo, Arafat also endorsed the call for the lifting of sanctions on the "suffering Iraqi people." Pro-Iraqi sentiments, including the fervent call of demonstrators for Saddam Hussein to "hit, hit Tel Aviv" (with chemical warheads), are indeed rife among Palestinians even now, despite the lessons learned from the disastrous choice in 1990–1991.
- Playing the dialogue with Israel (and the formal obligations detailed above) vs. [having] an ambivalent attitude towards the Hamas, terrorism, and the use of violence: the consequences of this way of keeping his options open and [of] avoiding any implication that he now "belongs" to Israel (like the former SLA [South Lebanon Army] in Lebanon) have become manifest in the recent crisis.

34. Palestine Papers: Olmert's Offer to Abu Mazen (August 31, 2008)*

EDITOR'S NOTE *In January 2011 the Arab news agency Al-Jazeera released about 1,700 documents from the files of Palestinian negotiators, leaked by a dissident member of the team. The documents dated from 1999 to 2010. Of special interest were the behind-the-scenes negotiations between Israeli Prime Minister Ehud Olmert and Palestinian Authority President Mahmoud Abbas (Abu Mazen) in 2007–2008, the second serious attempt to negotiate final status issues. Following is the Palestinian summary of Olmert's final offer to Abbas, as recorded in the documents published.*

General

- The preamble will state that the agreement represents the implementation of UNSC Res. 242 and 338, as well as fulfillment of the API [Arab Peace Initiative] (no mention of UNGA Res. 194).

Territory

- Israel would annex 6.8 percent of the West Bank, including the four main settlement "blocs" of Gush Etzion (with Efrata), Ma'ale Adumim, Giv'at Ze'ev and Ariel), as well as all of the settlements in East Jerusalem (with Har Homa), in exchange for the equivalent of 5.5 percent from Israeli territory.
- The "safe passage" (i.e., the territorial link) between Gaza and the West Bank would be under Israeli sovereignty, with Palestinian control, and is not included in the above percentages.
- There will be a special road connecting Bethlehem with Ramallah, thus bypassing East Jerusalem (most likely the same road currently planned around Adumim).
- East Jerusalem would be divided territorially along the lines of the Clinton Parameters, with the exception of the Holy Basin, whose sovereignty would be delayed to a later stage (see Jerusalem below).
- There was no mention of the Jordan Valley.

---

* "Summary of Olmert's 'Package' Offer to Abu Mazen (made on August 31, 2008)," available at http://www.ajtransparency.com/files/4736.pdf.

Jerusalem

- Sovereignty over the Holy Basin, which Olmert said comprises 0.04 percent of the West Bank (approximately 2.2 km²), would be delayed to a later stage.
- The issue would continue to be negotiated bilaterally between Israel and Palestine with the involvement of the United States, Saudi Arabia, Jordan, and Egypt, but without the ability of these third parties to force an agreement on the parties.

Refugees

- Israel would acknowledge the *suffering* of—but not responsibility for—Palestinian refugees (language is in the preamble). In parallel, there must also be a mention of Israeli (or Jewish) suffering.
- Israel would take in 1,000 refugees per year for a period of 5 years on "humanitarian" grounds. In addition, programs of "family reunification" would continue.
- Israel would contribute to the compensation of the refugees through the mechanism and [on the basis of] suffering.
- Not clear what the heads of damage for compensation would be, just that there would be no acknowledgement of responsibility for the refugees, and that compensation, and not restitution or return (apart from the 5,000), would be the only remedy.

Security

- The "package" apparently made no mention of security.

35. "My Offer to Abbas"

Ehud Olmert*

EDITOR'S NOTE Ehud Olmert (1945–) was prime minister of Israel from 2006 to 2009, leading the centrist Kadima party that had been founded by Ariel Sharon when he split from the right-wing Likud. Following the Annapolis Conference in late 2007, Olmert and PA President Abbas engaged in extended private negotiations over a final resolution of the conflict—as noted, this was only the second such sustained effort between accredited leaders of the two core parties. In response to the publication of the Palestine Papers (Reading 34), Olmert published his own account of the same exchange, taken from memoirs that were published several years later (Ehud Olmert, "Beguf Rishon" ["In First Person"], Yidiot Ahronot, 2018).

I had a meeting scheduled with Abu Mazen [Mahmoud Abbas] for September 16, [2008]; I began by presenting the principles of the arrangement that I was proposing. After I finished, Abu Mazen sighed deeply and asked to see the map that I had prepared. I spread it out. He looked at it, and I looked at him.

He was silent.

Never before had any Israeli prime minister presented such a crystallized and detailed position about resolving the conflict as was presented to him on that day. For the first time since the negotiations began, I was very tense. For the first time since I had become prime minister, I truly felt the weight of Jewish history on my shoulders, and despite the fact that I was confident that I was doing the right thing, the negotiations were very heavy.

Abu Mazen said that he could not decide and that he needed time. I told him that he was making an historic mistake.

"Give me the map so that I can consult with my colleagues," he said to me. "No," I replied. "Take the pen and sign now. You'll never get an offer that is more fair or more just. Don't hesitate. This is hard for me too, but we don't have an option of not resolving [the conflict]."

I saw that he was agonizing [over it]. In the end he said to me: "Give me a few days. I don't know my way around maps. I propose that tomorrow we meet with two map experts, one from your side and one from our side. If they tell me that everything is all right, we can sign." The next day they called and said that Abu Mazen had forgotten that they needed to be in Amman that day, and they asked to postpone the meeting by a week.

I haven't met with Abu Mazen since then. The map stayed with me.

---

* From "Ehud Olmert Gives Account of Key Meeting with Palestinian President," Guardian, January 27, 2011, translated from Yidiot Ahronot, January 27, 2011.

36. "Conditions for a Two-State Solution"

Benjamin Netanyahu*

EDITOR'S NOTE *Benjamin Netanyahu (1949–), leader of Israel's right-wing Likud Party, served as prime minister in 1996–1999 and returned to that post following the Knesset elections of February 2009. Netanyahu's governing center-right coalition included proponents of the renewed negotiation and acceptance of an independent Palestinian state alongside Israel—the two-state solution. Given the pressure in this direction both within Israel and from abroad, much attention was paid to Netanyahu's first major policy statement on these issues, laid out in a speech at Bar-Ilan University on June 14, 2009.*

Honored guests, citizens of Israel,

Peace has always been our people's most ardent desire. Our prophets gave the world the vision of peace, we greet one another with wishes of peace, and our prayers conclude with the word peace.

We are gathered this evening in an institution named after two pioneers of peace, Menachem Begin and Anwar Sadat, and we share in their vision.

Two and half months ago, I took the oath of office as the Prime Minister of Israel. I pledged to establish a national unity government—and I did. I believed, and I still believe, that unity was essential for us now more than ever, as we face three immense challenges—the Iranian threat, the economic crisis, and the advancement of peace. [...]

And the third challenge, so exceedingly important, is the advancement of peace. I also spoke about this with President Obama, and I fully support the idea of a regional peace that he is leading.

I share the president's desire to bring about a new era of reconciliation in our region. To this end, I met with President Mubarak in Egypt and King Abdullah in Jordan, to elicit the support of these leaders in expanding the circle of peace in our region. I turn to all Arab leaders tonight and I say: "Let us meet. Let us speak of peace and let us make peace." I am ready to meet with you at any time. I am willing to go to Damascus, to Riyadh, to Beirut, to any place— including Jerusalem. [...]

---

* Abridgement of Address by Prime Minister Netanyahu at Bar-Ilan University, June 14, 2009, available at http://mfa.gov.il/MFA/PressRoom/2009/Pages/Address_PM_Netanyahu_Bar-Ilan_University_14-Jun-2009.aspx.

I turn to you, our Palestinian neighbors, led by the Palestinian Authority, and I say: Let's begin negotiations immediately without preconditions.

Israel is obligated by its international commitments and expects all parties to keep their commitments. We want to live with you in peace, as good neighbors. We want our children and your children to never again experience war: that parents, brothers, and sisters will never again know the agony of losing loved ones in battle; that our children will be able to dream of a better future and realize that dream; and that together we will invest our energies in plowshares and pruning hooks, not swords and spears.

I know the face of war. I have experienced battle. I lost close friends, I lost a brother. I have seen the pain of bereaved families. I do not want war. No one in Israel wants war.

If we join hands and work together for peace, there is no limit to the development and prosperity we can achieve for our two peoples—in the economy, agriculture, trade, tourism, and education—most importantly, in providing our youth [with] a better world in which to live a life full of tranquility, creativity, opportunity, and hope.

If the advantages of peace are so evident, we must ask ourselves why peace remains so remote, even as our hand remains outstretched for peace. Why has this conflict continued for more than sixty years?

In order to bring an end to the conflict, we must give an honest and forthright answer to the question: What is the root of the conflict?

In his speech to the first Zionist Conference in Basel, the founder of the Zionist movement, Theodor Herzl, said about the Jewish national home: "This idea is so big that we must speak of it only in the simplest terms." Today I will speak about the immense challenge of peace in the simplest words possible.

Even as we look toward the horizon, we must be firmly connected to reality, to the truth. And the simple truth is that the root of the conflict was, and remains, the refusal to recognize the right of the Jewish people to a state of their own, in their historical homeland.

In 1947, when the United Nations proposed the partition plan of a Jewish state and an Arab state, the entire Arab world rejected the resolution. The Jewish community, by contrast, welcomed it by dancing and rejoicing. The Arabs rejected any Jewish state, within any borders.

Those who think that the continued enmity toward Israel is a product of our presence in Judea, Samaria, and Gaza [are] confusing cause and consequence.

The attacks against us began in the 1920s, escalated into a comprehensive attack in 1948 with the declaration of Israel's independence, continued with the *fedayeen* attacks in the 1950s, and climaxed in 1967, on the eve of the Six-Day War, in an attempt to tighten the noose around the neck of the State of Israel.

All this occurred during the fifty years before a single Israeli soldier ever set foot in Judea and Samaria.

Fortunately, Egypt and Jordan left this circle of enmity. The signing of peace treaties [has] brought about an end to their claims against Israel, an end to the conflict. But, to our regret, this is not the case with the Palestinians. The closer we get to an agreement with them, the further they retreat and raise demands that are inconsistent with a true desire to end the conflict.

Many good people have told us that withdrawal from territories is the key to peace with the Palestinians. Well, we withdrew. But the fact is that every withdrawal was met with massive waves of terror, by suicide bombers and thousands of missiles.

We tried to withdraw with an agreement and without an agreement. We tried a partial withdrawal and a full withdrawal. In 2000, and again last year, Israel proposed an almost total withdrawal in exchange for an end to the conflict, and twice our offers were rejected. We evacuated every last inch of the Gaza strip, we uprooted tens of settlements and evicted of Israelis from their homes; and, in response, we received a hail of missiles on our cities, towns, and children.

The claim that territorial withdrawals will bring peace with the Palestinians, or at least will advance the peace, has up till now not stood the test of reality. In addition to this, Hamas in the south, like Hizbullah in the north, repeatedly proclaims their commitment to "liberate" the Israeli cities of Ashkelon, Beersheba, Acre, and Haifa.

Territorial withdrawals have not lessened the hatred and, to our regret, Palestinian moderates are not yet ready to say the simple words: "Israel is the nation-state of the Jewish people, and it will stay that way."

Achieving peace will require courage and candor from both sides, and not only from the Israeli side. The Palestinian leadership must [rise] and say: "Enough of this conflict. We recognize the right of the Jewish people to a state of their own in this land, and we are prepared to live beside you in true peace."

I am yearning for that moment; for, when Palestinian leaders say those words to our people and to their people, then a path will be opened to resolving all the problems between our peoples, no matter how complex they may be. Therefore a fundamental prerequisite for ending the conflict is a public, binding, and unequivocal Palestinian recognition of Israel as the nation-state of the Jewish people. To invest this declaration with practical meaning, there must also be a clear understanding that the Palestinian refugee problem will be resolved outside Israel's borders. For it is clear that any demand for resettling Palestinian refugees within Israel undermines Israel's continued existence as the state of the Jewish people.

The Palestinian refugee problem must be solved, and it can be solved, as we ourselves proved in a similar situation. Tiny Israel successfully absorbed hundreds of thousands of Jewish refugees who left their homes and belongings in Arab countries. Therefore justice and logic demand that the Palestinian refugee problem be solved outside Israel's borders. On this point there is a broad national consensus. I believe that, with goodwill and international investment, this humanitarian problem can be permanently resolved.

So far I have spoken about the need for Palestinians to recognize our rights. In a moment, I will speak openly about our need to recognize their rights. But let me first say that the connection between the Jewish people and the Land of Israel has lasted for more than 3,500 years. Judea and Samaria, the places where Abraham, Isaac, and Jacob, David and Solomon, and Isaiah and Jeremiah lived, are not alien to us. This is the land of our forefathers.

The right of the Jewish people to a state in the Land of Israel does not derive from the catastrophes that have plagued our people. True, for 2,000 years the Jewish people suffered expulsions, pogroms, blood libels, and massacres which culminated in a Holocaust—a suffering which has no parallel in human history. There are those who say that, if the Holocaust had not occurred, the state of Israel would never have been established. But I say that, if the state of Israel [had] been established earlier, the Holocaust would not have occurred.

This tragic history of powerlessness explains why the Jewish people need a sovereign power of self-defense. But our right to build our sovereign state here, in the Land of Israel, arises from one simple fact: this is the homeland of the Jewish people, this is where our identity was forged.

As Israel's first Prime Minister David Ben-Gurion proclaimed in Israel's Declaration of Independence: "The Jewish people arose in the land of Israel and it was here that its spiritual, religious and political character was shaped. Here they attained their sovereignty, and here they bequeathed to the world their national and cultural treasures, and the most eternal of books."

But we must also tell the truth in its entirety: within this homeland lives a large Palestinian community. We do not want to rule over them, we do not want to govern their lives, we do not want to impose either our flag or our culture on them.

In my vision of peace, in this small land of ours, two peoples live freely, side by side, in amity and mutual respect. Each will have its own flag, its own national anthem, its own government. Neither will threaten the security or survival of the other. These two realities—our connection to the Land of Israel, and the Palestinian population living within it—have created deep divisions in Israeli society. But the truth is that we have much more that unites us than divides us.

I have come tonight to give expression to that unity and to the principles of peace and security, on which there is broad agreement within Israeli society. These are the principles that guide our policy. This policy must take into account the international situation that has recently developed. We must recognize this reality and at the same time stand firmly on those principles essential for Israel.

I have already stressed the first principle—recognition. Palestinians must clearly and unambiguously recognize Israel as the state of the Jewish people.

The second principle is demilitarization. The territory under Palestinian control must be demilitarized, with ironclad security provisions for Israel. Without these two conditions, there is a real danger that an armed Palestinian state would emerge that would become another terrorist base against the Jewish state, such as the one in Gaza. We don't want Kassam rockets on Petah Tikva, Grad rockets on Tel Aviv, or missiles on Ben-Gurion airport. We want peace.

In order to achieve peace, we must ensure that Palestinians will not be able to import missiles into their territory, to field an army, to close their airspace to us, or to make pacts with the likes of Hizbullah and Iran. On this point as well, there is wide consensus within Israel. It is impossible to expect us to agree in advance to the principle of a Palestinian state without assurances that this state will be demilitarized. On a matter so critical to the existence of Israel, we must first have our security needs addressed.

Therefore, today we ask our friends in the international community, led by the United States, for what is critical to the security of Israel: clear commitments that, in a future peace agreement, the territory controlled by the Palestinians will be demilitarized, namely without an army, without control of its airspace, and with effective security measures to prevent weapons smuggling into the territory—real monitoring, and not what occurs in Gaza today. And, obviously, the Palestinians will not be able to forge military pacts. Without this, sooner or later, these territories will become another Hamastan. And that we cannot accept.

I told President Obama when I was in Washington that, if we could agree on the substance, then the terminology would not pose a problem. And here is the substance that I now state clearly:

If we receive this guarantee regarding demilitarization and Israel's security needs, and if the Palestinians recognize Israel as the state of the Jewish people, then we will be ready in a future peace agreement to reach a solution where a demilitarized Palestinian state exists alongside the Jewish state.

Regarding the remaining important issues that will be discussed as part of the final settlement, my positions are known: Israel needs defensible borders, and Jerusalem must remain the united capital of Israel with continued religious freedom for all faiths. The territorial question will be discussed as part of the final peace agreement. In the meantime we have no intention of building new settlements or of expropriating additional land for existing settlements.

But there is a need to enable the residents to live normal lives, to allow mothers and fathers to raise their children like families elsewhere. The settlers are neither the enemies of the people nor the enemies of peace. Rather they are an integral part of our people, a principled, pioneering, and Zionist public.

Unity among us is essential and will help us achieve reconciliation with our neighbors. That reconciliation must already begin by altering existing realities. I believe that a strong Palestinian economy will strengthen peace.

If the Palestinians turn toward peace—in fighting terror, in strengthening governance and the rule of law, in educating their children for peace and in stopping incitement against Israel—we will do our part in making every effort to facilitate freedom of movement and access and to enable them to develop their economy. All of this will help us advance a peace treaty between us.

Above all else, the Palestinians must decide between the path of peace and the path of Hamas. The Palestinian Authority will have to establish the rule of law in Gaza and overcome Hamas. Israel will not sit at the negotiating table with terrorists who seek their destruction. [...]

With a Palestinian leadership committed to peace, with the active participation of the Arab world, and [with] the support of the United States and the international community, there is no reason why we cannot achieve a breakthrough to peace.

Our people have already proven that we can do the impossible. Over the past 61 years, while constantly defending our existence, we have performed wonders.

Our microchips are powering the world's computers. Our medicines are treating diseases once considered incurable. Our drip irrigation is bringing arid lands back to life across the globe. And Israeli scientists are expanding the boundaries of human knowledge. If only our neighbors would respond to our call—peace too will be in our reach.

I call on the leaders of the Arab world and on the Palestinian leadership, let us continue together on the path of Menahem Begin and Anwar Sadat, Yitzhak Rabin and King Hussein. Let us realize the vision of the prophet Isaiah, who, in Jerusalem, 2,700 years ago, said: "nations shall not lift up sword against nation, and they shall learn war no more."

With God's help, we will know no more war. We will know peace.

Chapter 8

The Downward Spiral

The new realities of the fourth stage of the Israeli–Palestinian conflict—non-state actors, asymmetric wars, and religious extremism—continued to mark the years that followed the Gaza War of 2008–2009. In this unsettled environment, Israeli elections in 2009, 2013, and 2015 produced hawkish government coalitions under Prime Minister Benjamin Netanyahu. Attempts to renew negotiations over "final status" issues foundered in the early part of this period over the Palestinian condition that Israel freeze construction of new settlements in the West Bank at a time when right-wing Israeli coalitions were giving higher priority to new settlement projects.

The fact that Hamas remained in control of the Gaza strip was yet another complication. Looking for other ways to advance Palestinian statehood, Palestinian Authority President Mahmoud Abbas reached a formal—and ultimately unimplemented—unity agreement with Hamas and applied in late 2011 for recognition of Palestine as a United Nations member state (Reading 37). In the end he achieved recognition only as an non-member observer state.

The diplomatic channel was, however, reopened by US Secretary of State John Kerry upon his assuming office in early 2013. Operating with a tight deadline of nine months, Kerry's mission collapsed and led to a renewal of Palestinian unilateralism—developments described by the chief US negotiator in these talks, Martin Indyk, in Reading 38.

"Asymmetric" wars between regular Israeli forces and the irregular Hamas fighters also occurred in 2012 and 2014. The legal and moral dilemmas raised by such combat are seen from the perspectives of both sides in Reading 39—a Palestinian condemnation of Israeli methods of warfare in 2014—and in Reading 40—Prime Minister Netanyahu's defense of Israel's policies and tactics.

Looking back at what he learned in his four years of close contact with Israeli–Palestinian diplomacy, Secretary of State Kerry, in his final days in office, sets out suggested principles for future negotiations (Reading 41).

Further online resources:

United Nations Report on 2010 Mavi Marmara Incident: http://www.un.org/News/dh/infocus/middle_east/Gaza_Flotilla_Panel_Report.pdf.

Resolution on Status of Palestine in the United Nations, 2012: https://unispal.un.org/DPA/DPR/unispal.nsf/0/C05528251EA6B4BD85257AE5005271B0.

Egyptian Cease-Fire Proposal (2014 Gaza conflict): https://www.haaretz.com/the-egyptian-cease-fire-proposal-1.5255539.

Fatah–Hamas Reconciliation Agreement, 2014: https://www.jpost.com/Arab–Israeli-Conflict/Text-of-Fatah-Hamas-agreement-376350.

US Secretary of State John Kerry Announcement of Iranian Nuclear Agreement, 2015: https://2009–2017.state.gov/p/nea/p5/index.htm.

Prime Minister Netanyahu's Response to Kerry Speech of December 2016: https://www.timesofisrael.com/full-text-of-netanyahus-response-to-kerry-speech-on-mideast-peace.

37. "Recognize Palestine as a UN Member State"

Mahmoud Abbas*

EDITOR'S NOTE *With diplomacy stalled, the Palestinian Authority under President Mahmoud Abbas in late 2011 launched an initiative aimed at gaining international recognition and support of Palestinian statehood. Fatah and Hamas had signed a unity agreement in May 2011, so Abbas was able to present the case for membership in the United Nations as a unified state, even though Hamas remained in actual control of Gaza. The United Nations was a favorable arena for Palestinians, since most UN members had recognized Palestinian statehood in some form since it was initially declared in 1988. Abbas made the formal application in an address to the UN General Assembly on September 23, 2011.*

Mr. Secretary-General of the United Nations,

Excellencies,

Ladies and Gentlemen,

The Question of Palestine is intricately linked with the United Nations via the resolutions adopted by its various organs and agencies and via the essential and lauded role of the United Nations Relief and Works Agency for Palestine Refugees in the Near East—UNRWA—which embodies the international responsibility towards the plight of Palestine refugees, who are the victims of Al-Nakba (Catastrophe) that occurred in 1948. We aspire for and seek a greater and more effective role for the United Nations in working to achieve a just and comprehensive peace in our region that ensures the inalienable, legitimate national rights of the Palestinian people, as defined by the resolutions of international legitimacy of the United Nations.

A year ago, at this same time, distinguished leaders in this hall addressed the stalled peace efforts in our region. Everyone had high hopes for a new round of final status negotiations, which had begun in early September in Washington under the direct auspices of President Barack Obama and with participation of the Quartet, and with Egyptian and Jordanian participation,

* Abridgement of speech by Mahmoud Abbas, United Nations General Assembly Official Records, 66th Session, 16th Plenary Meeting, September 23, 2011, A/66/PV.19.

to reach a peace agreement within one year. We entered those negotiations with open hearts and attentive ears and sincere intentions, and we were ready with our documents, papers, and proposals. But the negotiations broke down just weeks after their launch.

After this, we did not give up and did not cease our efforts for initiatives and contacts. Over the past year we did not leave a door to be knocked or channel to be tested or path to be taken and we did not ignore any formal or informal party of influence and stature to be addressed. We positively considered the various ideas and proposals and initiatives presented from many countries and parties. But all of these sincere efforts and endeavors undertaken by international parties were repeatedly wrecked by the positions of the Israeli government, which quickly dashed the hopes raised by the launch of negotiations last September.

The core issue here is that the Israeli government refuses to commit to terms of reference for the negotiations that are based on international law and United Nations resolutions, and that it frantically continues to intensify building of settlements on the territory of the State of Palestine. [...]

The occupation is racing against time to redraw the borders on our land according to what it wants and to impose a fait accompli on the ground that changes the realities and that is undermining the realistic potential for the existence of the State of Palestine. [...]

This policy will destroy the chances of achieving a two-state solution, upon which there is an international consensus, and here I caution aloud: this settlement policy threatens to also undermine the structure of the Palestinian National Authority and even end its existence.

In addition, we now face the imposition of new conditions not previously raised, conditions that will transform the raging conflict in our inflamed region into a religious conflict and a threat to the future of a million and a half Christian and Muslim Palestinians, citizens of Israel, a matter which we reject and which is impossible for us to accept being dragged into. [...]

Yet, because we believe in peace and because of our conviction in international legitimacy, and because we had the courage to make difficult decisions for our people, and in the absence of absolute justice, we decided to adopt the path of relative justice—justice that is possible and could correct part of the grave historical injustice committed against our people. Thus we agreed to establish the State of Palestine on only 22 percent of the territory of historical Palestine—on all the Palestinian Territory occupied by Israel in 1967. [...]

I confirm, on behalf of the Palestine Liberation Organization, the sole legitimate representative of the Palestinian people, which will remain so until the end of the conflict in all its aspects and until the resolution of all final status issues, the following:

1 The goal of the Palestinian people is the realization of their inalienable national rights in their independent State of Palestine, with East Jerusalem as its capital, on all the land of the West Bank, including East Jerusalem, and the Gaza Strip, which Israel occupied in the June 1967 war, in conformity with the resolutions of international legitimacy and with the achievement of a just and agreed upon solution to the Palestine refugee issue in accordance with resolution 194, as stipulated in the Arab Peace Initiative, which presented the consensus Arab vision to resolve the core the Arab–Israeli conflict and to achieve a just and comprehensive peace. To this we adhere and this is what we are working to achieve. Achieving this desired peace also requires the release of political prisoners and detainees in Israeli prisons without delay.

2 The Palestine Liberation Organization and the Palestinian people adhere to the renouncement of violence and rejection and condemning of terrorism in all its forms, especially state terrorism, and adhere to all agreements signed between the Palestine Liberation Organization and Israel.

3 We adhere to the option of negotiating a lasting solution to the conflict, in accordance with resolutions of international legitimacy. Here I declare that the Palestine Liberation Organization is ready to return immediately to the negotiating table on the basis of the adopted terms of reference based on international legitimacy and a complete cessation of settlement activities.

4 Our people will continue their popular peaceful resistance to the Israeli occupation and its settlement and apartheid policies and its construction of the racist annexation Wall, and they receive support for their resistance, which is consistent with international humanitarian law and international conventions and has the support of peace activists from Israel and around the world, reflecting an impressive, inspiring, and courageous example of the strength of this defenseless people, armed only with their dreams, courage, hope, and slogans in the face of bullets, tanks, tear gas, and bulldozers.

5 When we bring our plight and our case to this international podium, it is a confirmation of our reliance on the political and diplomatic option and a confirmation that we do not undertake unilateral steps. Our efforts are not aimed at isolating Israel or delegitimizing it; rather we want to gain legitimacy for the cause of the people of Palestine. We only aim to delegitimize the settlement activities and the occupation and apartheid and the logic of ruthless force, and we believe that all the countries of the world stand with us in this regard. [...]

Despite the unquestionable right of our people to self-determination and to the independence of our state as stipulated in international resolutions, we have accepted in the past few years to engage in what appeared to be a test of our worthiness, entitlement, and eligibility. During the last two years our national authority has implemented a program to build our state institutions. Despite the extraordinary situation and the Israeli obstacles imposed, a serious extensive project was launched that has included the implementation of plans to enhance and advance the judiciary and the apparatus for the maintenance of order and security, to develop the administrative, financial, and oversight systems, to upgrade the performance of institutions, and to enhance self-reliance to reduce the need for foreign aid. [...]

When division struck the unity of our homeland, people, and institutions, we were determined to adopt dialogue for the restoration of our unity. We succeeded months ago in achieving national reconciliation, and we hope that its implementation will be accelerated in the coming weeks. The core pillar of this reconciliation was to turn to the people through legislative and presidential elections within a year, because the state we want will be a state characterized by the rule of law, democratic exercise and protection of the freedoms and equality of all citizens without any discrimination, and the transfer of power through the ballot box. [...]

I come before you today from the Holy Land, the land of Palestine, the land of divine messages, ascension of the Prophet Muhammad (peace be upon him) and the birthplace of Jesus Christ (peace be upon him), to speak on behalf of the Palestinian people in the homeland and in the diaspora, to say, after 63 years of suffering the ongoing Nakba: enough. It is time for the Palestinian people to gain their freedom and independence.

The time has come to end the suffering and the plight of millions of Palestine refugees in the homeland and the diaspora, to end their displacement, and to realize their rights; some of them were forced to take refuge more than once in different places of the world.

At a time when the Arab peoples affirm their quest for democracy—the Arab Spring—the time is now for the Palestinian Spring, the time for independence. [...]

I say: the time has come for my courageous and proud people, after decades of displacement and colonial occupation and ceaseless suffering, to live like other peoples of the earth, free in a sovereign and independent homeland.

I would like to inform you that, before delivering this statement, I submitted, in my capacity as the president of the State of Palestine and chairman of the Executive Committee of the Palestine Liberation Organization, to H. E. Mr. Ban Ki-moon, secretary-general of the United Nations, an application for the admission of Palestine, on the basis of the June 4, 1967 borders [sic], with Al-Quds Al-Sharif as its capital, as a full member of the United Nations.

I call upon Mr. secretary-general to expedite transmittal of our request to the Security Council, and I call upon the distinguished members of the Security Council to vote in favor of our full membership. I also call upon the states that have not recognized the State of Palestine as yet to do so. [...]

Your support for the establishment of the State of Palestine and for its admission to the United Nations as a full member is the greatest contribution to peacemaking in the Holy Land.

I thank you.

38. "Collapse of Kerry Initiative"

Martin Indyk*

EDITOR'S NOTE *Martin Indyk (1951–) is a US diplomat and scholar who served as special envoy for Israeli–Palestinian negotiations during the period of the Kerry initiative, 2013–2014. John Kerry (1943–) was US secretary of state during President Barack Obama's second term (2013–2017). Soon after assuming office, he initiated a full-scale effort to reach a final resolution of the Israeli–Palestinian conflict, with Indyk as chief US negotiator. Palestinians had refused to enter negotiations without a freeze on new Jewish settlements in the West Bank; this was set aside by a deal in which Palestinian prisoners in Israel were released in return for the Palestinian Authority putting off planned applications to join UN agencies. With a set deadline of April 2014, agreement on details proved impossible, so Kerry tried to reach a framework agreement: there would be two states; Palestine to be demilitarized; borders to be based on the 1967 lines, with land swaps and a shared Jerusalem; and there would be no mass return of refugees to Israel. But this goal could not be realized before the expiration of the deadline, and talks were suspended indefinitely. Shortly afterward Indyk offered his own appraisal of the circumstances that favored an agreement and, more importantly, of the obstacles that defeated this particular initiative.*

Last July, President Obama and Secretary of State John Kerry launched a vigorous effort to reach a final status agreement between Israelis and Palestinians. Now it is early May, we have passed the nine-month marker for these negotiations, and for the time being the talks have been suspended. Some have said this process is over. But that is not correct. As my little story testifies. As you all know well—in the Middle East, it's never over. [...]

In some ways things are easier in the Israeli–Palestinian context today than in the past.

The international context for peacemaking is better today. The Cold War and fear that a conflict in the Middle East would trigger a nuclear superpower confrontation [are] no longer there.

---

* From Martin Indyk, "Remarks on the Israeli–Palestinian Negotiations," Washington Institute's Weinberg Conference, Washington, DC, May 8, 2014, available at https://2009-2017.state.gov/p/nea/rls/rm/225840.htm.

The region has not faced an all-out Arab–Israeli war in 40 years. Peace treaties with Egypt and Jordan have held today despite very difficult circumstances—two Intifadas, conflicts with Hezbollah in Lebanon and Hamas in Gaza, and of course the Arab revolutions. Turmoil in the Mideast is bringing Israelis and Arab states closer together. Indeed, there is a virtual realignment taking place between the enemies of moderation on the one side and the proponents of moderation on the other that crossed the Arab–Israeli divide. As Israeli Prime Minister Netanyahu has noted, "many Arab leaders today already realize that Israel is not their enemy, that peace with the Palestinians would turn our relations with them and with many Arab countries into open and thriving relationships."

In the Israeli–Palestinian domestic arena there is, in some ways, greater political realism than before. Back in Kissinger's day, Golda Meir said there was no such thing as a Palestinian people. Now a Likud prime minister says there [have] to be two states for two people. Back then, Yasser Arafat was committed to Israel's destruction. Today his successor, Abu Mazen, is committed to living alongside Israel in peace.

The US–Israel relationship has also changed in quite dramatic ways. Only those who know it from the inside—as I have had the privilege to do—can testify to how deep and strong are the ties that now bind our two nations. When President Obama speaks with justifiable pride about those bonds as "unbreakable," he means what he says. And he knows of what he speaks. Unlike the "reassessment" Kissinger did in the Ford Administration, there is one significant difference: President Obama and Secretary Kerry would never suspend US–Israel military relations, as their predecessors did back then. Those military relations are too important to both our nations.

However, in many respects, when it comes to peace negotiations, things have proven to be much harder today than in the 1970s.

Kissinger faced Israelis and Egyptians who were coming off the painful 1973 war. I was an Australian student in Israel at the time. I remember well the sense of existential dread in the country brought on by the scope of Israeli casualties, and I remember also a willingness to consider withdrawals from Sinai that had previously been ruled out. Few of you remember [that] Moshe Dayan stated before the 1973 war that he would rather have Sharm el Sheikh than peace. Egypt also had a sense of urgency, generated by Sadat's belief that only peace with Israel could change Egypt's dire circumstances and only US diplomacy could achieve that peace.

Yet where is this sense of urgency today? To be absolutely clear, I am not for a moment suggesting that violence is necessary to produce urgency and flexibility. That is abhorrent. We are very fortunate to have two leaders, in President Abbas and Prime Minister Netanyahu, who are committed to achieving a resolution of the Israeli–Palestinian conflict through peaceful means.

But one problem that revealed itself in these past nine months is that the parties, although both showing flexibility in the negotiations, do not feel the pressing need to make the gut-wrenching compromises necessary to achieve peace. It is easier for the Palestinians to sign conventions and appeal to international bodies in their supposed pursuit of "justice" and their "rights," a process which by definition requires no compromise. It is easier for Israeli politicians to avoid tension in the governing coalition and for the Israeli people to maintain the current comfortable status quo. It is safe to say that, if we, the United States, are the only party that has a sense of urgency, these negotiations will not succeed. [...]

On the Israeli–Palestinian front, the Oslo Accords provided for an interim process that was supposed to last five years. It has now been twenty years since Yitzhak Rabin and Yasser Arafat shook hands on the White House south lawn. Since then, thousands of Israelis and Palestinians have died and the interim process is now thoroughly stuck, with further redeployments and road maps turned into road kill along the way.

An interim period that was designed to build trust has in fact exacerbated mistrust: suicide bombings, the Second Intifada, and continuous settlement growth have led many people on both sides to lose faith. This is why Secretary Kerry, with the full backing of President Obama, decided to try this time around for a conflict-ending agreement.

There are other differences too. [...] The Palestinians are just now in the process of building their state and, given the bitter experience of the Second Intifada and the consequences of the unilateral withdrawal from Gaza, Israelis don't trust them to live up to any of their commitments. Even now, after a serious US-led endeavor to build credible Palestinian security services, after seven years of security cooperation that the IDF [Israeli Defense Forces] and the Shin Bet now highly appreciate, and [after] Abu Mazen's efforts to promote non-violence in the face of pressure from extremists, the fundamental mistrust remains.

The geographic context is different too. [...] Israelis and Palestinians live virtually on top of each other. Moreover, the geographic issues are at the heart of what it means to be a Palestinian or an Israeli. The core issues—land, refugees, Jerusalem—have defined both peoples for a very long time. [They are] part of their identity in a way that the Sinai desert was not.

Now as back in 1975, we face a breakdown in talks, with both sides trying to put the blame on the other party. The fact is both the Israelis and [the] Palestinians missed opportunities and took steps that undermined the process. We have spoken publicly about unhelpful Israeli steps that combined to undermine the negotiations. But it is important to be clear: we view steps the Palestinians took during the negotiations as unhelpful too. Signing accession letters to fifteen international treaties at the very moment when we were attempting to secure the release of the fourth tranche of prisoners was particularly counterproductive. And the final step that led to the suspension of the negotiations at the end of April was the announcement of a Fatah–Hamas reconciliation agreement while we were working intensively on an effort to extend the negotiations.

But it is much more important to focus on where we go from here. And it is critical that both sides now refrain from taking any steps that could lead to an escalation and dangerous spiral that could easily get out of control. Thus far, since the negotiations [have] been suspended, they have both shown restraint; and it is essential that this continue.

We have also spoken about the impact of settlement activity. Just during the past nine months of negotiations, tenders for building 4,800 units were announced and planning was advanced for another 8,000 units. It's true that most of the tendered units are slated to be built in areas that even Palestinian maps in the past have indicated would be part of Israel. Yet the planning units were largely outside that area in the West Bank. And from the Palestinian experience, there is no distinction between planning and building. Indeed, according to the Israeli Bureau of Census and Statistics, from 2012 to 2013 construction starts in West Bank settlements more than doubled. That's why Secretary Kerry believes it is essential to delineate the borders and establish the security arrangements in parallel with all the other permanent status issues. In that way, once a border is agreed, each party would be free to build in its own state.

I also worry about a more subtle threat to the character of the Jewish state. Prime Minister Netanyahu himself has made clear [that] the fundamental purpose of these negotiations is to ensure that Israel remains a Jewish and democratic state—not a de facto binational state. The settlement movement, on the other hand, may well drive Israel into an irreversible binational reality. If you care about Israel's future, as I know so many of you do and as I do, you should understand that rampant settlement activity—especially in the midst of negotiations—doesn't just undermine Palestinian trust in the purpose of the negotiations; it can undermine Israel's Jewish future. If this continues, it could mortally wound the idea of Israel as a Jewish state—and that would be a tragedy of historic proportions.

Public opinion was another element that we found very challenging over the past 9 months [...] Consistently over the last decade, polling on both sides reveals majority support for the two-state solution. But, as many of you know, neither side believes the other side wants it and neither seems to understand the concerns of the other. For example, Palestinians don't comprehend the negative impact of their incitement on the attitudes of Israelis. When Palestinians who murdered Israeli women and children are greeted as "heroes" in celebration of their release, who can blame the Israeli public—parents who lost children, and children who lost parents—for feeling despair? On the other side, Palestinians feel that Israelis don't even see their suffering any more, thanks to the success of the security barrier and the security cooperation. One Palestinian negotiator told his Israeli counterparts in one of our sessions: "You just don't see us; we are like ghosts to you."

Israelis don't seem to appreciate the highly negative impact on the Palestinian public of the IDF's demolition of Palestinian homes, or military operations in populated Palestinians towns that are supposed to be the sole security responsibility of the Palestinian Authority, or the perceived double standard applied to settlers involved in "price tag" attacks. Palestinians cannot imagine how offended and suspicious Israelis become when they call Jews only a religion and not a people. Israelis cannot understand why it took a Palestinian leader 65 years to acknowledge the enormity of the Holocaust; Palestinians cannot understand why their leader should have been denigrated rather than applauded for now doing so. And the list goes on and on.

The upshot of these competing narratives, grievances, and insensitivities is that they badly affected the environment for negotiations. While serious efforts were under way behind closed doors, we tried to get the leaders and their spokesmen to engage in synchronized positive messaging to their publics. Instead, Prime Minister Netanyahu was understandably infuriated by the outrageous claims of Saeb Erekat, the Palestinian chief negotiator no less, that the prime minister was plotting the assassination of the Palestinian president. And Abu Mazen was humiliated by false Israeli claims that he had agreed to increased settlement activity in return for the release of prisoners.

So why, then, in the face of all of this, do I believe that direct negotiations can still deliver peace? Because over the last nine months, behind the closed doors of the negotiating rooms, I've witnessed Israelis and Palestinians engaging in serious and intensive negotiations. I've seen Prime Minister Netanyahu straining against his deeply held beliefs to find ways to meet Palestinian requirements. I've seen Abu Mazen ready to put his state's security into American hands to overcome Israeli distrust of Palestinian intentions. I have seen moments where both sides have been unwilling to walk in each other's shoes. But I have also witnessed moments of recognition by both sides of what is necessary. I have seen moments when both sides talked past each other without being able to recognize it. But I have also seen moments of genuine camaraderie and engagement, in the negotiating room, to find a settlement to these vexing challenges.

The reality is that, aside from Camp David and Annapolis, serious permanent status talks have been a rarity since the signing of the Oslo Accords in 1993.

For all of its flaws, this makes the past nine months important. In twenty rounds over the first six months, we managed to define clearly the gaps that separate the parties on all the core issues. And since then we have conducted intensive negotiations with the leaders and their teams, to try to bridge those gaps. Under the leadership of General Allen, we have done unprecedented work to determine how best to meet Israel's security requirements in the context of a two-state solution—which Secretary Kerry has emphasized from day one is absolutely essential to any meaningful resolution to this conflict. As a result, we are all now better informed about what it will take to achieve a permanent status agreement.

One thing that will never change and is as true today as it was during Kissinger's time is that peace is always worth pursuing, no matter how difficult the path. Indeed, until the very last minute it may seem impossible, as it did in Kissinger's day. The cynics and critics will sit on the sidelines and jeer. They will say "I told you so." They are doing it already. They will even claim that the United States is disengaging from the world, even as we have been deeply engaged in this issue that matters so much to so many of our partners around the globe. But we will make no apologies for pursuing the goal of peace. Secretary Kerry certainly won't. And President Obama won't. To quote Secretary Kerry, "the United States has a responsibility to lead, not to find the pessimism and negativity that's so easily prevalent in the world today."

And the benefits are just too important to let go. For Palestinians, a sovereign state of their own; a dignified future; a just solution for the refugees. For Israelis, a more secure Jewish and democratic homeland; an opportunity to tap into the potential for a strategic alliance and deep economic relations with its Arab neighbors. For all of us, for all of the children of Abraham, an opportunity for a more prosperous, peaceful, and secure future. [...]

Let's hope it won't take a five-month pause this time. Let's hope that President Abbas and Prime Minister Netanyahu are able to overcome the hurdles that now lie on that path back to the negotiating table. When they are ready, they will certainly find in Secretary Kerry and President Obama willing partners in the effort to try again—if they are prepared to do so in a serious way. The obvious truth is that neither Israelis nor Palestinians are going away. They must find a way to live together in peace, respecting each other, side by side, in two independent states. There is no other solution. The United States stands ready to assist in this task, to help the leaders take their peoples to where they have never been, but where they still dream of going.

39. "2014 Gaza War: Palestinian View"

*Diana Buttu**

EDITOR'S NOTE *Diana Buttu is a Canadian Palestinian lawyer and a former spokesperson for the Palestine Liberation Organization (PLO). Her perspective on the fifty-day armed clash in 2014 between Israel and Hamas forces in Gaza appeared, shortly after the event, in the* Journal of Palestine Studies, *the leading publication of the Palestinian academic community.*

Israel's crimes—whether the expulsion of Palestinians in 1948, the military occupation and colonization of Palestinian (and other) territory, or periodic massacres—are invariably accompanied by a media discourse designed to explain, justify, and obfuscate the facts. After more than sixty-six years, and despite abundant factual evidence and extensive academic scholarship giving them the lie, tired, old Israeli mantras that demonize Palestinians and deny their existence as a people continue to live on. The massive attack on the Gaza strip in the summer of 2014 was no exception, with Israel now using both the media and its own discourse to legitimate the Dahiya doctrine—a policy deliberately targeting civilians and civilian infrastructure to induce such suffering among the population that it creates deterrence.

The Dahiya doctrine

In the summer of 2006, during Israel's so-called Lebanon War, Israeli forces bombed Dahiya, a suburb south of Beirut, leveling much of it to the ground. At the time, Israel's chief of staff, Gen. Dan Halutz, bragged that the army's targeting of infrastructure would "turn back the clock in Lebanon twenty years"[1] and made the argument that inflicting gross damage on civilian areas would send a deterrent message to any armed group that was hostile to Israel. The purported justification for this massive bombing was the presence of Hiz-

---

* Abridgement of Diana Buttu, "Blaming the Victims," *Journal of Palestine Studies*, 44.1 (2014): 91–96.
[1] Chris McGreal, "Capture of Soldiers Was 'Act of War' Says Israel," *Guardian*, July 13, 2006, http://www.theguardian.com/world2006/jul/13/israelandthepalestinians.lebanon1.

ballah partisans, both combatants and noncombatants, in the area. At the time, human rights organizations condemned the Israeli attacks as "serious violations of international law," describing them as "indiscriminate, disproportionate, and otherwise unjustified";[2] but, as with other Israeli war crimes, the international community remained largely silent.

The policy of massive bombardment remained unnamed until the then head of the Northern Command, Gen. Gadi Eizenkot, articulated what became known as the Dahiya doctrine in a newspaper interview just months prior to Israel's 2008–2009 attack on the Gaza strip. "We will apply disproportionate force on [every village] and cause great damage and destruction there. From our standpoint, these are not civilian villages, they are military bases," Eizenkot told *Yedioth Ahronoth*. "This isn't a recommendation. This is a plan. And it has already been approved."[3]

The Dahiya doctrine is in clear violation of the international legal requirements of proportionality and discrimination. But, in order to obscure the killing of more than 2,100 Palestinians, the bombing of the Gaza strip's sole power plant, 62 hospitals and clinics, 220 schools, tens of thousands of homes, and countless mosques, the entire population of the Gaza strip needed to be transformed into enemies—faceless, nameless, irrational beings whose deaths were celebrated by their own, or who were deliberately killed to harm Israel's image. Israel's media campaign was a precise reflection of its military campaign, depicting Palestinians as irrational individuals who attacked Israel for no reason and who, ultimately, had only themselves to blame for their own deaths.

Eliding the occupation, the siege, and ongoing military attacks

As part of its effort to demonize Palestinians, the Israeli *hasbara* [public relations] machine singled out Hamas, portraying it as an irrational actor which, for no logical reason, was carrying out a military attack on Israel. In so doing, Israel stripped its narrative of any reference to the political context, portraying itself as an ordinary country facing a crazed enemy. Ignored by Israeli officials and, worse still, by mainstream media were any references to Israel's eight-year blockade of the Gaza strip, its persisting military occupation, and its own military actions and cease-fire violations in the lead-up to the massive onslaught. The omissions included a ferocious security sweep through the West Bank, in

---

[2] *Why They Died: Civilian Casualties in Lebanon during the 2006 War*, Human Rights Watch, vol. 19, no. 5(E), September 2007, p. 13, http://www.hrw.org/sites/default/files/reports/lebanon0907.pdf.
[3] "Israel Warns Hizbullah War Would Invite Destruction," *Ynet*, October 3, 2008, http://www.ynetnews.com/articles/0,7340,L-3604893,00.html.

which hundreds of Palestinians were detained, injured, and even killed, as well as multiple air strikes on the Gaza strip that killed more than ten Palestinians before a single rocket was fired from the territory. [...]

[The] Israeli establishment, whose narrative echoes Prime Minister Netanyahu's oft-repeated view that Hamas "is another instance of Islamist extremism, violent extremism that *has no resolvable grievance*" (emphasis added).[4] Not only were Palestinians (and specifically Hamas) now irrational actors, attacking Israel for no good reason, they were further transformed from nationalist, political actors into an unhinged and extreme Islamist threat. At the same press conference where he uttered the words quoted above, Netanyahu added: "Hamas is like ISIS, Hamas is like al-Qaeda, Hamas is like Hizballah, Hamas is like Boko Haram." The Israeli prime minister even tweeted, "RT THIS: Hamas is ISIS. ISIS is Hamas. They're enemies of Peace [*sic*]. They're enemies of all civilized countries."[5]

These comparisons, particularly with ISIS [the Islamic State of Iraq and Syria], were both illogical and incorrect: Hamas has a nationalist agenda, while ISIS has an anti-nationalist agenda; and al-Qaeda has denounced Hamas on numerous occasions. But the comparisons were made anyway, to convince a largely ill-informed western audience that Israel faces the same "global terror" threat as the one being fought by the United States and to elicit support for Israel's brutal actions against Hamas-controlled Gaza. In the face of this irrational, demonic enemy, Israel could then claim it was acting in self-defense and portrayed itself as a victim of barrages of rockets. During another press appearance, Netanyahu noted that "there's only been one other instance where a democracy has been rocketed and pelleted with these projectiles of death, and that's Britain during World War II [...] Israel is undergoing a similar bombardment." [...]

Israeli statements to the western media omitted describing not only the crude quality and accuracy of the projectiles used on the Palestinian side, but also the high-tech Iron Dome system in place to stop them. Interestingly, and well in accordance with past habit, in the English-language media Israel portrayed itself as the underdog, whereas in the Arabic-language media it presented itself as the strong and almighty nation that was impervious to Hamas's weak and "useless" rockets. [...]

---

[4] "Netanyahu: Hamas Is Islamist Extremism Like al Qaeda, ISIS," NBC News, July 22, 2014, http://www.nbcnews.com/storyline/middle-east-unrest/netanyahu-hamas-islamist-extremism-al-qaeda-isis-n162076.

[5] Joshua Mitnick, "Israel Does About-Face over Hamas-ISIS Tweet," *Wall Street Journal*, updated August 22, 2014, http://online.wsj.com/articles/Israel-does-about-face-over-hamas-isis-tweet-1408724928.

Blaming Palestinians for their own deaths

Alongside its portrayal of Hamas as an irrational, demonic actor, Israel needed a means to explain away bombing hospitals, schools, mosques, shelters, medical clinics, and ambulances, as well as entire residential neighborhoods. As with the 2008–2009 assault on Gaza, once again the high Palestinian death toll proved to be the Israelis' Achilles' heel: twenty-one hundred Palestinians killed, 70 percent of whom were classified as noncombatants, including over five hundred children. To counter what former US secretary of state Madeleine Albright deemed an "image" problem, Israeli officials adopted a new approach that consisted in blaming Palestinians–specifically Hamas–for their own deaths. Thus, according to that view, Hamas was responsible because they fired rockets from areas that Israel subsequently bombed, or because Hamas gave specific orders for civilians to remain in areas that were about to be bombed. In other words, Palestinian civilians were unknowingly serving as Hamas's human shields. Despite the fact that countless journalists and others refuted these allegations and despite the fact that it has since been established that Israel has continued its own practice of using Palestinians as human shields, Israel's vocal allegation was repeated ceaselessly.

Palestinian civilians used by Hamas as human shields [were] a talking point in the 2008–2009 Operation Cast Lead, but this time around the Israeli media machine took it one step further: as a means of further dehumanizing Palestinians, Israel cynically began focusing (and repeating) claims that Palestinians enjoyed a "culture of martyrdom" and hence did not care whether civilians were killed, provided that they had the effect of harming Israel's image. In a CNN interview on July 27, Netanyahu asserted that Hamas "want to pile up more and more dead bodies of Palestinian civilians" and on another occasion he echoed the words of the *Washington Post* commentator, Charles Krauthammer, saying, "they [Hamas] use telegenically dead Palestinians for their cause. They want— the more dead, the better."[6] The dehumanization did not stop there, however. Soon *all* Palestinians, not merely Hamas, wanted to see more of their own dead, and no one was innocent. In other words, Palestinians became *knowing* human shields or, worse still, no longer civilians worthy of protection. [...]

These statements, like those uttered by leaders in other conflicts where mass atrocities have been committed, were made precisely to dehumanize Palestinians and to justify Israel's defiance of international law governing occupation and war. As Thomas Friedman explained in regard to Israel's 2006 attack on Lebanon, the strategy is

---

[6] "Netanyahu: Israel Seeks 'Sustainable Quiet' with Gaza," CNN, July 21, 2014, http://www.cnn.com/2014/07/20/world/meast/mideast-crisis-blitzer-netanyahu-interview.

to inflict substantial property damage and collateral casualties on Lebanon at large. It was not pretty, but it was logical. Israel basically said that when dealing with a non-state actor, Hezbollah, nested among civilians, the only long-term source of deterrence was to exact enough pain on the civilians—the families and employers of the militants—to restrain Hezbollah in the future.[7]

Thus it became easy for Israel to justify the killing of noncombatants—they were either members of Hamas or human shields of Hamas—and to explain away the wholesale destruction of Palestinian infrastructure in Gaza by arguing that it was used by Hamas or for the benefit of Hamas.

The dehumanization did not simply come from Israel's *hasbara* machine; journalists and even the Palestinian leadership inadvertently aided the endeavor. In the belief that they had to add "balance" to a lopsided war and lopsided civilian casualties, several reporters covered an injured owl in Israel's zoo and recounted the elephants' distress at the sound of the high-pitched sirens. Palestinian children with body parts scattered among the rubble were apparently too commonplace to be journalistically relevant. [...]

My personal experience with the mainstream media required me to devote significant time and energy to challenging the unquestioned characterizations according to which Palestinians both wanted and deserved to be the victims of Israeli bombs. In the dozens of interviews I gave, virtually every one featured an interviewer asking me questions that cemented rather than challenged Israel's media discourse. Without missing a beat, reporters asked questions about Hamas's charter, Palestinian textbooks, and streets named after "martyrs," as though the charter, the textbooks, and the streets in question were responsible for the dropping of 20,000 tons of bombs on 1.8 million beleaguered individuals and as if every person in Gaza were a combatant. The fallout from the interviews was no less bad, with pro-Israel activists sending me death and rape threats after a media appearance in which I said that oppressed peoples around the world, including Jews in the Warsaw Ghetto, had dug tunnels for their survival.

One can only hope that there will be no more massacres in the Gaza strip, that the news media will learn to question Israel's outlandish claims, and that the Mahmud Abbas-led Fatah and Palestinian Authority will realize that Gaza and its residents are not the enemy. Absent such changes, I fear that Palestinians will, once again, have to defend their very right to exist and Israel will further entrench the Dahiya doctrine.

---

[7] Thomas L. Friedman, "Israel's Goals in Gaza?" *New York Times*, January 13, 2009, http://www.nytimes.com/2009/01/14/opinion/14friedman.html?ref=opinion&_r=0.

40. "2014 Gaza War: Israeli View"

Benjamin Netanyahu*

EDITOR'S NOTE *Israeli Prime Minister Benjamin Netanyahu defended his government's conduct of the 2014 clash with Hamas in his annual address to the United Nations General Assembly shortly after the fighting ended. Netanyahu's defense of Israel's conduct of the war demonstrates the complexity of applying traditional laws of war to modern, non-traditional forms of warfare. At the same time, he appeals for international support by putting the Gaza conflict in a broader framework of worldwide clashes with religious extremism and terror.*

Ladies and Gentlemen,

The fight against militant Islam is indivisible. When militant Islam succeeds anywhere, it's emboldened everywhere. When it suffers a blow in one place, it's set back in every place.

That's why Israel's fight against Hamas is not just our fight. It's your fight. Israel is fighting a fanaticism today that your countries may be forced to fight tomorrow.

For 50 days this past summer, Hamas fired thousands of rockets at Israel, many of them supplied by Iran. I want you to think about what your countries would do if thousands of rockets were fired at your cities. Imagine millions of your citizens having seconds at most to scramble to bomb shelters, day after day. You wouldn't let terrorists fire rockets at your cities with impunity. Nor would you let terrorists dig dozens of terror tunnels under your borders to infiltrate your towns in order to murder and kidnap your citizens.

Israel justly defended itself against both rocket attacks and terror tunnels. Yet Israel also faced another challenge. We faced a propaganda war. Because, in an attempt to win the world's sympathy, Hamas cynically used Palestinian civilians as human shields. It used schools, not just schools—UN schools, private homes, mosques, even hospitals to store and fire rockets at Israel.

* Excerpt from Benjamin Netanyahu's Address to United Nations General Assembly, September 29, 2014, available at http://mfa.gov.il/MFA/PressRoom/2014/Pages/PM-Netanyahu-addresses-the-UN-General-Assembly-29-Sep-2014.aspx.

As Israel surgically struck at the rocket launchers and at the tunnels, Palestinian civilians were tragically but unintentionally killed. There are heartrending images that resulted, and these fueled libelous charges that Israel was deliberately targeting civilians.

We were not. We deeply regret every single civilian casualty. And the truth is this: Israel was doing everything to minimize Palestinian civilian casualties. Hamas was doing everything to maximize Israeli civilian casualties and Palestinian civilian casualties. Israel dropped flyers, made phone calls, sent text messages, broadcast warnings in Arabic on Palestinian television, always to enable Palestinian civilians to evacuate targeted areas.

No other country and no other army in history have gone to greater lengths to avoid casualties among the civilian population of their enemies. This concern for Palestinian life was all the more remarkable, given that Israeli civilians were being bombarded by rockets day after day, night after night. As their families were being rocketed by Hamas, Israel's citizen army—the brave soldiers of the IDF [Israel Defense Forces], our young boys and girls—they upheld the highest moral values of any army in the world. Israel's soldiers deserve not condemnation, but admiration. Admiration from decent people everywhere.

Now here's what Hamas did: Hamas embedded its missile batteries in residential areas and told Palestinians to ignore Israel's warnings to leave. And just in case people didn't get the message, they executed Palestinian civilians in Gaza who dared to protest.

No less reprehensible, Hamas deliberately placed its rockets where Palestinian children live and play. Let me show you a photograph. It was taken by a France 24 crew during the recent conflict. It shows two Hamas rocket launchers, which were used to attack us. You see three children playing next to them. Hamas deliberately put its rockets in hundreds of residential areas like this. Hundreds of them.

Ladies and gentlemen, this is a war crime. And I say to President Abbas, *these are the war crimes committed by your Hamas partners* in the national unity government which you head and you are responsible for. And these are the real war crimes you should have investigated, or spoken out against from this podium last week.

Ladies and gentlemen, as Israeli children huddled in bomb shelters and Israel's Iron Dome missile defense system knocked Hamas rockets out of the sky, the profound moral difference between Israel and Hamas couldn't have been clearer:

Israel was using its missiles to protect its children. Hamas was using its children to protect its missiles.

By investigating Israel rather than Hamas for war crimes, the UN Human Rights Council has betrayed its noble mission to protect the innocent. In fact, what it's doing is to turn the laws of war upside down. Israel, which took unprecedented steps to minimize civilian casualties, Israel is condemned. Hamas, which both targeted and hid behind civilians—that a double war crime—Hamas is given a pass.

The Human Rights Council is thus sending a clear message to terrorists everywhere: Use civilians as human shields. Use them again and again and again. You know why? Because, sadly, it works.

By granting international legitimacy to the use of human shields, the UN's Human Rights Council has thus become a Terrorist Rights Council, and it will have repercussions. It probably already has, about the use of civilians as human shields.

It's not just our interest. It's not just our values that are under attack. It's your interests and your values.

Ladies and gentlemen, we live in a world steeped in tyranny and terror, where gays are hanged from cranes in Tehran, political prisoners are executed in Gaza, young girls are abducted en masse in Nigeria, and hundreds of thousands are butchered in Syria, Libya, and Iraq. Yet nearly half, nearly half of the UN Human Rights Council's resolutions focusing on a single country have been directed against Israel, the one true democracy in the Middle East—Israel—where issues are openly debated in a boisterous parliament, where human rights are protected by independent courts, and where women, gays, and minorities live in a genuinely free society.

The Human Rights—that's an oxymoron, the UN Human Rights Council, but I'll use it just the same—the Council's biased treatment of Israel is only one manifestation of the return of the world's oldest prejudices. We hear mobs today in Europe call for the gassing of Jews. We hear some national leaders compare Israel to the Nazis. This is not a function of Israel's policies. It's a function of diseased minds. And that disease has a name. It's called antisemitism.

It is now spreading in polite society, where it masquerades as legitimate criticism of Israel. For centuries the Jewish people have been demonized with blood libels and charges of deicide. Today the Jewish state is demonized with the apartheid libel and charges of genocide.

Genocide? In what moral universe does genocide include warning the enemy's civilian population to get out of harm's way? Or ensuring that they receive tons, tons of humanitarian aid each day, even as thousands of rockets are being fired at us? Or setting up a field hospital to aid for their wounded?

Well, I suppose it's the same moral universe where a man who wrote a dissertation of lies about the Holocaust, and who insists on a Palestine free of Jews, *Judenrein*, can stand at this podium and shamelessly accuse Israel of genocide and ethnic cleansing.

In the past, outrageous lies against the Jews were the precursors to the wholesale slaughter of our people. But no more. Today we, the Jewish people, have the power to defend ourselves. We will defend ourselves against our enemies on the battlefield. We will expose their lies against us in the court of public opinion. Israel will continue to stand proud and unbowed.

41. "Saving the Two-State Solution"

*John Kerry**

EDITOR'S NOTE As the days of the Obama presidency drew to a close in late 2016, Secretary of State John Kerry delivered a major address that summarized the conclusions he reached in his efforts to negotiate an Israeli–Palestinian peace. While critical of both sides, Kerry ended his analysis with a statement of the core principles that, in his view, could and should form the basis for a durable resolution of the conflict.

Today I want to share candid thoughts about an issue which for decades has animated the foreign policy dialogue here and around the world: the Israeli–Palestinian conflict.

Throughout his Administration, President Obama has been deeply committed to Israel and its security, and that commitment has guided his pursuit of peace in the Middle East. This is an issue which, all of you know, I have worked on intensively during my time as secretary of state for one simple reason: because the two-state solution is the only way to achieve a just and lasting peace between Israelis and Palestinians. It is the only way to ensure Israel's future as a Jewish and democratic state, living in peace and security with its neighbors. It is the only way to ensure a future of freedom and dignity for the Palestinian people. And it is an important way of advancing United States interests in the region.

Now, I'd like to explain why that future is now in jeopardy, and provide some context for why we could not, in good conscience, stand in the way of a resolution at the United Nations that makes clear that both sides must act now to preserve the possibility of peace. [...]

Despite our best efforts over the years, the two-state solution is now in serious jeopardy.

The truth is that trends on the ground—violence, terrorism, incitement, settlement expansion, and the seemingly endless occupation—they are combining to destroy hopes for peace on both sides and increasingly cementing an irreversible one-state reality that most people do not actually want.

---

* Excerpts from John Kerry, "Remarks on Middle East Peace," December 28, 2016, available at https://2009-2017.state.gov/secretary/remarks/2016/12/266119.htm.

Today there [is] a number—there [is] a similar number—of Jews and Palestinians living between the Jordan River and the Mediterranean Sea. They have a choice. They can choose to live together in one state, or they can separate into two states. But here is a fundamental reality: if the choice is one state, Israel can either be Jewish or democratic—it cannot be both—and it won't ever really be at peace. Moreover, the Palestinians will never fully realize their vast potential in a homeland of their own with a one-state solution.

Now, most on both sides understand this basic choice, and that is why it is important that polls of Israelis and Palestinians show that there is still strong support for the two-state solution—in theory. They just don't believe that it can happen. [...]

It is in that spirit that we offer the following principles—not to prejudge or impose an outcome, but to provide a possible basis for serious negotiations when the parties are ready. Now, individual countries may have more detailed policies on these issues—as we do, by the way—but I believe there is a broad consensus that a final status agreement that could meet the needs of both sides would do the following.

PRINCIPLE NUMBER ONE: provide for secure and recognized international borders between Israel and a viable and contiguous Palestine, negotiated based on [sic] the 1967 lines, with mutually agreed equivalent swaps.

Resolution 242, which has been enshrined in international law for 50 years, provides for the withdrawal of Israel from territory it occupied in 1967 in return for peace with its neighbors and secure and recognized borders. It has long been accepted by both sides, and it remains the basis for an agreement today.

As secretary, one of the first issues that I worked out with the Arab League was their agreement that the reference in the Arab Peace Initiative to the 1967 lines would from now on include the concept of land swaps, which the Palestinians have acknowledged. And this is necessary to reflect practical realities on the ground and mutually agreed equivalent swaps that will ensure that the agreement is fair to both sides.

There is also broad recognition of Israel's need to ensure that the borders are secure and defensible and that the territory of Palestine is viable and contiguous. Virtually everyone that I have spoken to has been clear on this principle as well: no changes by Israel to the 1967 lines will be recognized by the international community unless agreed to by both sides.

PRINCIPLE TWO: fulfill the vision of the UN General Assembly Resolution 181 of two states for two peoples, one Jewish and one Arab, with mutual recognition and full equal rights for all their respective citizens.

This has been the fundamental—the foundational—principle of the two-state solution from the beginning: creating a state for the Jewish people and a state for the Palestinian people, where each can achieve their national aspirations. And Resolution 181 is incorporated into the foundational documents of both Israelis and Palestinians. Recognition of Israel as a Jewish state has been the US position for years, and, [on the basis of] my conversations in these last months, I am absolutely convinced that many others are now prepared to accept it as well—provided the need for a Palestinian state is also addressed. [...]

PRINCIPLE NUMBER THREE: provide for a just, agreed, fair, and realistic solution to the Palestinian refugee issue, with international assistance that includes compensation, options and assistance in finding permanent homes, acknowledgment of suffering, and other measures necessary for a comprehensive resolution, consistent with two states for two peoples.

The plight of many Palestinian refugees is heartbreaking, and all agree that their needs have to be addressed. As part of a comprehensive resolution, they must be provided with compensation, their suffering must be acknowledged, and there will be a need to have options and assistance in finding permanent homes. The international community can provide significant support and assistance. I know we are prepared to do that, including in raising money to help ensure the compensation and other needs of the refugees are met, and many have expressed a willingness to contribute to that effort, particularly if it brings peace. But there is a general recognition that the solution must be consistent with two states for two peoples, and cannot affect the fundamental character of Israel.

PRINCIPLE FOUR: provide an agreed resolution for Jerusalem as the internationally recognized capital of the two states, and protect and assure freedom of access to the holy sites consistent with the established status quo.

Now, Jerusalem is the most sensitive issue for both sides, and the solution will have to meet the needs not only of the parties, but of all three monotheistic faiths. That is why the holy sites that are sacred to billions of people around the world must be protected and remain accessible and the established status quo maintained. Most acknowledge that Jerusalem should not be divided again, like it was in 1967, and we believe that. At the same time, there is broad recognition that there will be no peace agreement without reconciling the basic aspirations of both sides to have capitals there.

PRINCIPLE FIVE: satisfy Israel's security needs and bring a full end, ultimately, to the occupation, while ensuring that Israel can defend itself effectively and that Palestine can provide security for its people in a sovereign and non-militarized state.

Security is the fundamental issue for Israel, together with a couple of others I've mentioned—but security is critical. Everyone understands that no Israeli government can ever accept an agreement that does not satisfy its security needs or that risks creating an enduring security threat, like Gaza transferred to the West Bank. And Israel must be able to defend itself effectively, including against terrorism and other regional threats. In fact, there is a real willingness by Egypt, Jordan, and others to work together with Israel on meeting key security challenges. And I believe that those collective efforts, including close coordination on border security, intelligence-sharing, joint operations, can all play a critical role in securing the peace.

At the same time, fully ending the occupation is the fundamental issue for the Palestinians. They need to know that the military occupation itself will really end after an agreed transitional process. They need to know they can live in freedom and dignity in a sovereign state, while providing security for their population even without a military of their own. This is widely accepted as well. And it is important to understand there are many different ways without occupation for Israel and Palestine and Jordan and Egypt and the United States and others to cooperate in providing that security. [...]

PRINCIPLE SIX: end the conflict and all outstanding claims, enabling normalized relations and enhanced regional security for all, as envisaged by the Arab Peace Initiative. It is essential for both sides that the final status agreement resolves all the outstanding issues and finally brings closure to this conflict, so that everyone can move ahead to a new era of peaceful coexistence and cooperation. For Israel, this must also bring broader peace with all of its Arab neighbors. That is the fundamental promise of the Arab Peace Initiative, which key Arab leaders have affirmed in these most recent days. [...]

So, ladies and gentlemen, that's why it is vital that we all work to keep open the possibility of peace, that we not lose hope in the two-state solution, no matter how difficult it may seem—because there really is no viable alternative. [...]

Chapter 9

The Impasse that Remains

The three sets of serious full-scale negotiations for an Israeli–Palestinian peace—2000–2001, 2007–2008, and 2013–2014—followed the two-state model of partition between the Jewish state and the Arab state as a point of departure. Alternatives to this model will be discussed in Chapter 10. But the experience of these talks furnishes some indication of what a two-state solution might look like and what gaps would still need to be bridged.

In all the talks to date, the 1949 armistice lines—also referred to as the pre-1967 borders—were the main point of reference. Palestinians argued that, since the 1949 lines left only 22 percent of Mandatory Palestine in Arab hands, they could not accept less than that. Any redrawing of these lines in order to put new Jewish settlements within the state of Israel would have to include "land swaps" of equal size from Israel to the Palestinian state. This is complicated by the presence of Jewish settlement blocs deep into Palestinian territory and by particular issues in Jerusalem, namely the difficulty of disentangling Jewish and Arab neighborhoods and opposed visions for the Old City and the Temple Mount/Noble Sanctuary. An overview of territorial issues is provided by Michael Herzog (Reading 42).

Arguments over the legality and practicality of Jewish settlements in the West Bank are intense, both between the parties and in the domestic arenas of each. Walid Salem presents a mainstream Palestinian case in Reading 43, while Hillel Halkin represents the pro-settlement position within Israel in Reading 44.

The other two major "final status" issues are security questions and the Palestinian refugees from 1948–1949; officially registered refugees and their descendants number over 5 million today. Negotiations over security issues have centered on the proposed demilitarization of the Palestinian state and on the deployment of Israeli troops on the Jordan River, its eastern border. The refugee issue, festering for close to 70 years, is often described as the most difficult remaining hurdle to overcome, since it pits the Palestinian right of return against the demographic threat of transforming Israel into a non-Jewish state. Again, there is a spectrum of opinion on both sides. Rashid Khalidi presents the argument for an "attainable" solution for Palestinians in Reading 45, while Efraim Karsh (Reading 46) represents an Israeli position that attacks the very basis of Palestinian claims.

Further online resources:

Beilin-Abu Mazen Draft Agreement (unofficial negotiations: the "Stockholm" talks), 1995: http://www.jewishvirtuallibrary.org/the-beilin-abu-mazen-document.

Geneva Accord (Beilin–Abd Rabbo unofficial negotiations), 2003: http://www.mideastweb.org/geneva1.htm.

UN Security Council Resolution 2334 Concerning Jerusalem, Settlements, and the Territories, 2016: http://www.un.org/webcast/pdfs/SRES2334–2016.pdf.

United Nations Relief and Works Agency (UNRWA), Annual Operational Report 2016: https://www.unrwa.org/resources/reports/annual-operational-report-2016.

Peace Index (Israeli monthly public opinion survey): https://en.idi.org.il/centers/1159/1520 (see subdirectory Full Questionnaires and Commentaries).

Palestinian Survey Research Polls, Palestinian Center for Survey and Policy Research: pcpsr.org.

42. "Territorial Issues"

*Michael Herzog**

EDITOR'S NOTE Michael Herzog is a retired Israeli brigadier general who served as head of the Israel Defense Forces Strategic Planning Division and was involved in Israeli negotiations with the Palestinians from 1993 to 2010. Herzog's analysis of the positions of both parties on territorial issues, written in 2011, remains valid for the period since then.

This paper analyzes the parties' differing positions on territory and borders, particularly as expressed in bilateral negotiations over the years. The author is careful not to suggest that these differences are unbridgeable or that a territorial deal is impossible; the gaps, however, will be very difficult to bridge, requiring strong resolve and leadership on both sides.

Major bones of contention

It is no coincidence that, unlike Abbas, President Obama referred to 1967 "lines," not to "borders." As discussed below, the boundaries in question were never recognized as borders. In essence, the 1967 lines essentially match the armistice lines reached with Jordan at the end of Israel's War of Independence and demarcated from 1949 to 1951. The Armistice Agreement stipulated that the territorial delineation was to be made "without prejudice to future territorial settlements or boundary lines." But history is tricky, unfolding in a way that has made these politically elusive lines the epicenter of Palestinian claims regarding their future state's border. Current Israeli and Palestinian contentions about territory and borders epitomize these conflicting perspectives on historical rights, legal claims, security, Jerusalem, and other sensitive issues.

Baseline for negotiation. The first order of debate, while largely symbolic, is nevertheless crucial. Namely, should the baseline for territorial negotiations be premised on the full area encompassed by the 1967 lines, as Palestinians demand—a formula that would obligate Israel to provide territorial compensation for any deviations? Or should it be predicated on adjustments to these

---

* Abridgement of Michael Herzog, "Minding the Gaps: Territorial Issues in Israeli–Palestinian Peacemaking," *Policy Focus* 116, December 2011, Washington Institute for Near East Policy.

lines based on Israel's security needs and related to post-1967 demographic developments—namely, the formation of Israeli settlement blocs? On the surface, this debate may appear purely semantical. In any "mutually agreed" territorial exchanges, the parties would have to reconcile their conflicting claims through bilateral negotiations in which each wields veto power. Once they do so, debate over the baseline formula becomes redundant. Nevertheless, one should not underestimate the huge symbolic and domestic significance that the baseline territorial formula carries for both parties. [...]

Legal argument. From a legal perspective, the official Israeli position has always been that the territory in question is disputed rather than occupied, since no internationally recognized sovereign state existed there when Israeli forces seized it in self-defense in June 1967. It should be noted that, while most of the international community recognizes the validity of Israeli security concerns, it rejects this legal argument and considers the territories occupied. As for borders, Israel claims that the armistice lines set by the arbitrary deployment of rival armies at the end of the 1948–1949 war have no legal significance. That is, because they were never formally established as borders, they cannot be legally considered as such. Moreover, UN Security Council Resolution 242 of November 1967—a document adopted only after much deliberation and that became the accepted guiding reference for all subsequent Arab–Israeli peacemaking—recognized Israeli security concerns by calling for "withdrawal from territories" (not "all" or "the" territories) to "secure, recognized boundaries free from threats or acts of force."

For their part, the Palestinians claim they are the legal heirs—from Jordan, which occupied the West Bank between 1949 and 1967—to the territories occupied by Israel in June 1967. And although they never liked Resolution 242 and did not formally accept it until the late 1980s, they claim that its withdrawal clause is legally subject to the principle of "inadmissibility of the acquisition of territory by war," as stated in the document's (nonbinding) preamble. They also cite as precedents Israel's full withdrawal from Egyptian and Jordanian territories occupied in 1967 in return for bilateral peace agreements with those countries, as well as its apparent willingness to do the same with Syria and Lebanon.

Yet every Israeli government has differentiated between these cases and the Palestinian situation, not only because of the historic affiliation to the West Bank and its lack of sovereign status when it was captured, but also because of Israel's strategic vulnerability from that territory. They have therefore interpreted Resolution 242's reference to "withdrawal from territories" as applying to the West Bank.

East Jerusalem. The fate of East Jerusalem is much entangled in the historical and legal debates. Palestinians (and most of the world) regard it as part of the territories occupied in 1967 and therefore as an integral part of the baseline for negotiations. Yet Israel has always maintained its entitlement to Jewish holy sites and historic quarters in East Jerusalem, and thus basically rejects the idea that it owes territorial compensation to the Palestinians for retention of these sites. In practice, all Israeli governments have made a distinction between East Jerusalem and the West Bank. Israel annexed a wider east Jerusalem—some 67 km²—after the 1967 war, a measure that most of the world does not recognize. In addition, all Israeli governments have refrained from designating the Jews in that part of the city as "settlers" or, with the exception of Prime Minister Ehud Olmert's peace proposals in 2008, from counting East Jerusalem in its West Bank territorial calculations.

Israel's essential security needs

Although no consensus exists among Israelis regarding the terms of reference for territorial negotiations, there is wide agreement that the country cannot return to the June 4, 1967 lines due to critical security considerations. In addition to being the product of a temporary armistice agreement, these lines deny Israel vital strategic depth in the face of potential military threats and are thus unsatisfactory as a permanent, defensible border. Specifically, such lines would leave Israel with a dangerously narrow waist along its coastal plain—about nine miles at the thinnest point and overlooked by the West Bank's commanding hills. This strip includes Israel's largest cities, some 70 percent of its population, its only international airport, and vital infrastructure, and industries that represent some 80 percent of its gross domestic product. Therefore Israel could be seriously threatened and perhaps paralyzed if a military conflict were to erupt along these lines. For Israelis, this represents an existential vulnerability, one that could tempt enemies to aim for the country's narrow "jugular" in order to inflict a fatal blow. Even Israel's strong military would have difficulty defending against such a threat without paying a very heavy, perhaps intolerable price. [...]

Palestinians have acknowledged certain Israeli security needs, but only reluctantly and after years of opposition. And they continue to reject the concessions on territory or sovereignty required by Israel to satisfy these needs. In past bilateral security negotiations, for example, Palestinians were amenable to the concept of demilitarization, but only if the other two Israeli pillars were not applied; they would accept only minor adjustments to the 1967 lines and rejected any Israeli military deployment on their soil, with the possible exception of a few early-warning sites. Indeed, Palestinians tend to adhere strictly to the formula of "land for peace" established in Resolution 242, maintaining that a peace agreement would provide security. Yet Israelis have always believed in "land for security and peace" because, however desirable peace may be, it cannot by itself guarantee security and must be fortified by solid security arrangements.

Settlement blocs

Notwithstanding fierce public debate in Israel regarding settlements, there is relatively wide consensus that the major blocs adjacent to the 1967 lines would significantly contribute to Israel's security requirements and should therefore be annexed in any two-state agreement. Indeed, during his 1992 election campaign for premiership the late Prime Minister Yitzhak Rabin referred to these blocs as "security settlements," distinguishing them from "political" or "ideological" settlements. And Prime Minister Binyamin Netanyahu recently spoke in the Knesset of the "widespread agreement that the settlement blocs must remain within the State of Israel," implying, for the first time in his tenure, that the remainder of the West Bank would be available for a territorial settlement.[1] Moreover, in Israel's view, President Bush's statement that "existing major Israeli population centers" would guide expectations for a future territorial settlement signified US recognition of that position. Obama's May 22 statement created similar Israeli expectations.

Israelis regard three major blocs and about five smaller settlement areas, stretching from the 1967 lines into the West Bank, as important for beefing up the previously discussed "narrow waist," fortifying the security of Jerusalem, and allowing military deployment in times of emergency. [...]

In territorial terms, the above-mentioned security barrier—parts of which are still under construction—demarcates blocs comprising somewhere between 8 percent and 8.5 percent of the West Bank territory. In comparison, Prime Minister Olmert's September 2008 proposal to Abbas called for Israeli annexation of approximately 6.5 percent of the territory. Thus there is some room for negotiation over the size of the blocs. Yet it is difficult to imagine any Israeli government drawing a map of the three major blocs that is significantly smaller than Olmert's.

In principle, the Palestinians view the settlement blocs as no different from the rest of the West Bank—Israeli possession of these lands is regarded as equally illegal. Given developments on the ground and the realization that no Israeli government is likely to conclude a deal without the blocs, however, the Palestinians have resigned themselves to a territorial agreement allocating

---

[1] Benjamin Netanyahu, Address at the Opening of the Knesset Summer Session, May 16, 2011, mfa.gov.il/MFA/.../2011/.../PM_Netanyahu_Knesset_summer_session_16-May-2011.

some blocs to Israel, to be offset through land swaps. Nevertheless, they have consistently demanded that the exchanges be minimal.

Specifically, the handful of maps that Palestinians have presented in bilateral negotiations through the years would allow Israel to annex, at most, somewhere between 2 percent and 3 percent of the West Bank. [...]

Land swaps

Israel first implemented the principle of territorial exchanges in its October 1994 peace treaty with Jordan. In the Palestinian context, the idea first surfaced in the unofficial October 1995 draft agreement between Israeli left-wing leader Yossi Beilin and Mahmoud Abbas, both of them senior officials at the time. This "Beilin–Abu Mazen Agreement" included a map with similar land swaps involving around 250 km^2 (or approximately 4.5 percent) of the West Bank. Neither side's leadership adopted this agreement, however.

The main premise behind land swaps has been to reconcile the Palestinian insistence on a state encompassing the entirety of the West Bank with Israel's insistence on accommodating security needs and allowing the majority of settlers to remain in their homes.

Israeli officials did not readily endorse the concept at first because they did not accept the basic Palestinian premise of entitlement to 100 percent of the West Bank. In their view, such a premise implicitly denied any Israeli claim to land seized in 1967. Even as late as 2000, Prime Minister Ehud Barak rejected the concept of swaps at the outset of the Camp David talks, accepting it only toward the summit's end, upon President Clinton's insistence. Barak then proposed a land swap based on a 9:1 ratio in Israel's favor: that is, for 9 percent of the West Bank to be annexed to Israel, the Palestinian state would receive Israeli territory equivalent to 1 percent of the West Bank.

Subsequent Israeli offers have come considerably closer to Palestinian demands, yet no Israeli government to date has accepted the Palestinian stipulation that land swaps be fully equal in size and "quality." From the Israeli perspective, equal swaps would deviate from the letter and spirit of UN Security Council Resolution 242, which calls for withdrawal "from territories" (not "the" or "all" territories) to "secure, recognized boundaries." Nevertheless, Ehud Olmert did approach a 1:1 ratio in his September 2008 proposal to Abbas, offering to exchange 5.8 percent of Israeli territory for 6.5 percent of the West Bank. [...]

Conclusion

In his 1979 book *White House Years*, Henry Kissinger recalled that, when he first encountered UN Resolution 242 and its conflicting interpretations, he did not appreciate the extent to which it obscured rather than illuminated the parties' fundamentally clashing positions. The same can be said of the current US baseline for territorial negotiations—it masks a deep divide. At the same time, however, its final interpretation is in the eye of the beholder. To borrow another Kissinger phrase, time will tell whether "the 1967 lines with mutually agreed swaps" proves to be constructive rather than destructive ambiguity.

As far as substance is concerned, the parties have come to agree on several important points throughout years of negotiations. Since 2000, Israel has essentially agreed to regard the 1967 lines as a reference point—even if not a "baseline"—for territorial deliberations, without prejudice to its call for significant adjustments to these lines. The Palestinians have come to accept Israeli retention of some settlement blocs. And both sides have agreed to bridge gaps through territorial exchange. But the basic narratives guiding their territorial viewpoints are still deeply at odds, as are the practical implications of these views. [...]

Indeed, territory and borders are make-or-break issues. A breakthrough in territorial negotiations could open the door to other core issues and catalyze progress, yet reaching such a breakthrough may require trade-offs on those very issues. And a deadlock in territorial talks would certainly block negotiations writ large.

43. "West Bank Settlements: A Palestinian View"

*Walid Salem**

EDITOR'S NOTE *Walid Salem is director of the Center for Democracy and Community Development and teaches at Al-Quds University; both institutions are located in Arab East Jerusalem. The article excerpted here was published in the* Palestine–Israel Journal, *a jointly edited Palestinian–Israeli periodical that promotes rapprochement between the two sides.*

After 50 years of the Israeli occupation of the Palestinian territories of the West Bank, East Jerusalem and the Gaza strip, the situation on the ground cannot be described as being any less than catastrophic for the Palestinians. This is a situation that can reasonably be described as a continuation of the 1948 Nakba. [...]

In brief, an Israeli one-state solution in all the historical land of Palestine is in the making, while the Palestinians are facing a growing ignorance of their right to self-determination in an independent state on the 1967 borders. The PLO [Palestine Liberation Organization] has accepted this compromise in 1988, a two-state solution to live side by side, in peace and security with Israel. However, Israel is no longer interested in the two-state solution. [...]

A further problem is that these dispossessions of the Palestinians are followed by the establishment of military camps and, in most cases, Israeli settlements. In the literature of political science and international relations, this combined process of displacement and replacement is called "settler colonialism." In the Israeli–Palestinian case, this process is also planned and supported by the Israeli governments, while being protected by the Israeli occupying army. What complicated such a situation even more is the denial of such a process at both the official and the public levels of the State of Israel.

At the official level, the term "occupation" was not, and still is not, accepted. Neither are the descriptions of the Israeli settlers as colonials. Instead of using the term "occupation," the Israeli government decided in 1967 to call the Pal-

---

* Abridgement of Walid Salem, "Apartheid, Settler Colonialism and the Palestinian State 50 Years On," *Palestine–Israel Journal* 22.2/3 (2017): 112–118.

estinian territories occupied in 1967 as "areas administered by Israel." The "legal" justification used for such a name is that these areas have never been territories of a Palestinian state, but were instead occupied by Jordan and Egypt in the period between 1948 and 1967. Upon this justification, which cannot be accepted by the international law of war, the areas were dealt with neither as being occupied, nor as having an identity. [...]

After the 1993 Oslo Declaration of Principles (DOP), the Israeli government changed the term it used from "areas administered by Israel" to "areas under dispute." This means that they consider Israel to have equal claims to the territories as those held by the Palestinians. This change in terminology represented the Israeli interpretation of the Oslo Declaration of Principles—and also of Oslo II in 1995—as if these agreements gave Israel the right to present ideas for territorial change through the annexation of some parts of West Bank to Israel, with or without a swap with the Palestinians. [...]

As such, the Israeli government's position regarding the 1967 occupied Palestinian territories (OPT) has already passed through three stages since 1967.

In the first stage, from 1967 to 1977, the occupied territories were temporarily considered as "areas administered by Israel" until a "territorial compromise" could be achieved regarding their future with Jordan. During this period the Israeli Mapai party-led governments started the Israeli settlement project in East Jerusalem (since 1967); Hebron, Gush Etzion and the Jordan Valley (since 1968); Gaza (from 1970); and around Nablus (from 1974–1975). The aim was to create Israeli facts on the ground that would influence the division of the "territories" between Israel and Jordan.

The second stage started in 1977, when the first right-wing government was composed, led by Prime Minister Menachem Begin; his government presented a different position: that the West Bank and East Jerusalem were part of the "Greater Land of Israel" and not just administered by it. [...] In the West Bank, this government decided to begin construction all over the OPT, including [in] areas that are densely populated by the Palestinians, [and] also in areas that did not fall within the parameters of the Alon Plan.

The 1977 Israeli government—and most of the governments that followed until 1987—proposed what was called "a functional distribution of tasks," in which Israel would maintain overall control of the OPT, while the management of the civil issues of the Palestinians would be handled by Jordan. The Palestinian Intifada of 1987 ended this approach. As a result, Jordan decided to disengage from the West Bank on July 31, 1988. That same year, the PLO accepted the two-state solution, and the Palestinian National Council declared the Palestinian State on Nov. 15. [...]

With these developments, Israel was obliged to start considering talking directly to the Palestinians, either as part of a Jordanian–Palestinian delegation

(Madrid Conference of 1991 formula) or directly (Oslo secret negotiations of 1992–93). Until these negotiations, the Israeli position regarding the Palestinian territories occupied in 1967 ranged between the Israeli Zionist left position, which considered them to be areas under dispute to be divided between Israel and Jordan, and the Zionist right, which wanted to create a gradual de facto annexation of them to Israel.

Some observers consider the Israeli official recognition of the PLO in 1993 as a turning point that represents a third-stage development in the Israeli position regarding the OPT.

However, the negotiation strategy of the Israeli Zionist left-wing governments continued to be the same regarding territorial compromise, albeit this time with the PLO instead of Jordan. On one hand, the Israeli Zionist right-wing governments kept their positions about Gaza being a Palestinian entity (the withdrawal by Ariel Sharon's right-wing government of the Israeli Forces and dismantling of the Israeli settlements there in 2005). On the other hand, they kept the ongoing process of de facto annexation of the West Bank to Israel.

Indeed, during the long negotiation period that proceeded, some leaders, such as Ehud Olmert, left the right-wing positions to adopt those of the left wing during his 2007–2008 negotiations with Palestinian Authority President Mahmoud Abbas (Abu Mazen). The fact still remains, however, that neither the Zionist left-wing nor the Zionist right-wing governments were ready to move beyond the recognition of the PLO; nor [were they ready to move beyond] the vague recognition of the "political rights of the Palestinians," as included in the preamble of the Oslo Agreement.

A positive shift might have occurred toward the Palestinians had the Israeli governments accepted the equal right of the Palestinian people [to] self-determination and the 1967 borders as the starting point for negotiations. Except for Olmert, none of the other Israeli negotiators accepted this second point.

Instead of having a positive third-stage development in the Israeli politics toward the Palestinians, another negative third stage took place with the Netanyahu governments, beginning in 2009, through to today. This third stage can be described as a stage of leaving aside the priority of peace with the Palestinians for the sake of a separate agenda. This agenda can be seen to range from those who want to keep the OPT in the hands of Israel for security reasons and those who want to keep it in the hands of Israel, based on historical and ideological claims.

The commonality between these two positions is Israel's enduring control of the Palestinian territories. Furthermore, the differences between the security-based and ideology-based agendas are narrowing day by day. For instance, Netanyahu, who initially adopted the security-based position, is now a strong advocate of the idea that Jews are not foreigners in the territories but they have indigenous historical rights to it. This position is similar to the position of his coalition partner from the Jewish Home party, Naftali Bennett. [...]

The preceding overview shows that, after 50 years of occupation, the Palestinians are facing three combined processes of domination and subordination. The first is of a belligerent occupation that kills, arrests, shells, and invades. The second is of an apartheid system of discrimination in favor of the settlers [and] at the expense of the Palestinians. This is in addition to all the restrictions on the Palestinians' freedom of movement and the "ghettoization" of their lives. The third is a growing settler colonial project that is territorialized at the expense of the Palestinian people, increasing deterritorialization.

Between these three components, the balance falls in favor of the settlers, whom the Israeli army protects and the government legislates for. Moreover, one of the aims of the restrictions that are imposed on the Palestinians is the preservation of the settlers' safety and security.

Within this framework, a typical settler colonial project can be identified, Israel representing the mother state and the colonial settlements as its daughter. [...] Two communities—one indigenous and one colonial-settler—are competing over the same territory. The indigenous community comprises 3 million living in West Bank and East Jerusalem, and the colonial-settler community consists of around 627,000 as of the end of 2016, representing more than one-fifth of the Palestinian population. The colonial settlers are more powerful than the Palestinians, due to Israeli army and government support and the fact that they have their own militias and security patrols. [...]

That being said, one does not require special powers of prediction to see that it is only a matter of time before the big confrontation will start between the settlers and the Palestinians. The rehearsal for such confrontation is already represented by the daily attacks of the settlers against the Palestinians in the West Bank, which are usually carried under the Israeli army protection of the settlers. The UN Office of Coordination of Humanitarian Assistance (OCHA) and other organizations are doing a good job documenting these attacks.

What will be the results of such a confrontation? Will it be the Algerian model, in which the settlers are defeated and obliged to leave? Or will it be the Israeli 1948 model of expelling the Palestinians from their homeland, this time partially to Jordan, or to "the Palestinian state" of Gaza? It is difficult to predict, but at the same time one thing is quite clear, and that is that the Israeli–Palestinian context is becoming chronic, and it is already too late [for it] to be solved just by negotiations. In order to solve it and to alter the path of events, there is a need to deploy other means of empowerment to the Palestinians toward achieving Palestinian statehood on the 1967 borders. [...]

44. "West Bank Settlements: An Israeli View"

Hillel Halkin*

EDITOR'S NOTE *Hillel Halkin (1939–) is an Israeli writer and translator and a regular contributor in the Jewish press to public debates over Arab–Israeli issues. This article summarizes the major arguments—advanced in debates within Israel—that defend the legality and practicality of the settlements, either under current conditions or in the framework of a final settlement. It was published during the Second Intifada, following the Camp David and Taba talks, when the issue became especially prominent.*

That the settlements *are* illegal, the conventional wisdom says, is obvious. But it is far from obvious—even if, like many a commonplace, it has been remarked upon so often that it has attained the status of a universally acknowledged truth.

The case for the illegality of the Jewish settlements in the West Bank rests largely on a single source: Article 49(6) in the fourth Geneva Convention of 1949. This article states that an occupying military power "shall not deport or transfer part of its own civilian population into the territory it occupies." Yet, as a number of international jurists have pointed out, not only has Israel "deported" or "transferred" no one to the settlements, whose inhabitants are there of their own free will; it is by no means clear that Israel was ever, legally, in the position of being an occupying power.

This is because, in 1967, Israel had as good a claim as anyone to the West Bank, which in effect belonged to no government. The Jordanian annexation of the area, while acquiesced in by the same Palestinian leadership that had rejected the 1947 UN partition resolution, was unrecognized by most of the world, and Jordan itself had refused to make peace with Israel or to consider their joint border more than a temporary cease-fire line. A reasonable case could thus he made that, as the sole sovereign state to have emerged from British-mandated Palestine, Israel had not only the right but the duty to act as the West Bank's civil administrator, pending determination of the area's status.

* Abridgement of Hillel Halkin, "Why the Settlements Should Stay," *Commentary* 113.6 (2002): 21–27.

The conventional wisdom is also wrong in asserting—a frequently made claim—that continued settlement activity on the part of Israel is a violation of the 1993 Oslo accords. The plain fact of the matter is that nowhere in that agreement was there any reference to the settlements, apart from a single paragraph stating that—along with Jerusalem, refugees, and "other issues of common interest"—their fate was to be settled in final-status negotiations. This was hardly an oversight. The Palestinians wanted a settlement freeze and fought for one at Oslo; if they did not get it, this is only because in the end they accepted the Israeli refusal to agree to one. In repeatedly demanding one anyway over the ensuing years, it is they, not the Israelis, who have gone back on the document they signed.

And yet, whatever the legality of the settlements, the debate over it is incapable of adjudication, since international law, especially with regard to disputes between countries, remains in large measure a fiction lacking courts to interpret it impartially. Nor, it must be admitted, did questions of legality especially exercise Israel when it established the settlements in the first place. It is therefore worth recalling why, when, and where it did establish them. [...]

*   *   *

At the time of the momentous defeat of Labor in the elections of 1977 by Menachem Begin's Likud Party, there were barely ten thousand Jews living in the West Bank. Soon after these elections, Egypt's President Anwar Sadat came to Jerusalem on his peace overture. Had there been at this time the slightest willingness on the part of Jordanians or Palestinians to join the Egyptian–Israeli peace talks, these few settlers would have been an obstacle to nothing. (Their number was indeed only slightly greater than the number of Israelis in the Sinai that would be evacuated by the Begin government in 1981.) But the Jordanians stood aloof from the proposal for West Bank autonomy made by Begin to Sadat; the Palestine Liberation Organization assailed it; and more and more settlers, encouraged by Likud policy, began moving into the West Bank.

Were they an obstacle to peace with the Palestinians? The historical record shows that, at least up to the Oslo Agreement of 1993, they were the opposite: not an obstacle but an impetus to peace.

This can be continued, first of all, empirically. From 1977 on, as West Bank settlement grew by leaps and bounds, passing the 100,000 mark in 1990, Arab and Palestinian attitudes toward Israel became steadily more flexible. The year 1979 marked the signing of the Israeli–Egyptian peace treaty. In 1985 the PLO, which had hitherto called for the destruction of Israel and the establishment of a "secular, democratic" (i.e., non-Jewish) state in all of Palestine, suggested forming a joint delegation with Jordan to negotiate the return of the West Bank and Gaza strip alone; in 1988, it announced its acceptance of Resolution 242 and its willingness to recognize Israel; in 1992, it went to Oslo with the Rabin government.

Of course, there were other reasons for this, too. They included the peace between Israel and Egypt; the defeat of the PLO in Lebanon in 1982; the PLO's financial and political debacle in the Gulf War; the waning of the First Intifada, which broke out in 1987 and had begun to subside by the early 1990s; and the growing popularity, in the occupied territories, of Islamic groups challenging PLO supremacy. But, of all these factors, it may be that nothing convinced the PLO that time was against it so much as the growth of the settlements. [...]

*   *   *

There is something unacceptable about telling Jews that, although they may live anywhere they wish, in New York and London, in Moscow and Buenos Aires, there is one part of the world they may not live in—namely, Judea and Samaria, those regions of the land of Israel most intimately connected with the Bible, with the Second Temple period, and with Jewish historical memory, and most longed-for by the Jewish people over the ages. [...]

Be that as it may, Jordan, Israel's main military adversary in 1948, saw to it that the West Bank it annexed had not a Jew in it. It was thus inevitable, following the 1967 victory, that there should have been widespread sentiment in Israel for opening Judea and Samaria to Jewish settlement. [...]

To sum up: the great majority of the Israeli settlements in the West Bank are not there because of Israel's original post-1967 policy and would not have been built at all had the Arabs been prepared to negotiate a peace treaty in the aftermath of the 1967 war. They are not necessarily illegal, and they have probably, over the years, furthered peace more than they have hindered it. Relocating their inhabitants would cost enormous sums. Moreover, they express a deep Jewish imperative that cannot be challenged without calling into question the Jewish historical attachment to Palestine that validates the state of Israel. And, although many of them are built on land taken from the Palestinians against their will, their physical dimension is not intolerable from a Palestinian point of view.

What is intolerable is both the discriminatory asymmetry behind the settlements—that is, the assumption that, whereas Jews have a right to live in all of the historical land of Israel, Palestinian refugees do not have a right to live in all of historic Palestine—and the practical consequences of Palestinian hostility to them. If not for such hostility, no Israeli army would be needed to defend them, and if no Israeli army were needed to defend them, they could exist in a Palestinian state.

* * *

Over a year-and-a-half into the cruelest fighting that the Jewish–Arab conflict in Palestine has known, and in which the settlers have been a main target of Palestinian violence, the notion that they could live in a Palestinian state may seem laughably quixotic.

This may be what it is. But if it is, so is the notion of a genuine Israeli–Palestinian peace (as opposed to either a permanently ongoing conflict or a tense state of non-belligerency with closed borders and no economic or other relationships). Is it possible, after all, to imagine a Palestine and Israel with friendly relations and open borders, tourism and trade, Palestinian workers coming every day to earn their livelihood in Israel, Israeli and Palestinian products being exchanged back and forth, and over a million Palestinian citizens of Israel regularly hosting and visiting friends and families in a Palestinian West Bank in which no Jews are allowed to live?

It has been suggested that, although Jews might indeed live in a Palestinian state some day, the currently inflamed emotions on both sides and the extreme anti-settler sentiments of the Palestinians make speaking of this at the present moment an instance of placing the cart before the horse. First, the two peoples must be separated, with Israelis on one side of a recognized border and Palestinians on the other. Then, as the old passions subside and the wounds of enmity are healed, they can begin to mix again.

Good fences, in other words, will make good neighbors. And yet the idea that the best way of enabling Jews to live in Judea and Samaria is to begin by removing 225,000 of them from there is not only curiously Rube Goldbergish, it will not even lead to the desired separation, since there will still be over a million Palestinians, most of them identified with the Palestinian state, living in Israel. If the purpose of evacuating Jewish settlers to the Israeli side of the border is an amicable divorce, this should logically be accompanied by moving Israel's Arabs to the Palestinian side. Those who attack the asymmetrical injustice of granting Jewish settlers a historical right denied to Palestinian refugees overlook the similar injustice of relocating the settlers alone.

Perfect symmetry between Israelis and Palestinians is no longer attainable. It was proposed in 1947 by the United Nations, which voted to divide Mandate Palestine in half, and rejected then by the Arabs. But, without some symmetry, an Israeli–Palestinian reconciliation is unattainable, too. One element in achieving it might therefore be to let the 225,000 settlers remain in a Palestinian state while allowing a similar number of Palestinian refugees to return to Israel and fairly compensating all those who cannot. (This might also be a far better use of $20 billion.) To prevent the returnees from adversely affecting Israel's demographic balance, it would then be necessary to create another symmetry: just as the Jewish settlers and their offspring in a Palestinian state could live there as permanent residents while remaining Israeli citizens and voting in Israeli elections, so returning Palestinian refugees resettled in Israel would remain citizens of Palestine. [...]

*   *   *

One thing should be clear. A West Bank without Jews means a Palestine and an Israel without a normal relationship. If *this* is what it comes to, Israel will have to ask many or most of the settlers to pack their bags and will then withdraw to a defensive line of its own choosing, which will not be that of 1967 and will not meet Palestinian demands. After that, the fences will go up. They will not make good neighbors.

45. "The Refugee Issue: A Palestinian View"

*Rashid Khalidi**

EDITOR'S NOTE *Rashid Khalidi (1948–) is a prominent Palestinian American scholar, serving as the Edward Said Professor of Arab Studies at Columbia University and editor of the* Journal of Palestine Studies. *Most of his academic work has focused on the Arab–Israeli conflict. In this article, written at the peak of the Oslo peace process, when final status issues were being put on the table, Khalidi identifies the elements of a solution to the refugee problem deemed essential in Palestinian opinion.*

Many difficult and complex issues must be resolved before there can be a just, comprehensive, and final settlement of the question of Palestine and of the Arab–Israel conflict. The most basic among them is undoubtedly the problem of more than 700,000 Palestinians who became refugees during the fighting in 1947–1949—more than half of the Arab population of Palestine at the time. It will probably also be the most intractable issue to resolve, more so even than the formidably difficult question of Jerusalem. [...]

Many proposals have been made over the past fifty years for solving the problem of Palestinian refugees. Some involved full or partial return of the refugees to their homes and compensation for their losses; others were based on resettlement of the refugees in other Arab countries; still others involved combinations of these and other proposed elements of a solution. One element missing from most of these proposals, however, is a recognition that the key to resolution of this issue lies in Israel finally accepting, after fifty years, the major share of the responsibility for the creation of the Palestinian refugee problem. [...]

Over the past fifteen years a wealth of serious historical scholarship has greatly clarified the events of 1948 and the period leading up to them, particularly the creation of the refugee problem. It builds upon and confirms the conclusions of a few pioneering researchers who many years earlier began to establish how and why as many as three quarters of a million Palestinians left their homes. [...] Without exception, all of them, whether Israeli or not, have

---

* Abridgement of Rashid Khalidi, "Attainable Justice: Elements of a Solution to the Palestinian Refugee Issue," *International Journal* 53.2 (1998): 233–251.

determined that the flight of the vast majority was the result not of orders from their leaders (many of whom urged them to stay as soon as the scope of the exodus was revealed), but rather of forcible eviction by Israeli forces, fear and terror, and disorganization and lack of leadership among the Palestinians. [...]

Thus, when this issue is finally addressed, the outcome will depend upon an acceptance by Israel of a share of the responsibility for these events. That means some form of official recognition that the deliberate actions of Israel's founding fathers turned more than half of the Palestinian people into refugees between 1947 and 1949. This will not be easy, given the fact that the 1948 war, in which some 6,000 Israelis (or about 1 per cent of the country's Jewish population) died, is heroically inscribed in the Israeli national narrative as the War of Independence. It is a seminal event in Israeli history, which many older Israelis remember, and all have learned about in a sanitized nationalist version. [...]

As has already been mentioned, General Assembly resolution 194 III of 11 December 1948 sets forth a clear basis for the settlement of the refugee question. In summary, it would permit those refugees wishing to return to their homes and live at peace with their neighbours to do so, and those who did not wish to return would be compensated for their property. All refugees would be compensated for lost or damaged property. This is a simple formula, and one which was reiterated annually by the General Assembly for several decades after 1948.

The implementation of this fifty-year-old resolution will not be simple, however, in part because Israel has for many decades absolutely rejected this formula. [...] There are, therefore, virtually no empty homes to which Palestinian refugees could return, and, in that sense, the specific language of Resolution 194 ('refugees wishing to return to their homes') simply cannot be implemented. In any case, refugees and their descendants today number several times the 700,000-plus people who were driven from their homes in 1948, and it is therefore impossible even to contemplate their 'return' in strictly literal terms. Moreover, in practical, political terms, the return of three million Palestinians to the areas of what is now Israel, where they (or their forbears) lived, would overturn the demographic transformation which made possible the establishment of Israel as a state with a substantial Jewish majority in 1948. It is highly unlikely—if not completely inconceivable—that this would be acceptable to any Israeli government under any circumstances. While in moral terms this may not be a powerful argument (it hinges on a highly subjective calculation of the value of a Jewish state in Palestine, as against the cost which the existence of such a state imposes on the Palestinians), in practical political terms it certainly is. For where is the political will to come which will persuade a majority of citizens of a powerful country like Israel to accept something to which they are deeply opposed? It is highly doubtful that the will to do so exists today or is likely to exist in the future in the international community.

Even if such a return were acceptable in whole or in part, would Palestinian returnees accept the only possible interpretation of the qualifying language of the same paragraph of the resolution, which calls upon them to 'live at peace with their neighbours'? Would returnees be willing to live as minority Arab citizens of the Jewish State of Israel and in accordance with its laws? Would not the availability and levels of compensation offered affect directly the numbers of refugees and their descendants choosing not to return? It is clear from these and other possible questions that acceptance, even of the principles embodied in Resolution 194, will leave many practical and political difficulties in the way of implementation. [...]

In conclusion, what is the best that those who were made refugees in 1948, and their descendants, can look forward to today, fifty years after their dispossession? The following are five elements of a solution which, while not fully or absolutely just, embody an attempt to weigh justice for those who have been victims of injustice for half a century against the formidable practical and political difficulties just reviewed and the potential for doing injustice to others.

1   First, Israel must accept primary responsibility for the creation of the Palestinian refugee problem in 1948. This might occur in the context of the conclusions of a truth and justice commission or a truth and reconciliation commission, which if convened forthwith might still be able to collect testimony from a few of the refugees themselves and some of those who contributed to making them refugees. [...]

2   Second, that all Palestinian refugees and their descendants have a right to return to their homes must be accepted in principle, although the modalities of such return are necessarily subject to negotiation. In practice many will be unable to exercise this right, whether as a result of Israel's refusal to allow all of them to do so, the disappearance of their homes and villages, or the sheer number of people involved. However, in principle as many refugees as possible should be allowed to return to what is now Israel. [...] If the principle of return of a number of Palestinian refugees is accepted, some might be able to come back under a process of family reunification, if their home villages still exist inside Israel (about 100 Arab villages do), if they have family living there, and if they are willing to become law-abiding citizens of the state of Israel. It should be possible under these circumstances to secure the regulated entry of several tens of thousands of people per year over several years. [...]

3   A third element of a lasting resolution is reparations for all those who choose not to return or are not allowed to do so, and compensation for all those who lost property in 1948. Property losses alone, according to one detailed study, range from US$92 billion to US$147 billion at 1984 prices,

the year in which the study was done. Using an entirely different approach to calculate reparations, $30,000 per person for an arbitrarily chosen figure of 3 million eligible refugees and their descendants yields a total of US$90 billion. Lest this seem like a great deal of money, we should recall that it is less than the amount transferred by the United States to Israel in the form of grants, loans, and loan guarantees over the past seven years. [...]

4 A fourth element is the right to live in the Palestinian state-to-be and to carry its passport. This right was already putatively extended to all Palestinians by the 1988 Palestinian declaration of independence, which stated that the state of Palestine was the state of all the Palestinians. The right to live in this state—the collective right of return to Palestine, as it were—should not be subject to negotiation with Israel or any other power: it would be a sovereign right of any independent Palestinian state, whenever such a state is established. However, this 'right' will in practice necessarily be restricted by the country's absorptive capacity, which is limited, but which could be increased by determined efforts by the Palestinian public and private sectors and by international donors.

5 Finally, there are two groups which require special attention: Palestinian refugees in Jordan and those in Lebanon (and, to some measure, in Syria as well). Each group has special requirements.

Palestinians in Jordan, beyond those who choose to return to the areas under control of the Palestinian Authority today or [of] the Palestinian state tomorrow, and beyond any reparations they may receive, require a final and equitable resolution of their legal and national status as both Palestinians and Jordanians. [...] As far as Lebanon is concerned, a resolution of the status of Palestinians is extremely urgent, both because of the precarious economic, social, and political situation of the Palestinian population and because it has a direct impact on internal Lebanese equilibrium. [...] The status of those who remain in Lebanon is in urgent need of revision, which will at the very least involve issuing them with Palestinian passports and nationality and granting them permanent resident status and the right to work. This will involve long and difficult negotiations. [...].

For Palestinians, what is attainable includes recognition of the wrong done to them, return to their homeland or part of it, and reparations and restitution for the suffering they have endured and the property they have lost. For Israelis, it includes the peace of mind which comes from confronting an uncomfortable reality which all know still lurks after fifty years in the rubble, the old olive trees, and the cactus plants of 418 ruined Arab villages, and the comprehensive peace with their neighbours which can be achieved only if the refugee issue is resolved to the satisfaction of both sides.

46. "The Refugee Issue: An Israeli View"

Efraim Karsh[*]

EDITOR'S NOTE *Efraim Karsh (1953–) is an Israeli scholar and historian, who since 2013 has been director of the Begin–Sadat Center for Strategic Studies at Bar-Ilan University. At the time he wrote the article below, he was head of Mediterranean Studies at King's College, University of London. The article reflects the heightened debate over "final status" issues following the collapse of the Camp David summit and the onset of the Second Intifada. The quotations are unreferenced in the original.*

Whatever the strengths and weaknesses of the Palestinians' legal case, their foremost argument for a "right of return" has always rested on a claim of unprovoked victimhood. In the Palestinians' account, they were and remain the hapless targets of a Zionist grand design to dispossess them from their land, a historical wrong for which they are entitled to redress. In the words of Mahmoud Abbas (aka Abu Mazen), Yasir Arafat's second-in-command and a chief architect of the 1993 Oslo Accords: "When we talk about the right of return, we talk about the return of refugees to Israel, because Israel was the one who deported them." [...]

The claim of premeditated dispossession is itself not only baseless, but the inverse of the truth. Far from being the hapless victims of a predatory Zionist assault, the Palestinians were themselves the aggressors in the 1948–1949 war, and it was they who attempted, albeit unsuccessfully, to "cleanse" a neighboring ethnic community. Had the Palestinians and the Arab world accepted the United Nations resolution of November 29, 1947, calling for the establishment of two states in Palestine, and not sought to subvert it by force of arms, there would have been no refugee problem in the first place.

It is no coincidence that neither Arab propagandists nor Israeli "new historians" have ever produced any evidence of a Zionist master plan to expel the Palestinians during the 1948 war. For such a plan never existed. In accepting the UN partition resolution, the Jewish leadership in Palestine acquiesced in

---

[*] Abridgement of Efraim Karsh, "The Palestinians and the 'Right of Return,'" *Commentary* 111.5 (2001): 25–30.

the principle of a two-state solution, and all subsequent deliberations were based on the assumption that Palestine's Arabs would remain as equal citizens in the Jewish state that would arise with the termination of the British Mandate. [...]

Why did such vast numbers of Palestinians take to the road? There were the obvious reasons commonly associated with war: fear, disorientation, economic privation. But to these must be added the local Palestinians' disillusionment with their own leadership, the role taken by that leadership *in forcing* widespread evacuations, and, perhaps above all, a lack of communal cohesion or of a willingness, especially at the highest levels, to subordinate personal interest to the general good. [...]

In 1948 both the Jewish and the Arab communities in Palestine were thrown into a whirlpool of hardship, dislocation, and all-out war—conditions that no society can survive without the absolute commitment of its most vital elites. Yet while the Jewish community (or Yishuv), a cohesive national movement, managed to weather the storm by extreme effort, the atomized Palestinian community, lacking an equivalent sense of corporate identity, fragmented into small pieces. The moment its leading members chose to place their own safety ahead of all other considerations, the exodus became a foregone conclusion. [...]

The desertion of the elites had a stampede effect on the middle classes and the peasantry. But huge numbers of Palestinians were also *driven* out of their homes by their own leaders and/or by Arab military forces, whether out of military considerations or, more actively, to prevent them [sic] from becoming citizens of the Jewish state. [...]

None of this is to deny that Israeli forces did on occasion expel Palestinians. But this occurred not within the framework of a premeditated plan but in the heat of battle, and was dictated predominantly by ad hoc military considerations (notably the need to deny strategic sites to the enemy if there were no available Jewish forces to hold them). Even the largest of these expulsions— during the battle over the town of Lydda in July 1948—emanated from a string of unexpected developments on the ground and was in no way foreseen in military plans for the capture of the town. Finally, whatever the extent of the Israeli expulsions, they accounted for only a small fraction of the total exodus. [...]

But the appeal to history—to what did or did not happen in 1948–1949—is only one arrow in the Palestinian quiver. Another is the appeal to international law, and in particular to the United Nations resolution that, as Hanan Ashrawi sternly reminds us, "has been affirmed annually by the UN member states."

The resolution in question, number 194, was passed by the UN General Assembly on December 11, 1948, in the midst of the Arab–Israeli War. The first thing to be noted about it is that, like all General Assembly resolutions (and unlike Security Council resolutions), it is an expression of sentiment and carries no binding force whatsoever. The second thing to be noted is that its primary purpose was not to address the refugee problem but rather to create a "conciliation commission" aimed at facilitating a comprehensive peace between Israel and its Arab neighbors. Only one of its fifteen paragraphs alludes to refugees in general—not "Arab refugees"—in language that could as readily apply to the hundreds of thousands of Jews who were then being driven from the Arab states in revenge for the situation in Palestine. [...]

Given the Palestinians' far higher birth rate, the implementation of a "right of return," even by the most conservative estimates, would be tantamount to Israel's destruction.

Not that this stark scenario should surprise anyone. As early as October 1949, the Egyptian politician Muhammad Salah al-Din, soon to become his country's foreign minister, wrote in the influential Egyptian daily *al-Misri* that, "in demanding the restoration of the refugees to Palestine, the Arabs intend that they shall return as the masters of the homeland and not as slaves. More specifically, they intend to annihilate the state of Israel."

In subsequent years, this frank understanding of what the "right of return" was all about would be reiterated by most Arab leaders, from Gamal Abdel Nasser, to Hafez al-Assad, to Yasir Arafat. [...]

Indeed, if one were to insist on the applicability of international law, here is one instance where it speaks unequivocally. In 1948–1949, the Palestinians and Arab states launched a war of aggression against the Jewish community and the newly proclaimed state of Israel, in the process driving out from their territories hundreds of thousands of innocent Jews and seizing their worldly goods. Ever since, these same aggressors have been suing to be made whole for the consequences of their own failed aggression. Imagine a defeated Nazi Germany demanding reparations from Britain and the United States, or Iraq demanding compensation for losses it suffered during the 1991 Gulf War. Both legally and morally, the idea is grotesque.

But in the end none of this matters. What is at issue in the dispute over the "right of return" is not practicality, not demography, not legality, and certainly not history. What is at issue is not even the refugees themselves, shamefully left in homelessness and destitution, and nourished on hatred and false dreams, while all over the world tens of millions of individuals in similar or much worse straits have been resettled and have rebuilt their lives. What is at issue is quite simply the existence of Israel—or, to put it in the more honest terms of Muhammed Salah al-Din, the still vibrant hope among many Arabs and Palestinians of annihilating that existence, if not by one means then by another.

Tactically, "we may win or lose," declared Faysal al-Husseini, the "moderate" minister for Jerusalem affairs in Yasir Arafat's Palestinian Authority, in late

March of this year [2001]; "but our eyes will continue to aspire to the strategic goal, namely, to Palestine from the [Jordan] river to the [Mediterranean] sea"— that is, to a Palestine in place of an Israel. "Whatever we get now," he continued, "cannot make us forget this supreme truth." Until this "supreme truth" is buried once and for all, no amount of Israeli good will, partial compensation, or symbolic acceptance of responsibility can hope to create anything but an appetite for more.

Chapter 10

The Perfect Conflict

One reason why the Israeli–Palestinian conflict is so difficult to resolve—why it is a "perfect" conflict in the sense of a "perfect" storm—is that there is still no consensus on the basic framework for resolution. Should it remain one state, as defined by the former British Mandate of Palestine, or should it be divided somehow into a Jewish and an Arab state? If it is to be one state, will it be one dominated by one side, or will powers be shared somehow, be it according to a "binational" model or as in a decentralized federal system? If it is to be two states, is it still possible to disentangle the complicated webs that have been woven since 1967?

Supporters of a one-state solution, on both sides, are usually either very moderate parties, promoting cooperation with the like-minded on the other side, or from the most militant factions, naturally supporting the model of predominance. Ghada Karmi presents a Palestinian case for one state that includes both the cooperative option—binationalism—and the idea of a "secular democratic" state without communal features, a state that would inevitably become an Arab-majority state (Reading 47). Naftali Bennett, leader of a right-wing Israeli party, presents an equivalent Israeli version of a one-state solution based on Jewish predominance, with autonomy for most Arabs (Reading 48).

The two-state solution remains the course favored by the mainstream on both sides, though each side questions the sincerity of the other's commitment to it. David Unger, an American observer, presents the case for the inevitability of two states (Reading 49).

Another difficulty in getting to a final resolution is the fact that both sides see themselves, with some reason, as victims. It is impossible to talk about solutions without talking about justice, which involves deeper issues of historical wrongs. The late Yaacov Bar-Siman-Tov (1946–2013), an Israeli academic, addresses this issue and its implications for the debate over the framework for a durable peace (Reading 50).

Further online resources:

Israel Basic Law: Requirement of Referendum for Territorial Changes, 2014: https://www.haaretz.com/.premium-israel-passes-referendum-law-1.5332904, https://www.jpost.com/National-News/Knesset-passes-first-Basic-Law-in-22-years-Referendum-on-land-concessions-345169, https://www.timesofisrael.com/knesset-passes-referendum-bill-for-land-swaps.

Report of the Middle East Quartet: Need for a Two-State Solution, 2016: http://www.un.org/News/dh/infocus/middle_east/Report-of-the-Middle-East-Quartet.pdf.

Remarks by President Donald Trump at the Israel Museum, 2017: https://www.whitehouse.gov/briefings-statements/remarks-president-trump-israel-museum.

Israel Prime Minister Benjamin Netanyahu's Speech to the UN General Assembly, 2017:https://www.timesofisrael.com/full-text-of-prime-minister-benjamin-netanyahus-un-speech.

Palestinian National Authority President Mahmoud Abbas's Speech to the UN General Assembly, 2017: https://www.nad.ps/en/media-room/speeches/he-president-mahmoud-abbas-statement-un-general-assembly-72nd-session-2017.

Text of Fatah–Hamas Reconciliation Agreement, 2017: https://www.timesofisrael.com/translation-of-leaked-hamas-fatah-agreement, https://www.jpost.com/Arab–Israeli-Conflict/Leaked-the-six-clauses-of-the-Fatah-Hamas-rapprochement-deal-507401.

Noam Sheizaf, "One- Or Two-State Solution? The Answer is Both (Or Neither)," September 2, 2014: https://972mag.com/one-or-two-state-solution-the-answer-is-both-or-neither/96263.

Dov Waxman and Dahlia Scheindlin, "Hope Fades for a Two-State Solution: Is There Another Path to Middle East Peace?" May 7, 2016: https://www.theguardian.com/commentisfree/2016/may/07/israel-palestine-two-state-solution-another-path-to-peace.

47. "The One-State Solution: A Palestinian Version"

*Ghada Karmi**

EDITOR'S NOTE Ghada Karmi (1939–) is a Palestinian-born physician, academic, and research fellow at the Institute of Arab and Islamic Studies, University of Exeter, UK. The following article, published in 2011 in the leading Palestinian academic journal, was written in the aftermath of ten years of failed negotiations for a final settlement. It reflects an upsurge of interest in alternatives to the two-state solution, particularly among Palestinian activists.

Changes on the ground in the occupied Palestinian territories since 1993 threaten to make [a two-state] solution unlikely, if not impossible. The Israeli colonization of the West Bank and East Jerusalem has so advanced as to make questionable the logistical possibility of creating a viable Palestinian state on the territory that remains. Yet there is an extraordinary reluctance on the part of most politicians concerned with the conflict to look the facts in the face and draw the obvious conclusion: a two-state solution that complies even with minimalist Palestinian requirements cannot emerge from the existing situation. Rather as [in] Hans Christian Andersen's tale of the emperor's new clothes, none of them is willing to see the naked truth.

As the feasibility of the two-state solution recedes, the debate has turned to the one-state alternative, often as an undesirable outcome of last resort, failing implementation of the preferred option. [...] In fact the idea of sharing the land between Arabs and Jews is older than that of the two-state solution, which is a recent notion in Palestinian history that emerged in response to a series of defeats for the Palestinian national movement. Though never totally absent from the debate about a solution, the unitary state has increasingly become part of mainstream political discourse. [...]

The two-state solution has become something of a mantra for all those involved in the peace process. But the proposition that it is the ultimate solution, to the point of obviating the need to consider others, is neither true nor consonant with elementary notions of justice. Not only does it divide the Palestinians' historic homeland into grossly unequal parts, made possible by coer-

---

* Abridgement of Ghada Karmi, "The One-State Solution: An Alternative Vision for Israeli-Palestinian Peace," *Journal of Palestine Studies* 40.2 (2011): 62–76.

cion and force of arms, it also forecloses any meaningful return for the refugees driven out. The idea that it could reasonably settle a conflict whose very basis is dispossession and injustice without addressing those issues is, to say the least, unrealistic.

The two-state solution is in fact a recent position for Palestinians, who always rejected the idea of partition as a device used by Britain and later [by] the UN and Western states for accommodating Zionist ambitions in the country. [...]

Support for the two-state solution among Palestinians did not arise initially from a belief that it was in itself ideal, or even desirable. Rather, the appeal came from the desire for the occupation to end—even at the expense of dividing the historic homeland into two states—and because they thought it [was] the only way to save the last remnants of Palestine, where they could recoup Palestinian national identity and social integrity. Many diaspora Palestinians saw the state as the first step on the journey home, envisioning, within the context of two neighboring states at peace, the possibility of an exchange that could have provided a sort of return for the refugees.

The apparent attainability of the two-state solution in the immediate aftermath of Oslo added to its appeal. [...] Yet it has been clear for some time that implementation of a two-state solution has become logistically impossible on terms that could satisfy even the most minimal Palestinian aspirations, let alone rights. Israeli colonization and segmentation of the West Bank, unimpeded since 1967, have reduced what was supposed to form the Palestinian state to nonviability. The conclusion reached by numerous studies analyzing this problem is that a two-state outcome has been superseded. [...]

The one-state proposal represents a fundamentally different approach to solving the conflict. The two-state solution has as its sole object the termination of Israel's 1967 occupation and the establishment of a Palestinian state on the occupied land. It deals exclusively with the consequences of the 1967 war, as if the conflict with Israel began then and the territory that became Israel in 1948 had not been occupied Palestinian land whose owners had been expelled. The two-state proposal therefore leaves untouched the very nature of the Israeli state.

The one-state solution, by contrast, goes to the heart of the matter: the existence of Israel as a Zionist state. If the imposition of Zionism on the Arabs was the cause of the Palestinians' dispossession, the denial of their rights, and the constant state of conflict between Israel and its neighbors, it makes no sense for a peace agreement to preserve this status quo. For Palestinians, the key date in the conflict is 1948, and the occupation of the 1967 territories is a symptom of the disease, not its cause. The problem is that the two-state solution does not merely confine itself to dealing with the symptoms; it actively helps to maintain the cause.

The roots of the Israeli–Palestinian conflict lie in an ongoing belligerent and expansionist Zionist project. Zionism has not adapted to its environment in more than sixty years, nor [has it] accepted limits on its aspirations. On the contrary, the more Israel has been able to take from the Palestinians with impunity, the more it has wanted to take, [and this has resulted] in a self-perpetuating cycle of aggression and expansionism.

The one-state solution means the creation of a single entity of Israel–Palestine in which the two peoples would live together without borders or partitions, thereby avoiding a division of resources that could [be] neither workable nor fair. Only a one-state solution can address all the basic issues that perpetuate the conflict—land, resources, settlements, Jerusalem, and refugees—in an equitable framework. In the last analysis, the one-state solution is actually just a way of restoring a land deformed by half a century of division and colonization to an approximation of the whole country it once was, a rejection of disunity in favor of unity.

There is a perception that the one-state option is monolithically unitary, all or nothing. In fact, there are several models for sharing Palestine: principally the binational model, where the two groups share the country but remain ethnically separate; and the secular, democratic, "one person–one vote" model based on individual citizenship and equal rights irrespective of race, religion, or gender. The binational model preserves the structure of two religious/ethnic communities, while the secular democratic model emphasizes the individual rather than the community, in the style of Western liberal democracies. [...]

Under the simplest form of binational state, each community would be autonomous in terms of language, education, and cultural life, with an administrative council to run its communal affairs. Matters of common concern, such as national policy, defense, and the economy, would be handled by joint institutions and a joint parliament with equal representation. A binational state could be configured as cantonal, federal, or [...] as "dual states" superimposed on one another. Instead of two states side by side, Israelis and Palestinians would live in parallel states but [would] have the right, as citizens of each, to settle anywhere between the Mediterranean Sea and the Jordan River. Other models include a federation of separate Jewish and Arab administrative units linked to a central government, as in the United States, and two sovereign states in political and economic union, in a kind of rejuvenated UN Partition Plan. [...]

Support for the secular unitary state idea comes mainly from diaspora Palestinians, anti-Zionist Israelis, and left-wing intellectuals opposed on principle to ethnic or religious states. Many of these, however, have devoted their energies to promoting the principle, leaving for a later stage the design of what a unitary state would look like. [...]

As Israel's unwillingness to give up Palestinian land or comply with international law has become increasingly evident over the last decade, interest in the unitary state idea as a way out of the impasse has grown. [...] It would seem that the barriers to thinking the unthinkable have been breached. But it is important to remember that, with a few modest exceptions, no major institution or mass movement has adopted any variant of the one-state solution to date. [...] Certainly, there are objective reasons for reluctance over the one-state option. Both sides identify themselves as national communities with a right to self-determination, and the Palestinians especially would not willingly abandon their struggle for independence in order to struggle anew for equality in a joint state where Israel would inevitably have the upper hand; given the greater development of Israelis, Palestinian fears of being kept in a permanent underclass should not be dismissed. As for the Israelis, though they fear Palestinians in their midst, they have become accustomed to unfettered exploitation of Palestinian land and resources and would fight to keep their free hand. More generally, the level of distrust, grievance, and ill will between the parties is such that the very idea of sharing the land would be anathema to both.

The obstacle that dwarfs all others, however, is the mortal threat posed by the one-state solution to Israel's identity and indeed existence as a Jewish state. Zionism has become an integral part of the Jewish *Weltanschauung*, if only as a bulwark against Jewish insecurity, real or imagined. Keeping Israel secure has become an immutable international obligation, not open to question or challenge. [...]

Despite these compelling arguments and seemingly insurmountable obstacles, a small but growing number of dedicated advocates of the one-state solution remain undaunted, and the burgeoning interest in the idea continues to gather momentum. Clearly, a very long road lies ahead, with formidable barriers to building a Palestinian consensus on the idea, much less an agreed position on the issue. And yet, taking a long view of the history of the conflict and observing the current situation on the ground, some form of a one-state solution seems inevitable. [...]

For Palestinians, the refugees' right to return is not a minor issue, despite Israel's ceaseless and relentless efforts since 1948 to make it so. Indeed, if there were only one justification for the one-state solution, it would be this. In 2007, the number of forcibly expelled Palestinians and their descendants was estimated by the Bethlehem-based BADIL Resource Center for Residency and Refugee Rights at 7.6 million, 4.6 million of whom are UN-registered refugees. Especially in light of the international role in their plight, these people have an unequivocal right to a settlement of their claims in accordance with justice and the law. Instead, a raft of proposals—collective or individual compensation, settlement in host societies, transfer abroad—put forward by Israel and Western countries aims precisely at preventing the right of Palestinian return to Israel. Such attempts are of course inevitable in the context of a two-state solution. [...]

The one-state solution is as yet a political idea, which, like others (including Zionism at one time), has to be accepted in principle before it can be implemented. The fact that it may be impracticable at various historical junctures does not invalidate the idea itself. This essay has focused principally on that idea, with the aim of making it better understood and therefore more widely accepted. An implementation strategy that at least identifies the relevant forces to support the idea must now follow, and one-state supporters need urgently to elaborate an implementation plan. Not doing so would earn them dismissal as utopian or hopeless dreamers.

48. "The One-State Solution: An Israeli Version"

*Naftali Bennett**

EDITOR'S NOTE *Naftali Bennett (1972–) is leader of the right-wing religious party the Jewish Home (HaBayit HaYehudi), serving as minister of diaspora affairs since 2013 and as minister of education since 2015, in governments led by Likud's Benjamin Netanyahu. Bennett and his party have opposed a two-state solution to the conflict, proposing instead a solution based on the Israeli annexation of Area C (about 60 percent) of the West Bank, the sparsely populated area left under Israeli control by the Oslo Accords, and autonomy for Areas A and B, where most Palestinians live.*

Currently, in Israel's marketplace of ideas, only two solutions are being proposed for resolving the Israeli–Palestinian conflict. They are:

1 the establishment of a Palestinian State on the majority of the territory of Judea and Samaria; or
2 the full annexation of Judea and Samaria, including [their] two million Arab residents.

Yet the public understands that both of these solutions are impractical and would threaten Israel's security, demography, and humanitarian standing.

The time has come to provide a workable and rational solution which serves Israel's interests.

This program, which is still a work in progress, does not attempt to solve all of Israel's problems once and for all, recognizing that no such panacea exists.

The initiative, while far more modest in its aims, gives Israel three key advantages:

1 Israel will receive vital territories and assets.
2 It will strengthen our standing in the international community by completely neutralizing the "Apartheid" argument.

---

* Naftali Bennett, "The Israel Stability Initiative: A Practical Program for Managing the Israeli–Palestinian Conflict," posted February 2012 at www.onestateisrael.com.

3 It will create stability on the ground, and among the people, for decades to come. The plan relies on a number of senior government ministers (Saar, Kahlon, Katz, and Edelstein), [who] have already called for Israel's annexation of specific territories in Judea and Samaria, to actualize their words through concrete action.

What separates this plan from others is that it's practical.

The 7-point plan for managing the Arab–Israeli conflict in Judea and Samaria

1 **Israel unilaterally extending sovereignty over Area C**   Through this initiative, Israel will secure vital interests: providing security to Jerusalem and the Gush Dan [greater Tel Aviv] region, protecting Israeli communities, and maintaining sovereignty over our National Heritage Sites. The world will not recognize our claim to sovereignty, as it does not recognize our sovereignty over the Western Wall, the Ramot and Gilo neighborhoods of Jerusalem, and the Golan Heights. Yet eventually the world will adjust to the de facto reality. Further, the areas coming under Israel's sovereignty will create territorial contiguity and will include the Jordan Valley, the Dead Sea, Ariel, Maale Adumim, the mountains above Ben Gurion Airport, and all of the Israeli communities in Judea and Samaria. As a result, residents of Tel Aviv, the Gush Dan Region, Jerusalem, and Israel will live in full security, protected against threats from the east.

2 **Full naturalization of the 50,000 Arabs living in Area C**   This will counter any claims of apartheid. Currently there are 350,000 Jewish residents, and only 50,000 Arab residents, of Area C. Irrespective of religion [*sic*], all residents of the area will receive full citizenship. Based on this outline, no Arabs or Jews will be evicted or expelled from their properties.

3 **Full PA autonomy in Areas A and B, with the free flow of people and goods between all PA-controlled territories**   Palestinians will be able to travel freely anywhere in Judea and Samaria, without checkpoints and soldiers stopping them. We don't like long traffic jams, and understandably neither do they. This contiguity can be achieved with a one-time investment of hundreds of millions of dollars. This will not create separate roads for Jews and Arabs. Instead, it will eliminate all obstructions to the free flow of traffic at critical junctions, in a safe and secure manner. Today Arabs and Jews in Judea and Samaria use the same roads, and this should continue. As this will also improve the lives of the Palestinians, it will deflect unnecessary international and humanitarian pressure off Israel.

4 **Palestinian refugees from Arab countries will not enter into Judea and Samaria**   This is in contrast to the currently discussed framework, under which millions of Palestinian refugees from Arab countries would be absorbed into a Palestinian state. Unfortunately, Prime Minister Netanyahu, in his Bar Ilan speech, accepted this notion. This is a fatal mistake that will lead to an irreversible demographic disaster. As soon as millions of refugees from Lebanon, Syria, Egypt, and other Arab countries flood into Judea and Samaria, there will be no going back. Descendants of the refugees should be absorbed into the countries where they currently reside and will not be allowed to move west of the Jordan River.

5 **A full Israeli security umbrella for all of Judea and Samaria**   The success of the initiative is conditional on keeping the territories peaceful and quiet. Peace can only be achieved with the IDF [Israel Defense Force] maintaining a strong presence in, and complete security control over, Judea and Samaria. If the IDF leaves, Hamas will rapidly infiltrate the area. This is how Hamas took control of Gaza, and how Hezbollah took control of southern Lebanon.

6 **The separation of Gaza from Judea and Samaria**   In contrast to the idea of creating a "safe passage," we must recognize that there is no connection between Gaza and Judea and Samaria. If such a connection were forged, it would bring the violence, instability, and problems of Gaza into the currently calm areas of Judea and Samaria. Gaza is also gradually becoming closer to, and more dependent on, Egypt. This process is ongoing and Gaza is not our responsibility. After all, when Israel expelled 8,000 Jews forcibly from their homes in Gush Katif and pulled back to the last inch, Israel received a Hamas state and thousands of rockets in return. Now the burden is being passed to Egypt.

7 **Massive economic investment in coexistence on the ground**   This would include building interchanges, the improvement of infrastructure, and the supporting of joint industrial zones. Peace is a bottom-up initiative that can best be achieved through people who want to live their everyday lives. Instead of money going to the fruitless diplomatic cocktails of Oslo, Geneva, and Camp David, it could be used to produce substantial change and improvements on the ground.

One prominent example would be at the Hizma Junction, in the Benjamin Region, which has long been lacking a proper interchange. As a result, every morning thousands of Israelis and Palestinians sit though unnecessary traffic jams, while the neglectful uptake of such roads is also the cause of many traffic accidents.

Today there is no great love between the Arabs and [the] Jews of Judea and Samaria. Yet both sides have already come to the understanding that the other isn't going away. Therefore, instead of continuing to spend our time, energy, and resources on solutions that only lead to frustration and violence, we can instead focus on practical steps that will improve people's lives and stabilize the situation. The time has come for fresh ideas that shift from conflict resolution to conflict management.

The time has come for Israel to take the initiative.

49. "The Two-State Solution"

*David C. Unger**

EDITOR'S NOTE *David C. Unger (1947–) is an American journalist and academic who, at the time this article was published, was a member of the* New York Times *editorial board. Unger's case for the two-state solution reflects prevailing views within the foreign policy establishment, including emphasis on the problematic aspects of the alternatives that have been proposed.*

By 2033, two states, Israel and Palestine, will be living side by side in an uneasy peace, with the risk of war between them and terrorism across their common border diminishing year by year. This two-state solution will not be imposed by the United States or the Arab world. It will be freely chosen by the Israelis and Palestinians themselves. The growing Palestinian majority living between the Mediterranean and the Jordan River will continue to insist on nothing less. And a solid majority of Israelis will by then have come to see a two-state partition of Palestine as essential to Israel's survival as a tolerable place to live and raise their families. That is not the only outcome possible for 2033. But it is the most likely—and it is the most attractive one for Israelis, Palestinians and the outside world.

Consider the alternatives. [...]

In the absence of a comprehensive two-state solution, there is little chance that Israel can muster the political will to dismantle vulnerable West Bank settlements lying well beyond the green line over the next quarter century. The security barriers needed to protect them, in the face of an increasingly adverse demographic balance, will stifle any hope of real economic development in the West Bank. The Gaza strip, presumably still under the control of Hamas or [of] an even more radical successor, will remain economically blockaded.

The nearly seven million Arabs of Palestine will be poor, desperate, and with little to lose by 2033. Permanent insurgency, with terrorist and rocket attacks on Jewish settlements, Israeli soldiers, and Israelis living across the green line are a certainty. Israel has the military capability of suppressing an occupied

---

* Abridgement of David C. Unger, "The Inevitable Two-State Solution," *World Policy Journal* (Summer 2002): 59–67.

Palestinian majority indefinitely—provided [that] three crucial conditions continue to be met.

First, Israelis would have to continue to be willing to provide their sons, daughters, and political support for [sic] the kind of all-out repression that would frequently include killing children and other innocent civilians, systematic torture, and international obloquy. Second, in the face of this, Washington and American public opinion would have to remain willing to provide the kind of uncritical diplomatic support and military and economic aid that George W. Bush has provided the governments of Ariel Sharon and Ehud Olmert—without regard to Israeli policies, negotiating positions, or defiance of American requests.

Third, all or most of Israel's land borders—with Egypt, Jordan, Syria, and Lebanon—would have to remain under the control of governments willing and able to deny passage to Palestinian fighters and arms. [...]

All three of these conditions are subject to change over the next 25 years. In fact, all three are more likely to change than not. [...]

Theoretically, there exists another choice besides the two-state solution or indefinite military occupation. Palestinians, whether they live inside the green line, in Greater Jerusalem, or in the West Bank and Gaza strip, could simply be granted the full range of legal rights enjoyed by Jewish Israelis, including the right to live anywhere they choose between the Mediterranean and the Jordan, the right to serve in the armed forces, and the right of those living anywhere in the diaspora to return to live in Palestine. [...]

Superficially, this would seem the perfect liberal solution—assuming, and this is a very big assumption, that a future Palestinian majority (inevitable by 2033, giving the demographic realities) would not impose its own restrictions on the legal rights of the Jewish minority and [on] the rights of Jews elsewhere to immigrate to a binational Palestine. The record of the Arab world, indeed of most of the world, is not very encouraging on this score.

A binational state would negate Zionism, even Zionism's raison d'être—a Jewish majority government as a guarantee of Jewish security, Jewish political and civil rights, and the right of any Jew in the world to resettle in a Jewish-controlled homeland in Palestine. At best, a binational Palestine would offer the conditions Jews now enjoy in the United States—a Jewish minority living in peace, prosperity, and harmony with its non-Jewish neighbors. At worst, it would reproduce conditions resembling those of pre-1939 Poland or present-day Iran—a Jewish minority living in fear of mob violence, economic expropriation, and physical expulsion.

If Israeli Jews are going to commit their future to that range of possibilities, it is hard to see much reason for having an Israel at all. And that is exactly the point. A binational state means the end of the State of Israel.

That leaves a two-state solution as the only realistic possibility for 2033. But it still leaves the problem of getting from a here in which the territorial integrity of the West Bank keeps receding, communitarian boundaries in Jerusalem become increasingly scrambled, internal Palestinian political divisions solidify, and trust between the population on both sides diminishes to a there in which an economically and politically viable Palestinian state emerges and both peoples agree to live side by side, in peace forevermore.

How would the difficult and frustrating details of Jerusalem, borders, Palestinian refugees, and Israeli security finally be resolved? And, more fundamentally, how would Israeli society and Palestinian society each arrive at their own stable consensus that whatever deal is finally struck on these issues is not subject to future reopening, but is for keeps and thus the legal and legitimate end of their historic conflict over the land of Palestine?

Apart from these all-important details, the broad parameters of a two-state solution have to some extent already been worked out. Bill Clinton's attempt to get Yasir Arafat and Ehud Barak to agree on final terms at Camp David in the summer of 2000 broke down in recriminations, followed by the outbreak of the Second Intifada. But President Clinton persisted and, in December 2000, he offered a detailed set of American parameters that can still serve as a useful starting point for a final status agreement. It provides for Palestinian sovereignty over 94 to 96 percent of the West Bank (allowing Israel to keep a compact bloc of settlements around the green line). An area roughly equivalent to what Israel retains in the West Bank would be ceded to the Palestinians from inside the green line. Israel would retain sovereignty over Jewish areas of Jerusalem, while Palestine would have sovereignty over Arab areas. The most religiously significant areas of the Temple Mount complex would be similarly divided. Palestinian refugees would have an absolute right of return to Palestine, but no specific right of return to Israel. [...]

But let's not get ahead of ourselves. There is little point to fleshing out the details of these 2000–2002 near-solutions when none of them is currently on the negotiating table between Israeli and Palestinian leaders. Those partial frameworks were thrashed out between the most dovish elements of the Israeli and Palestinian political classes. They have never been accepted by the top political leadership on either side. And, while polls taken in times of relative tranquility suggest majorities of both societies might accept such arrangements in the abstract, there is a big difference between being polled about abstract ideas and agreeing to give up land or refugee rights, particularly when there will be no shortage of rejectionist politicians on both sides, urging intransigence. [...]

What would much more clearly build peace [is] steps that would visibly change the lives of ordinary Palestinians—like dismantling internal security barriers and roadblocks between West Bank cities, except for those clearly and directly related to the security of Israelis living inside the border fence.

The single most important step any Israeli government could take to rebuild Palestinian faith in progress toward a two-state solution is an absolute freeze on all settlement expansion. The number of Jewish settlers on the West Bank (excluding East Jerusalem) has more than doubled since the Oslo Agreements were signed. [...] How can Palestinians ever be expected to believe that Israel will agree to a viable two-state solution unless this process is immediately brought to a complete halt, and all settlement outposts created in violation of Israeli law are dismantled?

This is much harder for any Israeli government to do than release prisoners, not just because of the size and political power of the settler community, but because such a decision would rightly be seen by Israelis and Palestinians alike as the most significant concrete step that could be taken today toward preparing the way for a two-state solution.

Achieving a two-state solution by 2033 means that the current impasses must somehow be overcome. Outside powers, especially the United States, can help by stepping in with credible security guarantees, conferring international legitimacy on courageous and innovative Israeli and Palestinian leaders, and withholding it from timeservers and obstructionists. Arab leaders can help by legitimating necessary Palestinian compromises, helping configure internationalized solutions for Jerusalem's religious sites, and facilitating the resettlement of Palestinian refugees.

But outsiders can only help. The main work will have to be done by Israelis and Palestinians themselves. Ultimately Israelis will decide their own fate. So will the Palestinians.

Even long before 2033, however, Israel's available options will be reduced to a nation besieged in continued occupation, a Jewish population of Palestine submerged in a binational state, or a political agreement between stable majorities of Israelis and Palestinians on a compromise two-state solution. Both sides will surely see that historic compromise as less than ideal. But they will also see it as clearly superior to any of the available alternatives for two populations determined to build and defend their homelands in the same narrow strip of land.

50. "Linking Justice to Peace"

Yaacov Bar-Siman-Tov[*]

EDITOR'S NOTE *Yaacov Bar-Siman-Tov (1946–2013) was professor of international relations at the Hebrew University, Jerusalem, where he also held the chair for the study of peace and regional cooperation. The following reading represents the summary of a lifetime of study of the conflict, as expressed in his last book. Although Bar-Siman-Tov is writing from an Israeli perspective, his work is marked by an effort to encompass the narratives of both sides and to identify paths through which justice might be achieved for both.*

This concluding chapter has two aims: (1) to summarize the role of the parties' justice narratives in the peace process and to argue that the gap between the contending narratives has been a major barrier for resolving the conflict; (2) to look for alternative solutions for linking justice to peace, among them linking justice to reconciliation, to a two-state solution, and to a one-state solution.

Linking justice to peace as a barrier to conflict resolution

The Palestinian demands for justice have two layers: a demand for procedural justice and a demand for transitional and corrective justice. The demand for procedural justice relates primarily to the Israeli recognition of the Palestinians as an equal partner in the peace process, despite the asymmetry in the power relations between the two parties and the occupier–occupied relations between them. The demand for transitional and corrective justice focuses mainly on the Israeli acknowledgment of its responsibility in perpetuating injustice against the Palestinian people and [on] its remedy by implementing the right of return for Palestinian refugees.

The Palestinian demand for procedural justice was acceptable to some of the Israeli negotiators in the Oslo process, though they had trouble in carrying it out in practice, so that the relations between the parties were not grounded in

[*] Abridgement of Chapter 7, "Linking Justice to Peace in the Israeli-Palestinian Conflict: Looking for Solutions," in Yaacov Bar-Siman-Tov, *Justice and Peace in the Israeli-Palestinian Conflict*, ed. Arie M. Kacowicz (London: Routledge, 2014), pp. 133–148.

real equality. Moreover, after the outbreak of the Second Intifada in September 2000, Israel found it difficult to recognize Arafat or Abu-Mazen as sincere and reliable negotiating partners, the former because of the loss of trust in him and the latter because of what was perceived as his weakness. Indeed, the Israeli unilateral disengagement from the Gaza strip in August 2005 was a direct outcome of Israeli disappointment about the possibility of resolving the conflict through peaceful negotiations. Nevertheless, the resumption of the peace negotiations via the Annapolis process in 2007–2008 took place after Israel recognized Abu-Mazen as a serious partner. Hence it seems that the relations between the Israelis and Palestinians, especially between Ehud Olmert and Abu-Mazen, were grounded in a better sense of equality and a certain degree of empathy. However, the asymmetrical power relations persist nowadays, so they will continue to influence the current and future negotiations. In this sense, most of the burden is on the Israeli side, and especially on the United States as a mediator to balance the asymmetrical power relations in the peace negotiations.

The Palestinian demands for transitional and corrective justice are principally linked to the outcomes of the 1947–1949 war and less so to the outcomes of the 1967 war. The Palestinians require that Israel acknowledges its responsibility for the expulsion of the Palestinians and for the creation of the refugee problem, and that it agrees to the implementation of the right of return within its borders. The Palestinians, for their part, do not acknowledge their responsibility for rejecting the Partition Plan of November 1947 and for initiating the 1947–1949 war. Similarly, they do not accept the Israeli standpoint on justice, which is focused on the right of Jews to establish a Jewish state in the Land of Israel and/or to recognize Israel as the state of the Jewish people. In the Palestinian view, such acknowledgment would add to the injustice that the Zionist movement inflicted upon them through the establishment of Israel on their land, and it has the potential to deny their right of return and undermine the rights of Palestinians living in Israel.

The Palestinians presented their demands for procedural, transitional, and corrective justice at the beginning of the Oslo process, but Israel completely rejected them. The Israelis conditioned the peace process on its focusing on the outcomes of the 1967 war rather than [on] those of the 1947–1949 war. Israel objected to dealing with injustice and its remedy as defined by the Palestinians and, in fact, imposed the negotiating framework that it wanted, [which was] based on a gradual and multi-phased process, including an interim arrangement (Palestinian self-government for five years in the occupied territories) before the parties engage in reaching a final and permanent peace treaty, with the core issues postponed to the permanent status negotiations. The Palestinians were then forced to accept the Israeli position at Oslo, recognizing that, in light of the power asymmetry between the parties, their insistence on having their demands for justice fulfilled could be a barrier to peace and to the establishment of an independent Palestinian state. Nonetheless, the Palestinians did not reconcile themselves to the removal of the justice issues from the agenda; and they saw the peace process as unjust and unfair and [as] the result of Israel exploiting its power during the negotiations.

The Palestinian demands for justice were renewed more adamantly at the Camp David Summit in July 2000, following the massive criticism leveled against Arafat and the Palestinian negotiating team by other Palestinians, especially the intellectuals, for abandoning their demands for justice, and particularly the right of return. Although the Palestinian demands for justice were not the only cause for the failure of this summit, [they] did contribute significantly to it.

The Israeli negotiating team at Camp David was surprised by the renewal of the Palestinian demands for justice and by their intensity, and they saw it as a barrier to peace. They had the impression that the Palestinian demands for justice [not only] included the right of return, which had the potential to endanger Israel as a Jewish state, but also in fact denied the very existence of Israel as the state of the Jewish people, because its establishment, on 14 May 1948, was considered the primary source of injustice perpetrated against the Palestinians. Israel refused to accept any responsibility for the creation of the refugee problem, though it expressed its sorrow for the Palestinian suffering; and it was ready to receive a limited number of refugees on a humanitarian basis in the framework of family reunification, but under no circumstances on the basis of a right of return. From the Israeli standpoint, the right of return should be implemented only within the Palestinian state. [...]

The failure of the Israeli–Palestinian peace process so far can be attributed mostly to the failure of both sides to reach an agreed formula for linking justice to peace. Thus the relationship between peace and justice has been at the heart of the peace process. As a matter of fact, the peace process sharply reflected and even enlarged the wide gap between both sides' narratives and the difficulty, if not the impossibility, of bridging the gap between them. Both parties continue to be guided by their historical narratives, which are protected values, that is, sacred and mystical values intertwined with national identity and therefore not subject to negotiation, bargaining, or compromise of any sort. Each side continues to be guided by [the] perceived injustices committed by the other side and by a high sense of justice and righteousness in its cause, while delegitimizing the justice of the other side. [...]

The basic conclusion of this complex reality is that justice cannot be absolute, but relative, and that it will be permanently incomplete. Any demand for linking justice to peace [that is] based solely on one's narrative is impossible and becomes a formidable barrier to conflict resolution. The central problem in the case of two conflicting views of justice is that both sides are partly right, in terms of one or another aspect of their claims, and therefore it cannot be expected that a peace agreement will fully and satisfactorily address all of the problems related to justice. Justice has then to be compromised if the sides have an interest in resolving the conflict.

Balancing between justice and peace: Between theory and practice

It would appear that the theoretical arguments we presented [...] could help in dealing with the problems of justice in the Israeli–Palestinian conflict as follows:

1 Reviewing the different approaches that consider the linking of justice to peace suggests that an explicit concern for justice must be included in the peace negotiations and in the peace agreement. [...]
2 Given that every peace process includes concessions, compromises, and costs, these should apply to questions of justice as well. [...]
3 Dealing with the current injustice of the Israeli occupation and the fact that the Palestinians still do not have an independent state is more urgent and significant than the injustice linked to the past.
4 The accepted tenet in the theoretical literature, that there is a trade-off to make between protected values as a compromise that combines justice with peace, has been so far formally rejected by the Palestinians. [...]
5 Issues of justice should be framed in terms of interests rather than values. [...]
6 Another reasonable compromise would involve distinguishing between the [Palestinians'] demands for transitional justice and their demands for corrective justice. [...]

The two-state solution as a form of compromised justice

With respect to the demands for corrective justice, the two-state solution and the establishment of an independent Palestinian state alongside Israel should be seen as an Israeli and Palestinian fair compromise, and as a fulfillment of the demands for corrective justice. Furthermore, the Israeli and American proposals—that the Palestinian refugees be also relocated to territories that Israel would exchange ("swap") with the Palestinians, and that relocation [be] then considered as realizing their right of return—can also be regarded as a kind of compromise.

The establishment of a Palestinian state would not only put an end to the current Israeli occupation of the West Bank and to the Palestinian suffering, but it would also allow the fulfillment of the right of return within the Palestinian state. So far, the Palestinians have rejected solutions that did not in their view address their demands for a right of return (to Israel itself). Yet the Palestinian demand for a right of return to Israel proper conflicts with the idea of establishing a Palestinian state. While returning Palestinian refugees to Israel is not possible, the establishment of an independent Palestinian state could offer a rational, moral, and reasonable solution to the refugee problem. Palestinian insistence on the right of return to Israel will not only prevent the achievement of a peace agreement and the creation of a Palestinian state, but will also cause more suffering to refugees and residents of the West Bank and Gaza strip and would increase the sense of grievance and injustice among Palestinian refugees in the Palestinian diaspora. The Palestinian demands for transitional and corrective justice in the form of demanding a comprehensive right of return are, therefore, a formidable barrier to peace.

The basic principle of a compromised justice should be based on mutual recognition of the rights of both sides for self-determination, nationhood, and statehood. The only possible solution that can accomplish this basic principle is the "two-state solution," which calls for "two states for two peoples." This solution is not a new one and was proposed first by the Peel Commission in 1937 and then by the 1947 UN Partition Plan. The Jewish side in the conflict accepted both proposals, whereas the Arab side rejected them. The Arab side initiated the 1947–1949 war in order to prevent the implementation of the UN Partition Plan and the establishment of a Jewish state. Following the war, Israel as the Jewish state was established, while the Palestinians lost their opportunity to establish their own independent state.

Following the 1947–1949 war and until 1988, the Palestinians continued to oppose the two-state solution. The Palestinian Declaration of Independence of November 1988 could be considered as the beginning of a sea change; it was interpreted as an indirect recognition of the State of Israel and expressed support for a two-state solution. Israel, which had occupied the West Bank and the Gaza strip after 1967, opposed that solution, maintaining that the establishment of a Palestinian state alongside of Israel in the West Bank and Gaza strip could pose an existential threat to it.

The Oslo process of 1993–2001 opened the road for the two-state solution, although the Oslo Accord did not explicitly refer to it. The main Palestinian goal during the Oslo process was to promote a two-state solution that will bring about the establishment of an independent Palestinian state in the West Bank and in the Gaza Strip within the pre-1967 war borders (i.e. the Armistice lines or "green line" of 1949), including East Jerusalem as the capital of the Palestinian state and implementation of the right of return to the State of Israel. This Palestinian goal has remained constant throughout the peace process and has formally not changed substantially until today.

During the Oslo process, Israel's position remained ambiguous vis-à-vis the establishment of a Palestinian state; in formal terms, the most that Israel was ready to accept was the establishment of a Palestinian entity which would be less than an independent state in the Gaza strip and in part of the West Bank, while keeping Jerusalem unified under Israel sovereignty and rejecting the right of return. Only at the Camp David Summit, in July 2000, Israel accepted for the first time the two-state solution, making it conditional upon the demand that the right of return be implemented only in the Palestinian state. In the 2000s, both Israeli prime ministers, Ariel Sharon and Ehud Olmert, also accepted the two-state solution. Even the current Israeli prime minister, Binyamin Netanyahu, endorsed the two-state solution in June 2009. Nevertheless, the parties have failed so far to reach an agreement on the two-state solution because they have been divided on several core issues, including borders, Jerusalem, refugees, and settlements. It seems that both parties are not ready yet to make the necessary concessions for reaching the two-state solution.

In our view, a two-state solution, despite all the difficulties involved in its realization, is probably the best compromise and just solution for the two sides. This solution requires both sides to make very painful concessions. Israel has to recognize the right of the Palestinian people to have their own state, while the Palestinians have to recognize the right of the Jewish people to have their own state. Furthermore, the formula of the two-state solution requires Israel to give up its dream of a Greater Israel (Land of Israel) and its occupation of the Palestinians. [...]

One-state solution as a just solution

The one-state or the binational solution was proposed several times by people on both sides and by outsiders throughout the long Israeli–Palestinian conflict. Proponents of that solution advocate a single state in Mandatory (Western) Palestine that will include the State of Israel, the West Bank, and the Gaza strip. In general, this solution refers to the establishment of a unitary, federal, or confederate Israeli–Palestinian state in the entire territory west of the Jordan River. This solution will provide citizenship and equal rights for all the inhabitants in the combined entity, [on the basis of] the principle of "one person–one vote." The advocates of the binational solution are mainly intellectuals, whereas this proposed solution is not very popular in both societies, not in the official circles and not with the general public. This solution gains some momentum mainly in periods of crisis and stalemate in the peace process, as a default and as an inevitable outcome of the failure of reaching a two-state solution. [...]

Other observers point out that the one-state solution is the only practical one because of the realities developed on the ground since the 1967 war, when Israel occupied the Palestinian territories. This solution appears to various people from both sides as the only feasible one, as the irreversible and inexorable outcome of the continuous expansion of the Israeli settlements in the West Bank and in East Jerusalem. This development prevents a viable, contiguous, sovereign, independent Palestinian state with East Jerusalem as its capital. Moreover, Israel and the Palestinian territories already function as a single political unit. They share the same resources, such as aquifers, the same highway network, the same electricity grid, and the same international borders, which can no longer be separated. [...]

In contrast, the one-state solution is perceived by most of the Israeli Jews and by the Jewish people around the world as a nightmare development that would bring about the end of the Jewish state. Within a few years, there will be a Palestinian majority between the Jordan River and the Mediterranean Sea, and the result will be another Arab state, in which the Jews will remain a small minority. Thus the majority of the Israeli Jews and the Jewish people in the diaspora interpret the one-state solution as a suicidal act and as the end of Zionism. Moreover, such a solution is defined as an injustice by itself for the Jewish people. [...]

Although not termed as such, the first formal Palestinian support for a binational state appeared in February 1969 with a resolution adopted by the fifth National Council of the PLO [Palestine Liberation Organization] that called for establishment of a "secular and democratic state" in the entire territory west of the Jordan River, including the Gaza strip, instead of the State of Israel. In that secular and democratic state Muslims, Christians, and Jews [would] enjoy equal civilian rights. Over the years, this idea failed eventually to attract substantial support on both sides, so in the 1988 Palestinian Independence Declaration the PLO gave up the idea of a one-state solution in favor of the two-state solution. [...]

Both parties realize that the binational solution cannot necessarily resolve the conflict and secure a peaceful coexistence between Israelis and Palestinians. Indeed, most of the proposals do not present concrete specific formulas regarding the future constitutional arrangement of the one-state solution, or its implications for both sides living in a single state. For instance, how will a single state resolve the mistrust and the mutual negative feelings between the parties? How will such a solution cope with the national aspirations, narratives, and identities of both sides? [...]

Conclusions

The negotiations in the Israeli–Palestinian peace process have demonstrated that narratives of justice on both sides played a significant and negative role in foiling the conclusion of a peace agreement. Both sides are motivated by the shadows of the past and [are] victims of them. Thus, narratives of justice proved to be formidable barriers to peace, if both sides sustain clashing narratives.

The major lesson and conclusion of this book is that the only way to conclude a peace agreement requires that both sides should put aside the pursuit for a just peace according to their absolute narratives of justice and strive for peace in the first place. In other words, *justice should be compromised for the sake of peace.* A two-state solution is the only solution that can be defined as an imperfect but relatively just peace, since it reflects both sides' right for self-determination on the one hand, while easing or even ending the long suffering of both parties throughout the conflict on the other hand. Unfortunately time is not working for the benefit of any of the parties, as new rounds of violence will just accelerate the grievances and lead to new victims in the name of "just peace."

Index